Noble Youth

Adventures of Fourteen Siblings
Growing Up on a Polish Estate
1919–1939

D1245835

Noble Youth

Adventures of Fourteen Siblings
Growing Up on a Polish Estate
1919 – 1939

Teresa Bisping Gniewosz
with
Christopher Gniewosz

CHRISCO Trading — Publication Division

www.nobleyouth.com

Printed and bound in the United States of America
First Printing 2002
Second Printing 2002

Cover and design by Brian Diehm

Publisher's Cataloging-in-Publication information:

Gniewosz, Teresa Bisping
        Noble youth : adventures of fourteen siblings growing
up on a Polish estate, 1919-1939 / Teresa Bisping
Gniewosz with Christopher Gniewosz. — 1st ed.
        p. cm.
        Includes bibliographical references and index.
        ICCN 2001119866
        ISBN 0-9711628-6-7
    1 . Bisping family. 2. Nobility—Poland—Biography.
    3. Poland—Biography. I. Gniewosz, Christopher.
    II. Title.
DK4419.G65 2002 943.8'04'092'2
QBI33-315

Bisping Family, ca. 1927

*Jan **Bisping**, 1880–*

*1ˢᵗ wife: Ewa **Dusiacka Rudomino**, 1876–1904*
Adam, 1904–1904

*2ⁿᵈ wife: Marynia **Zamoyski**, 1887–*
*(1ˢᵗ husband: Karol **Radziwill**, 1874–1906)*
*Michal **Radziwill**, 1907–*

Marysia, 1912–
Krzysztof, 1914–
Ela, 1915–
Stas, 1916–1919
Jas, 1917–
Terenia, 1919–
Ewa, 1922–
Adam, 1923–
Andrzej, 1924–
Piotr, 1925–
Jozek, 1926–
Ludwik, 1926–1926
Kryla, 1927–

MASSALANY ESTATE MANSION
CA. 1939

TERESA GNIEWOSZ, NÉE BISPING
"TERENIA"
FROM A PASTEL STUDY, CA. 1938

CHAPTER 1

D EEP IN the frigid winter of 1919, a plain coarse wood wagon stopped before a dilapidated cottage. It was heavily laden with round-topped, leather-strapped trunks. An elegant carriage followed. Energetically bounding down upon the frozen dirt drive from the carriage's protective boot, where he had been seated beside the teamster, the anxious gentleman's words disappeared into a biting wind.

Swinging open the carriage door, he heard a passenger inside delicately ask, "Is this it?"

Not taking time for extensive explanation, he offered his hand and replied, "Yes, the locals are completing preparations for childbirth."

Taking his hand, she abandoned the carriage with difficulty. A magnificent fur coat enshrouded the fine features of her face and gently swiped a light dusting of fresh snow as they made their way to shelter. Three children, equally concealed in fur, alighted to follow her and scurried toward the low cottage closely followed by their governess.

They arrived as the door opened and a workman with tools in hand emerged from within. He simply stated to the gentleman, "The *piec* is fixed. We started a fire and it's starting to warm up inside."

The gentleman, his face instantly showing relief, expressed a heartfelt "Thank you!"

It was indeed a simple shelter. A bed dominated the center of one sparsely furnished room where a woman was just completing the tucking in of its linen. Against one of the two windows was a simple plank table with two chairs. Beyond was a door to another room intended for the children and their governess. Filling the space between the bed and the door was the large furnace,

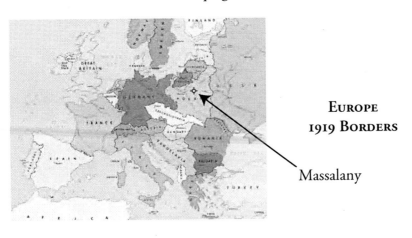

EUROPE
1919 BORDERS

Massalany

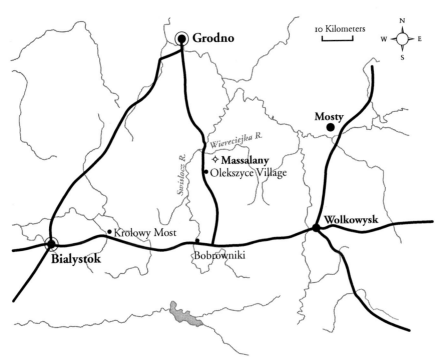

MASSALANY ESTATE AND REGION

so characteristic in Eastern Europe, which the workman had spoken of. It had apparently been repaired well, for its ceramic tiles were already radiating their pleasant heat.

The gentleman hastened the children with their governess to the second room, and helped his wife remove her bulky fur. "Marynia," he softly said, "I have to ride back immediately and take care of the sick children." Fleeing before marauding Bolsheviks,[1] they had left two children, ill with diphtheria, at home in the care of a trusted woman. The children would not have survived the trip.

Marynia's face expressed sadness upon hearing his words, and she replied hopefully, "Jan, maybe you could wait. You would know the outcome of my delivery." Jan was happy to oblige. It was late. There was little travel time left in the day and the horses needed rest.

They sat at the table, silently immersed in thought. Jan, owner of huge estates and a beautiful manor, thought about the last weeks where he had organized troops for the defense of his and his neighbors' estates against the bands of Bolshevik raiders.

The raiders attacked estates, savagely ravaging all that they came across, murdering owners and their families. Jan was distressed about the children left at home, but his immediate concern was for his wife, who was about to give birth. He was deeply apprehensive about the future of his family, the future of his people, and the future of his homeland.

The events of the last few months crossed Marynia's mind as though they were a series of pictures. The Russian revolution did not at first threaten traditional eastern Polish territories. Unfortunately, it was not long before local gangs were organized which openly threatened their lives. Anticipating the worst, Jan and Marynia had organized preparations throughout the estate. Weapons constantly required cleaning and needed to be kept at their sides at all times. Ammunition was stockpiled.

Marynia, with a passion for history and having been raised among historic collections and art, with her husband's support decided to send their extensive library, archives and art collections to a familiar convent deep within Polish territories. Overseeing the packing, it was through her personal efforts that the family treasures had all been successfully shipped to safety in the last weeks.

---

[1] Bolsheviks: Members of the Russian Communist party, constituted in 1903 by the majority faction of the congress of the Russian Social Democratic party.

Her husband would not have had time for such details. His efforts were concentrated on organizing the defense of his family, neighbors and numerous folk who had worked on the estate for generations.

Marynia contemplated the future of her child about to be born, theorizing that the interests and activities of a mother during pregnancy heavily influence the child. What would she have, a son or daughter? What would become of a child born of a mother who, throughout her pregnancy, lived in such turbulent times?

Their contemplations were cut off by the sudden onset of labor pains. Marynia stood and started to pace the worn wooden floor. This being her seventh child, she anticipated a quick labor. She asked Jan to call the doctor who had already been informed of their arrival in town and of their imminent need for assistance. The doctor arrived soon after, just in time to aid the swift delivery. The parents were overjoyed at the birth of a baby girl they named Terenia.

After a few days, Marynia, her three children and the new baby resumed the journey to the heart of Poland and the safety of her family. During the next months they were enveloped at Marynia's Aunt Marysia and Uncle Jan Zamoyski's estate, Trzebien, with warmth, concern and congenial care. Jan had returned home to the estate the morning following Terenia's birth, having promised Marynia to follow her upon the recovery of their two sick children. Marynia's entourage included not only her carriage and the wagon loaded with their possessions, but also a small herd of cattle and horses and several family dogs. The caravan arrived at its destination without additional delay. Later in the season Jan was able to rejoin them, but he came with one child. Three-year-old Stas had succumbed to diphtheria.

The infant Terenia quickly developed into a strong and healthy baby. She was often kept out in the fresh air offered by the veranda or the garden. By the bassinet, Wum, a great dog commanded to guard her, kept vigil. Wum never left Terenia's side. No one could approach until the parents ordered Wum to stand down.

It was under these circumstances that Marynia's brother Franciszek came to visit. Walking up to the house, he spotted the bassinet on the veranda and approached to see the baby. Suddenly, what seemed to be a great wolf rose from the ground, baring threatening, sharp, vicious fangs! Instantly Franciszek stopped, knowing full well the hazard he faced. Backing away from the ferocious creature, he entered the house, where Marynia greeted him joyfully.

"Come see my baby," she said warmly, inviting him back toward the veranda.

"I won't go out there," he replied upon her invitation. "There is one of Jan's wild wolves out there!"

Marynia, with a bemused smile, said, "That is the best guard for my child. Without my permission no one will approach, let alone try to touch Terenia."

Franciszek looked at the dog with a new appreciation. Jan's kennel, known throughout the region, bred shepherds with the great wild wolves that roamed the timberlands. Wum was an exceptional product of Jan's kennel. He was not only large, but magnificently built and had a long powerful tail.

At Marynia's approach the dog rose, and Marynia pet its shining coat. Wum accepted her praise for his good work and returned to lie in his chosen place by the bassinet to keep an eye on any activity. "You can go to the bassinet now, Franciszek. He knows that I allow you to touch the baby."

With an uncertain expression and keeping an eye on the dog, Franciszek cautiously, hesitatingly approached. Seeing that the dog did not react, he picked up the baby. "This is a beautiful child," he said. "She has such big blue eyes! I wonder what this innocent child will see in her life?"

The following year, 1920, was a difficult one for Poland, upon the heels of a hundred difficult years. On the 15th of August the Polish army faced invading Bolsheviks who, having tasted victory in their revolution in Russia, were moving westward to conquer Europe. Despite vastly inferior odds, Poland was victorious at the battle called "The Miracle on the Wisla River." Their stunning victory saved Europe from being inundated with Bolshevik communist ideology.

A proud nation for a millennium, in 1795 Poland was partitioned by her neighbors—Prussia, Austria and Russia—and ceased to exist as a country. In 1919, at the Treaty of Versailles, Poland was re-established from the Prussian and Austrian portions. This latest victory allowed Poland to reclaim its eastern territories from Russia. Jan, together with the other Polish people living on and around his estates, joyfully reunited with Poland.

Several months later, with the eastern lands once more a part of Poland, Jan and Marynia decided it was safe to return home. Departing from her dear family with mixed emotions of gratitude and anticipation, Marynia and their children climbed into the carriage for the journey. Jan ascended to the carriage boot, eagerly driving the team personally. Following them came the wagon with their belongings. Then came the servants, walking, as they drove the cattle and horses. Dogs nipped at the livestock's heels, while Wum proudly trotted beside the carriage, head held high with an eye out for Terenia. During the trip they passed several manors burned to the ground. Concern mounted for what they would find at home.

After several days, the caravan approached Jan's estate, Massalany, which had been established in 1853 by two wealthy but childless sisters, Alexandra (Bisping) Swetschein (1785–1853) and Jozefa (Bisping) Woyczynski (1786–1878). The sisters had legally established an inter-generational estate, or "majorat."[2] The estate could not be sold. Rather, it was to be passed down from the head of one generation to the next, thus avoiding dilution of the estate. Jan was the fourth Ordynat[3], having taken over the estate at age 17 upon the death of his father.

The manor, designed by the Italian architect Andriolli, was built in 1853. The pillared house, built in the shape of a horseshoe, was made of white painted masonry with a red ceramic tile roof. It was in a beautiful setting facing a lake. In the back, lanes fanned out through a wooded park of several acres.

From a distance, it looked as though the manor had escaped the devastation that was apparent at other estates they had passed throughout the trip. Standing, Jan called to the wagon driver to stop at the house and directed the servants to pen the stock. Not stopping, he hastened the carriage horses down the lane, passing the kitchen with its cooks' quarters above, the stalls and carriage house, the fisher's house and the hospice that Jan's great-aunts had built for retired or ill workers. When finally he did stop, it was before the family chapel. Wordlessly, he climbed down from the carriage and walked toward the chapel. He pulled out a twenty-centimeter-long bronze key, unlocked and opened the front door and entered. Marynia, who had instructed the governess to watch the children, followed silently. She found Jan, head bowed, kneeling before the altar. She, too, advanced to the altar, knelt beside her husband, closed her eyes and crossed herself.

After giving thanks to God for their safe return, they went out into the hot sun to find the children playing exuberantly by the water's edge. The governess, collecting their shoes and socks, looked as though she yearned also to be able to enjoy the coolness of the water.

---

[2]Majorat: Entailed (landed property settled in such a way that it cannot be sold and must be inherited and bequeathed in a certain way) estate with the right of primogeniture (being firstborn; conferring the right to inherit).
[3]Ordynat: Heir, Lord of the manor and estate.

Jan and Marynia looked out toward the manor backed by trees and deep blue sky mirrored in the lake. Eager to unpack and to see how the house had weathered their absence, Jan assisted Marynia back into the carriage and helped the reluctant children follow her.

Shocked surprise awaited them when they opened the front door to the house. It was empty! Looking at the large entry room and beyond to the living and dining rooms, they saw that everything was gone. The table that could seat twenty, with its hand-carved chairs emblazoned with the family crest and rich leather seats, treasured Gdansk cupboards, table service, silver and crystal, paintings and the salon furniture—all were missing.

Walking outside, Jan saw his trusted steward, Antoni Szemiot, approaching. The man's father, his grandfather and great grandfather had all served Jan's family well. Without a word of greeting Jan stated, "Tell them to bring it all back! I don't care who, what or how. Everything is to be placed on the veranda. If they are embarrassed or ashamed, they can bring it after nightfall. However, if after three days I find anything in the villages, they will face the consequences!"

"Welcome home, Sir," quietly replied the man.

Jan and Marynia could see they would need to get to work. Jan would need to reorganize the holdings, prepare fields and forests for the winter and make plans for the following spring. Marynia meanwhile, would need to direct the servants as she would work together with them to clean and restore the house.

They would need to install new windows, paint rooms and renew the parquet floors. The beautiful floors, made of black and white oak arranged in various designs, did not suffer too badly because of the straw covering that had been put on them at the last minute prior to the family's departure. Over the next several days of intensive long hours of work, with the help of several servants, Marynia was able to bring her home back to a more livable state.

The missing furnishings slowly started to show up. The house was just an empty shell without furniture, linen and tableware. In the middle-class American life that baby Terenia would one day enjoy, the manor and its possessions would seem few and simple. But each of them was important for the functioning of the estate that supported the region's population.

Often, upon waking, Jan and Marynia would find the veranda laden with a clutter of miscellaneous items. Marynia had the additional task of cleaning and repairing items, often dirty, damaged, or infested with vermin. The serious matter of the returns soon became a source of intrigue as they explored and uncovered new arrivals each morning. After three days had elapsed, much of what was missing had been returned. As Jan's words spread, items continued to trickle in for weeks, providing Marynia the pleasure of finding the missing odd piece of a set or some needed component. Each morning she would tell Jan of her findings and each evening they would share the progress made that day.

There were many strange occurrences during this time after the war. Late one evening, an unknown woman came to the yard at the back of the manor. Everyone was occupied preparing for evening activities. She had come without raising anyone's curiosity. Suddenly, the family, seated at dinner, heard a cry of alarm from a servant approaching from the kitchen. Running out they found the woman afire. They were horrified to find that she, having stripped to the flesh, had ignited gasoline she had poured over herself. An alert butler, running to the side cloakroom, grabbed a carriage plaid and was able to throw it over her, putting out the fire and saving her life.

Another time a different woman tried to enter the manor through a window. One of Wum's brood grasped her skirt in its teeth. Trembling, a shocked maid looked on as the mighty wolf pulled the intruder away from the window. Tearing herself free, the unknown woman fled.

Many such disturbed individuals roamed freely, having been cast out by their poor families. There were no organized public institutions during the governmental disorganization of the post-war period. These poor people posed a very real danger. Everyone was in fear of such people wandering about. Wum and a few of his siblings and offspring accompanied the family everywhere to safeguard them. Other dogs, wolves really, were tethered to doghouses by the side of the manor. Each had its own house and could freely roam around the house on its tether. At night, when no person was to be about, they were let loose, guarding the estate.

With hard work and care, and despite the unsettled times, Jan and Marynia were able to reestablish the pre-war stability of the estate. This in turn built the foundation of security for the region. The life baby Terenia was to know throughout her childhood began with the renewal of the Massalany estate.

CHAPTER 2

THIS WAS A HAPPY time for the children. Though their parents were heavily occupied, the family interacted frequently and affectionately. The children were under the constant care and tutelage of their excellent and experienced governess. The family also had a nanny from the British Isles, Miss O'Keefe.

At one point Marynia became concerned when she observed the older children speaking only English amongst themselves. She feared that she might be raising her Polish children to be unfamiliar with their native tongue. This problem, however, resolved itself soon enough.

Two years had passed since the birth of Terenia, and Marynia had not yet become pregnant again. Miss O'Keefe, who had come to care for infants, moved on to provide care for another family. After her departure, Marynia made a point of speaking only Polish with her children. Within a year she observed that the children had completely forgotten the English they had so recently spoken fluently. This was again a point of consternation as the knowledge of language was an important factor in the proper upbringing of children. She need not have been so concerned. As it was, one of the children, Ela, finding herself in England years later, amazed the English language instructors with her aptitude for learning English and the ease with which she spoke using the correct accent. This was often not the case for people from Slavic countries.

When Terenia was three, Jan and Marynia did have another child, a daughter they named Ewa. She was later acknowledged to be very intelligent and possessing a wonderful memory. Wet nurses, nannies and governesses raised many noble children, and Marynia's were no exception. She did, however, care for and nurture her babies by herself. As each succeeding child was born, a governess would take over the care of the older child. Since Ewa was not born until Terenia was three, Terenia benefited from the long period of care she received from her mother and therefore was very close to her.

A year after Ewa was born, Jan and Marynia had another son, Adam. A year after that they had another son, Andrzej. Then came son Piotr, and in 1926 twin boys, Jozek and Ludwik. The family was devastated when Ludwik died within hours of the twin's premature birth. Their last child was a daughter, which they named Krystyna, though she was always called Kryla.

Prior to her marriage with Jan, Marynia had been married to Prince Karol Radziwill, who died of scarlet fever just prior to the birth of their son Michal. Widowed at an early age, she married Jan several years after the death of Karol. In all, Marynia had fourteen children. Michal, the oldest, was separated in age from Kryla, the youngest, by twenty years. At age twenty-four, Michal had a son, Karol. The younger Karol often played with his aunt Kryla, who was only four years older than Karol. Often overheard during play was Kryla admonishing Karol, "If you are not nice, you will have to call me aunt."

The children soon reached school age. Marynia contacted the tutor who had educated her and her siblings, asking if she would agree to care for her school-age children. Niula, as the new governess came to be known, gladly agreed. Jan and Marynia decided, after a long discussion, that the children would receive a better education in Poznan, and since Niula was from there, she would be in familiar surroundings. They rented a large apartment in a desirable neighborhood. As the school year approached, Jan and Marynia took the three older children, Marysia, Krzysztof and Ela, to Poznan. The children were registered in their respective boys' and girls' schools.

Jan and Marynia completed arranging and furnishing the Poznan apartment. Niula selected two servants who would cook and take care of other household needs. As Marynia had known Niula from childhood, she knew that the children would be in nurturing, experienced hands.

Each September, as another child reached school age, he or she would accompany the older siblings to Poznan. Niula oversaw their intellectual and physical upbringing as well as making sure that they learned and used proper etiquette. For holidays and during summer vacations, they would all return home. All accepted Niula as if she were one of the family. She was loved and respected by the children. Of a noble family herself, she was respected by all. When she was a child, Niula's parents had died and she had been sent off to boarding school. She was one of the few women of her time to have completed not only her general studies, but also university studies, which she did

Niula, Governess

KRZYSZTOF AND MARYSIA,
FIRST HOLY COMMUNION, 1919

with top marks. Her first job was as a tutor for Marynia, where she had excellent results. Marynia did very well in history and mathematics, and became proficient in eight languages under Niula's tutelage.

Jan and Marynia's younger children, meanwhile, continued their normal, happy lives. Under the watchful eye of their loving parents they were constantly cared for by their nannies and governesses. They took daily walks and played in the wooded park behind the house. Toward the end of each confining winter they impatiently awaited the freedom afforded by warm weather. Picking the first wild violets and primroses, which announced the arrival of spring, they would present these treasures to their mother, who would arrange them on her bureau.

Announced from afar by their loud clacking, flocks of great storks soon arrived to reoccupy their massive nests in the grand old poplars. The children spent many hours playing games and climbing trees. Their caretakers sat on benches set out under ancient linden trees, arguing and gossiping amongst themselves when they weren't doling out instructions to the children or reciting the rosary.

The children called this favorite place *Pienki* (Stumps), because there were two great, old, round sections of oak tree trunks encircled with a soft yellow sand which their father ordered dumped there each year. The children were occupied for hours running sand through the wormhole-riddled stumps. Sculptures, fortresses and large cakes were shaped in the sand. When their castles were no longer alluring, each child would occupy their own tree, talking to one another from high perches. Two tall poles were set in the ground. From the crossbeam at the top hung a swing on which the children cooled themselves with long sweeps back and forth.

When old enough, each child had a private plot within the large garden for planting flowers and vegetables of their choice, with the help of the gardener, Jan Lis. He loved children and was always eager to reward a child's interest in the garden with seeds and seedlings. He patiently taught each child about the plants and how to care for them. The children learned much from him: how to encourage a plant or flower to grow better, how to pick and collect the plants at their prime for the kitchen, how to collect and store seeds to be used in the following season and how to be patient and give consistent care—requirements for succeeding with the plants they had chosen for their plots.

The children's parents further encouraged an interest in these endeavors by offering to pay for what each child could produce and deliver to the kitchen from their individual plot. At the end of the season the parents were in for a surprise. They encouraged the children to take upon themselves the responsibility and accounting for their enterprise, and so each highly treasured individual produce was enthusiastically valued as the child thought appropriate. When it came time for an accounting, the parents realized how expensive the produce was that they had been eating all summer. Doling out small fortunes to each child, the parents later laughed between themselves that their children would, indeed, someday make good business people.

As soon as the children could, around age five or six, they started riding horses under the watchful eyes of their father or the chief coachman. Jakub Krochmal was in charge of the manor's stable where horses and carriages were kept. Many a child's early riding memories were of sitting securely with their father, hanging on to the horse's mane, or starting to ride bareback on an older, trusted horse. They would often visit the stables, stroking a favored horse's head and neck, feeding them sugar cubes or corn husks. This led to a chorus of happy neighing in anticipation of treats when the children arrived. At times when the children found themselves around the carriages with their Papa, he would hoist them onto the boot, or inside the carriage, and tell them of experiences or stories connected with the particular carriage.

One such story was about the arrival of the Bishop in a particularly grand carriage kept for such special occasions. Coachman Krochmal, dressed in his best livery coat, had the honor of driving the team. The family, gathered in front of the manor, bowed to greet their guest as he approached. It so happened that at that moment, the team of four specially-selected, grain-fed horses were spooked — and they set off! The coachman, grasping the reins tighter, did well to maintain control while pulling them around the drive. The carriage, with the Bishop inside, encircled the drive in this way several times before the team was finally brought under control before the manor. The family bowed deeply to the Bishop each time the carriage passed by. Surmising that this was a special ceremonial welcoming, the Bishop grandly flourished his hat, bowing in return on each passing. Very pleased by the honor shown him, he was in an especially congenial mood throughout his visit.

The family often took advantage of pleasant summer evenings by playing tennis together. Both parents enjoyed the sport and soon the children learned to play as well. Raised to the game in this way, they competed in many tournaments. Years later, two of the boys found themselves in France. Impoverished due to the war, they collected balls to earn some cash. Barefoot and with no equipment, they were unable to play the game they enjoyed so much. Asked one day by a club member if they knew how to play, they eagerly said they could if only they had racquets. Handed racquets, the two boys enjoyed an athletic, skillful, aggressive game, thanked the member and left for the day.

Coming back the next morning, they were surprised to find several of the regulars playing barefoot. Asking what this was about, they were told that on the previous day two particularly skilled foreigners had played barefoot and everyone was eager to try playing in their style.

Each season provided its unique entertainment. Home from school during the summer, Terenia particularly liked to watch as fields of tall grass were scythed. She enjoyed rising early in the morning and running out to see the harvest. Men positioned themselves in an even line and with calm, even swings, the grass was cut. This coordinated teamwork resembled a choreographed dance. They would thus move uniformly down the field, until reaching the far edge of the field where scythes were stood, blade up before the men, for sharpening. Sharpening created a strange resonant, wailing cry, as files were expertly drawn across the length of the blade. This lasted a few minutes until the men staged themselves in a line once more and returned to scythe another swath across the field. As the tall grass fell to the side of each worker, morning dew glistened in the early sun and the scent of freshly cut grass filled the air. Birds alighted on the ground behind the men, scratching about to find newly exposed slugs and insects.

There were also fields of flax covered with a blanket of fine sky-blue flowers. Once the family had planted great fields of flax, but now only small peasant's plots were planted with it. It was labor-intensive work. As the flax grew it had to be weeded. Once it had flowered and ripened, women, sickle in hand, cut the flax and laid it down on the field to dry in the sun. When dry, it was gathered and the women would thrash the flax with wooden rods, breaking away the shell and exposing long fibers.

During long winter nights the women would work together at their spinning wheels turning these fibers into a fine yarn. They gathered, singing together late into the night, weaving the yarn into belts of arm-width fabric on handlooms. These long belts were rolled up, until the next summer when they were soaked in the river, then left to bleach on the shore. As soon as the sun grew hot, riverbanks were lined with the gray flax linen and slowly bleached until the river was edged as if by strips of snow. The women thus had a valuable and marketable commodity that was taken to market where it would fetch a good price.

This fabric could be effectively colored with bright dyes and made into clothing for women and their families. More experienced women often brought their best work to Marynia who paid a premium for superior yardage. The yardage Marynia purchased was stitched together to make bed sheets. Very durable, often outlasting a generation, the sheets were appreciated for the cool feel they provided in the heat of summer nights.

On many summer mornings Jan liked to ride out to see how the fields looked as work progressed. For these quick trips, he preferred to use his favorite carriage. It was a light, open carriage, with large wheels allowing a comfortable smooth ride, even over furrows and ditches. Pulling the carriage was a favorite team, Tarantela and Czelozja, whom he knew well, having used them for many years. Jan had purchased the horses when they were retired from the German army. A matched set, black but for dark brown speckled markings on the hindquarters, they would start, or stop, in response to his voice commands. If he were separated from the carriage, having moved off to take a closer look at something, a sharp whistle would bring the horses to him; he would climb onto the carriage and move on.

Jan often took one or more of the children along on his morning ride. Even the young children were occasionally given permission to drive his trusted team, adding to the adventure of the morning ride. He enjoyed telling them about the work being done in the fields, the forests he had planted and the birds and animals that lived amongst it all. He taught them how to identify the various grains growing in the fields, their various growth patterns and how to plan the right time to harvest.

"Two weeks after tassels start forming, the grain blooms and grows for two weeks," he often repeated, drumming this important principle into their minds. "The grain then needs two more weeks to mature before the time is right for harvest." The children not only enjoyed the opportunity to accompany their father, but also learned much from these explanations and the stories he told related to this land he knew so intimately. In this way, Jan passed on his love for the land as it had been passed to him by previous generations.

On some days Jan took the family to the cabin he had built in the woods nearby. It was a simple affair, one small room, a kitchen area and bathroom. Later, one wall was removed. The room was expanded with screens on three sides. It was furnished with a large central table and more than a dozen beds. The cabin was a favorite place to play or to enjoy the coolness of the fragrant forest on hot summer nights. The manor kitchen staff brought meals to the cabin whenever the family was there, making it a pleasant time for the family to play, relax and take walks through the forest together.

One morning the forester responsible for caring for this portion of the woods came to the children with a gift. He had found a fawn whose mother had been killed by poachers. The children were delighted. They took good

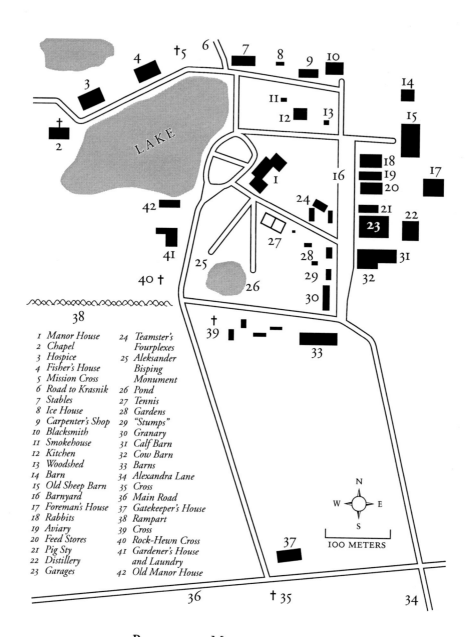

LAKE

N
W ☉ E
S
100 METERS

PLAN OF THE MASSALANY GROUNDS

care of their new pet and it in turn accepted its new family and delighted them with its antics. By the end of summer the deer had grown and rejoined its wild cousins.

Another hot summer day activity was to go swimming in the several-acre, man-made lake in front of the manor. One summer, when Krzysztof, the oldest, was fifteen, he designed a two-man canoe and helped the carpenter build it. It had a round bottom and proved rather unstable. As it would sink when tipped over—and it tipped over easily—the children were afraid to ride in it, even though they all knew how to swim. It became a challenge to see who would reach the submerged vessel and bring it up to be emptied and made available for use again.

The carpenter built two more canoes, this time with flat bottoms that proved far more stable. When not in use, the canoes were kept upside down on the grassy slope leading up to the manor. In time, Jan had a small dock built where the canoes and a large rowboat were kept. Adults would occasionally row around the lake in the boat. More often they would watch from the safety of the veranda as the children played on the lake.

Jas and Krzysztof built a diving board at the deep end of the lake, close to the chapel. At first the diving board was only built out from the embankment. As their skill and nerve grew, it was built up, finally reaching over three meters high. Here the boys proudly exhibited their virile, athletic diving skills.

Marynia oversaw the barnyard responsibilities. Frequently she, Jan, and the children, together with guests who chanced to be visiting, made the evening rounds. Taking the left lane through the wooded park they passed the tennis court, artesian well, vegetable garden on the right and fruit orchards on the left. Going through the gate, they reached the three teamsters' dwellings, each housing four teamsters and their families. Passing these, they entered the barnyard.

Crossing the road, they first went over to the hot, humid, estate cow barn. The sound of milk hitting metal pails and the aroma of fresh milk roused the senses of those entering. Children would gather their courage and wait until the large frightening bull, chained to the wall with his nose ring, turned away before they dared to pass. Just beyond stood forty Hollanders, with their distinctive black and white markings, being milked by the teamster's wives or daughters seated on short three-legged stools. The cows, eating contentedly, turned to inspect visitors with their large, gentle, brown eyes and were rewarded with a pat on their heads or were stroked upon being passed. Beyond, were calves being fed by the dairymen. Children enjoyed helping feed the younger calves the fresh, warm, rich milk from large bottles.

Next came the stables where the twelve pairs of workhorses were groomed and cared for, following a hard days work in the fields. Each teamster was responsible for a pair of horses that he worked with every day. He would usually become very attached to them and was concerned that they were well cared for, for the work to be done had to be a successful partnership of the teamster with the animals. At the end of the workday, during grooming, the horses enjoyed a rich blend of grain prior to being let loose in the field for the night.

Next was the pigsty with its superb sows and piglets. It was clean and bright and the pink piglets with their upward screwed tails gorged themselves enthusiastically. The aviary and food stores occupied the adjacent two buildings. Upon entering, hens abandoned nests exposing freshly laid eggs. Another space was reserved for ducks and geese that had not yet come in from the adjoining pond, preferring to wait out the last rays of light. Children favored the next building. It held soft, warm, cute rabbits that, upon entry, would hop over to be cuddled and fed.

By the time the tour was complete, it became dark. Geese waddled in from the pond. Upon seeing the children, the geese would move toward the children with their long, lowered necks extended in a loud honking offensive. With screams of terror, children hid behind adults. The geese were prone to painfully pinching young exposed legs. With this, the tour was over. Again passing the teamsters' fourplex dwellings and going through the gate, they returned home to the manor. It was a pleasant stroll after a long day.

The park was beautiful. Its various trails, raked regularly, were kept free of unwanted growth. Freshly scythed lawns added to the rich variety of fragrances emanating from the multitude of ornamental shrubs and trees. Upon entering the manor, each person spruced up before dinner. Nightingales commenced their nocturnal chorus at dusk, serenading all until the first rays of dawn.

Each night, the dogs were let loose to guard the manor and grounds. Once, having been let loose for the night, they disappeared until the next morning. The next evening a line of wagons approached the manor. The dogs' mischief of the previous night was heaped before the manor. One hundred twenty of the peasants' sheep had been killed that night. A young shepherd, seeing the flock under his care attacked by a pack of wolves, had climbed a tree for safety. He was surprised that a pack of wolves would descend upon the flock mid-summer. He observed them as they systematically killed the entire flock. Satisfied with the meat of one sheep, they departed. The shepherd and a group of older, experienced peasants were able to track Jan's animals. Jan paid dearly for the 120 sheep, which the family ate — continually — through the entire season. Afterward, the family was never again served mutton. Each offending dog had a bundle of rotten sheep carcass securely tied under its jowls for a good number of days. They too, lost their appetite for mutton, never repeating such an offense.

A few years later, an unknown dog joined the family's dogs. Unfortunately, it was rabid. In those days there was no inoculation for rabies. To the despair of Jan and the family, he had to put down all the dogs he had raised so carefully. His only consolation was that Wum, always his favorite, had died peacefully of old age a year earlier.

It was hard for the family to imagine life without their dogs. Jan purchased a black Labrador, well trained for hunting, and an Irish setter for the children. The lab was named Blackie and the setter Lord. Lord was as faithful to the children as Wum had been, putting up with all their mischief and always accompanying the boys when bird hunting.

Summer was a busy time filled with diverse tasks. July marked the start of grain harvests. A horse-drawn mower cut the dry stems crowned by a head of grain. Women followed, gathering armloads of the long stems, using a few of them to encircle bundles into sheaves. Sheaves were collected by tens, "ricks," which were stacked to sit out and dry until workers in wagons picked them up. The success of the harvest could be judged by observing the density of ricks across a field.

Grain was separated from stems at the side of the field, or sometimes, ricks were gathered and taken to a barn where grain would be separated from the stems later. Grain was bagged for transport and then emptied into the granary for storage or sale. During the post first-world-war period, grain was separated by immense, smoke-belching, steam-powered, belt-driven threshing machines. These machines were an awesome example of industrial might applied to agriculture that intrigued or frightened those who encountered them. Had not every able hand been urgently focused on harvest, the machines would have attracted quite a crowd.

As in all agricultural societies, this was a period of particular urgency. Harvesting, threshing and storage of the grain had to be accomplished within days of the grain's ripening. If rain were to come and wet the harvest, mildew and mold could set in, ruining that year's crop. At times, with rain approaching, the harvest might go on day and night. Sometimes, special dispensation from attending Holy Mass was given so workers could continue work even through Sunday.

Jan would always consult his trusted steward, Mr. Szemiot, about when to start the harvest. If Szemiot said that it would rain in the coming days, Jan held off. If he said this was a good time to start, for the weather would be dry, despite gray skies Jan trusted his judgment and the harvest began. Not only was this steward trusted, highly experienced and knowledgeable, he also had severe arthritis. If his bones ached, he predicted rain, thus delaying the start of harvest just to have it soaked. If his bones did not bother him and the grain was ripe, the harvest commenced. This system served the estate well.

Jan's estates, in Poland's northern region at longitude 55° north, had long summer days and short nights. The long summers were fully utilized with work starting at dawn and continuing into the late evening until workers could no longer see. Workers brought their meals with them to be eaten in the fields. Returning home after nightfall, they would only eat and sleep and then return to work again with the first light. The success of the harvest was important not only to the Lord of the manor, but to everyone, including each contracted peasant and his entire family. A successful harvest would mean a good life to be shared by all. A poor harvest could mean harsh conditions. Poland's climate was a good one and harvests, for the most part, bountiful. The estate's grain, lumber, produce and meat were shipped throughout Europe. These were good times.

Young and old could find work during harvest. Colorful family groups came out to the fields from roadside hamlets, singing local tunes. They wore richly colored clothing, dotting yellow fields with deep greens, the yellow-red of ochre and brilliant reds and blues.

Jan would ride out through the fields on his carriage, talking to various workers about progress of the harvest. "May God be praised," they would call out to Jan.

Jan would reply, "For ever and ever, Amen. How goes the harvest?"

"Tolerably," came the reply, or possibly, "It's a good harvest. We hope that it will not rain until we get it in." Not wanting to keep them from their work, Jan might agree, compliment them on their progress and ride on to another group.

The children often accompanied their father. If he stopped for a little while, they might affectionately join an older worker who was struggling to keep up and help her bundle her share of the grain.

The hard, seemingly unending harvest continued in this intense fashion for a few weeks. When the grain was in, the harvest festival ensued. This was a special time for all involved. The workers would dress in their most colorful attire. One beautiful maiden was selected to lead the jovial procession. Her head was adorned with a crown of flowers and rich tassels from various grains. The procession approached the main entrance of the manor. They sang, celebrating the successfully completed harvest. Having heard the revellers approach down the main entrance lane, Jan, Marynia, their children and guests went out onto the veranda.

Jan thanked the workers for their toil during the harvest. They received bonuses and were invited for an evening celebration with dancing and a feast to be held in the yard. At this invitation, the maiden approached Jan, removed her crown and handed it to him. This was the signal local boys waited for. The passing of the crown was the moment when the boys, with buckets of water held at the ready for this moment, proceeded to try to soak the pair. All those around, trying to avoid getting caught in the dousing, quickly dispersed amid shrieks and laughter.

With the late afternoon, as the day cooled, all gathered for the celebration. Tables were loaded with food and drinks. Local musicians played joyful tunes, inviting all to dance. Years later, peasant girls would recollect dancing with Jan's boys at these celebrations. The festivity continued into early morning hours. After a day of rest, life returned to the normal routine and the next harvest, of potatoes this time, was anticipated.

Between the harvests, there were many tasks to attend to. The fields needed to be plowed, breaking up the soil. Each teamster drove his horses that pulled the metal bladed, wood framed plow. After the field was plowed it was raked even. This had the added benefit of pulling up weeds. The planting cycle was carefully planned to maximize production. Each species needed or provided different nutrients. By selecting the planting sequence for any one field, the previous crop could help the next crop by adding the nutrients it would need rather than depleting the soil.

Once the soil was prepared, it was ready for planting. The fields were planted with various crops: wheat, rye, oats, barley, potatoes, beets, lupine, clover and vetch. Once again, each teamster seeded or plowed his own portion of the field. Each man was judged—and judged himself—by how straight a row he could plow. A momentary lapse in attention, or inattention to his horses, could result in the line veering, thus displaying the man's inexperience or ineptitude for all to see. Fields were often plowed in series. Each teamster was staggered slightly behind and just overlapping the one before him. As they cut the next line they cursed any waver of their cut and laughed at the fellow in front should his line not be straight. As the day progressed, the relationship between tired men and their tired teams was tested. The horses needed constant urging to continue and the men depended on the horses' experience and skill to keep on the line. With the end of a workday in sight, none wanted to delay finishing a field so that the horses could be cared for and all could get some rest.

Many of Jan's fields were planted with potatoes as Jan had three distilleries for making them into alcohol. As autumn approached, potato fields were plowed to raise the potatoes to the surface. Women followed the plow, gathering potatoes into wicker baskets that were in turn emptied into wagons. Then, as the wagons were filled, they were emptied into pits prepared in the fields. Each pit was lined with straw a third of a meter deep, onto which the potatoes were dumped. The potatoes were then covered with more straw and all of this was covered with half a meter of soil, leaving an elongated mound on the field. This way the potatoes were stored until needed at the distillery in the winter, or as seed when the next crop was planted in late spring.

During harvest, the musky scent of baked potatoes often wafted over the potato fields. Workers' families gathered round for the bake. Wood and the dried remains of potato plants were burned to provide a large mound of hot ashes. A generous quantity of potatoes was then inserted into the midst of these ashes and the fire kept alive on top. It was as the potatoes were seared and baked within this pile of ashes that the aroma would permeate the field with the promise of the eagerly anticipated meal. This scent and the taste of these baked potatoes remained a favorite recollection of the season.

Jan's boys looked forward to this season, as it was time for partridge hunting in the fields and duck hunting on lakes and in the marshes. Armed with single or double-barreled rifles and shotguns, they set off with the dogs. Partridges, fattened on fresh grain, were flushed by the dogs and fired upon by the boys. During evening hours, flocks of ducks set down on waters to feed prior to the night. On a good day, twenty of the highly favored birds would be deposited in the kitchen to be specially prepared by the manor's excellent cook. The cook and kitchen girls did not look forward to birds because they required much preparation: plucking feathers, stuffing, baking, as well as preparing specialty meats and pates. The family and their guests, however, appreciated the kitchen staff's efforts and would recall, many years later, the delicacies resulting from the hunt.

At the end of summer, with autumn approaching, the children faced the unhappy eventuality of having to leave home. It would soon be time to leave for Poznan. The school year was about to begin. Each child packed his or her individual needs for school, and organized or stored in chests belongings that would stay behind. The children would visit favorite places where they had played during the summer, bid farewell to individuals and take a final ride on a horse or play with a particular dog or puppy. Sad to be leaving home, they were gladdened with the thought that in only a few months they would be returning for the Christmas season. Wagons were loaded with chests of clothing and various supplies that would be used in Poznan. Early in the morning, saying their farewells to Jan, Marynia and younger siblings, the school-aged children set off by carriage to Grodno under the watchful care of Niula. In Grodno they would catch the train to Warsaw, make the connection to Poznan where they would finally arrive the next morning.

With the older children off to school, the household became quieter and much calmer. Dogs stretched out in the sun and riding horses lounged in their pasture. The house staff cleaned and prepared rooms for the winter.

The kitchen was situated some twenty meters from the manor. This was to separate the manor from the clamor and smell and the constant traffic of staff and workers about the kitchen, as well as for safety reasons. Above the kitchen was lodging for the cook and various administrators. The cook fed about fifty people daily. Excellent cooks were recruited for their diverse skills and training. Two or three locally hired girls assisted. The food was ample, nourishing and hearty. Manor food was specially prepared with gourmet attention, particularly when there were guests to entertain.

Three menus were prepared daily. The first for the manor, the second for administrators who did not have families, and the third for various staff and workers served at a large table in the kitchen. House girls carried the manor's food on trays to the manor's credenza,[4] where it was kept warm and then served on fine china and crystal in the dining room. Administrators could eat a quick meal in the kitchen, but more commonly would take a tray to their respective quarters. Except for sugar, salt and special spices, all the ingredients were grown, raised, or made on the estate.

Bread was baked twice weekly in an enormous rock oven. Three kinds of bread were baked. The most plentiful were huge rounds of black bread—baked on oak leaves that added a distinctive taste and aroma. These were best with honey and fresh butter. Baked in smaller quantities were the standard, hearty, rye breads and special white bread or rolls made of wheat.

The open oven covered one wall of the kitchen. The opening was over a meter wide, two meters high and almost two deep. It was large enough to roast an entire calf, or twenty loaves of bread simultaneously. These last were baked on special metal shelves. Enormous cakes, some half a meter in height, were baked here as well. On baking morning, the oven was fired with wood, which would heat up and radiate intense heat throughout the day.

---

[4]Credenza: butler's pantry adjoining dining room where food is prepared for serving.

All the fruit and vegetables came from the estate gardens and orchards. Next to the kitchen was a smoke house where a wide assortment of sausages, fish and meats were prepared year-round. Dried mushrooms, fruits and vegetables hung on strings from the ceiling of the nearby storehouse. All were kept in good supply, prepared under the direction of the stores-keeper. She was in charge of receiving, maintaining and dispersing inventories. Inventories included various items: bread, sausages, daily provisions for the kitchen and manor, eggs, cheese, canned fruit and berries, juices and various specialties, sweets and gourmet foods. The stores-keeper also canned fruit and berries in the storehouse. The house staff could be heard commenting to the stores-keeper when requisitioning the daily needs. "We don't need as much sausage, eggs, or bread today, the Lord's sons are off for a few days." Other times they said, "Their appetite is dulled, we don't need as much." Or, "We need a lot of preserves and white bread, they have visitors from France and those Frenchmen like the white bread."

An icehouse kept meat frozen from one winter all through summer to the next winter. It was situated near the stable, on the road to the carpenter's. The icehouse, made years earlier, had been dug about five meters deep and measured some ten meters by ten meters. The sides were lined with wood and insulated with a meter or more of straw. The roof, made of wooden rafters and planks, was also layered with over a meter of straw and covered with a meter of earth. The floor and sides were then lined to the thickness of over a meter with numerous blocks of ice. In the dead of winter, ice was cut from the lake in front of the manor. Access to the icehouse was down a set of steps, through a heavy wooden door and beyond a wall of straw.

Jan and Marynia were known for their exceptional fruit and berries. In early summer, cherries and a rich variety of berries were collected: strawberries, raspberries, blackberries, huckleberries, gooseberries and currants — red, white and black. Later in the season, apples, pears, peaches and apricots, as well as cantaloupe, pumpkin and watermelon, walnuts, pecans and hazelnuts were harvested. All that were not eaten fresh were canned or dried. Their seeds were collected for eating or reseeding. Apples and pears were specially cared for in the basement of the storehouse. They were placed individually, on special shelves, so that one would not touch or adversely affect another. Under constant observation, any spoiling fruit was removed immediately. In this way supplies lasted until the next crop.

CHAPTER 3

THE DAYS GREW shorter as fall approached. The young boys would sometimes accompany their father on afternoon hunts for hare, fox and partridges. They dressed in comfortable loose woolen coats and knickerbockers, high leather boots and woolen caps. Armed with light shotguns at the age of six or seven, they were taught by their father to become proficient young hunters. Crossing furrowed fields, sometimes obscured by wafts of low-lying clouds in the cool fall air, they followed attentively behind Jan's dog. Jan, following slightly behind, kept a sharp eye out to be sure that the boys directed their firearms safely. He instructed them to remain calm when game was spotted and to check the field of fire before taking aim. It was a momentous day when a young man would bag his first game on one of these hunts. The boys headed home proudly with a shoulder heavily laden with a hare or a few partridges to be deposited in the kitchen.

Marynia enjoyed playing the piano. The children would often come from the children's wing to listen. They encouraged her to play. She played the large grand beautifully, sometimes stopping to explain something to the children about the composition, or the composer, as they sat in the deep, soft, wall-to-wall sofa. When she had played enough, she often pulled down a memory album. Sitting among the children, she told stories about her or other families' trips throughout Europe, showing the sights on post cards in the albums. Other times she would talk about members of their large extended family while showing photographs from photo albums.

All females in the household embroidered ornate pillowcases and top sheets during long, quiet, winter days. Each year, Marynia utilized the bright morning winter light for precise embroidery of a design she had brought with her from Italy, where she had spent many winters during her youth. She worked on this project through the years of bearing her fourteen children and beyond. Upon completion, she sent her embroidery work to Italy, where it was gilded and sewn into fine priest's vestments. It was suggested that this extraordinary work be presented to the Pope, but she knew the Pope had many such treasures and she had other plans. The finished vestments were returned to the estate and she was able to present them to the priest at the family chapel, where they were first worn on the celebration of Jan and Marynia's twenty-fifth wedding anniversary.

And so, a typical afternoon would pass. As evening approached, the children would once more return to their wing. Children ate dinner in the children's wing dining room. Younger pre-school age children were only invited to eat with the adults on special occasions. By that time they were well acquainted with proper table manners, having been taught by the nannies and governesses while they ate in their separate dining room. After dinner the children were cleaned up and prepared for the evening. Under the care and tutelage of their nannies, they listened to books and fairy tales. Some of the favorites were various folk-tales common throughout Europe, such as those the brothers Grimm collected and published. Story time over, it was time for bed.

Wooden-framed beds and cribs had wool-stuffed mattresses. Sheets were sewn together from linen purchased each spring from local women. Bottom sheets covered mattresses, but top sheets were sewn, like pillowcases with openings at the top. Into the pockets quilts were stuffed. Quilts were made of colorful cloth filled with duck down. Pillows were of similar materials, measuring about one meter square. Dressed in long white nightshirts, the children knelt on rugs by their beds for prayer. They said common prayers as they knelt, starting with an "Our Father" and "Hail Mary." Then they prayed for each individual in the family, those who had died, any special concerns and then went securely to sleep after a busy day.

As they slept, terrors from tales that had been forthrightly read to them returned to haunt the night. They ran from the clutches of witches wanting to enclose them in gingerbread houses, awakening in a sweat just in time, with the relieved realization that they were in the safety of their beds at home and not in deep, dark, threatening forests.

Siberian winds brought on frigid winters. Moist Baltic clouds from the west dumped heavy snowfalls upon encountering the numbing Siberian cold from the east. Great sheepskin overcoats were worn over woolen jackets and wheeled wagons were replaced with sleighs. Window glass accumulated frost, forming enchanting shapes, which children interpreted as representing various images. Looking out from the warmth inside, they enjoyed viewing the winter scene outside. Horses, heavy with winter coats, faces encircled with frost from moist exhalation, pulled sleighs to the jingle of bells. The joyful Christmas season approached.

St. Nicholas day was celebrated on the sixth of December in most homes where children lived. The night before, children set shoes out beside their beds. Early the next morning, when they awoke, they would often find candy in the shoes. An uncooperative child might find only a lump of coal in his or her shoe. In some homes, St. Nicholas might come to the children in the evening. He had long, white hair and whiskers, wore a red coat and held a large bag over his shoulder. Each child would, in turn, approach St. Nicholas, who asked the child if he or she had been good throughout the year. He would then either reward them with candy or, as was the fear and dread of every child, he would hand over a switch with which their parents were to correct their behavior.

One year, Terenia, then about five years old, told her mother that St. Nicholas was very similar to her father, both by appearance and the sound of his voice. She wanted to pull on St. Nicholas' beard to see if it was real. She did not because she had been a good girl all year. She was afraid if she had pulled on his beard, he might be upset and not give her the candy she had earned for her good behavior.

Children were kept busy during the advent season. Weeks were spent learning poetry and preparing ornaments to be presented as Christmas gifts. Creating decorations brought out various talents. Carols were learned. Meals were kept simple during the advent season to encourage reflection on the coming of the infant Christ. The bitter cold outside and the need to bundle up extensively did not justify venturing into the frigid weather. Rather, the children preferred the view through the windows, close to the warmth of the radiant *piec.*

Celebration of Christmas was both solemn and festive. The household prepared for many guests. Chaos ensued. Dogs, their tails waging, barked to greet arrivals. School-aged children joyfully returned home. Niula accompanied those from Poznan. All had tales of school adventures. Sleigh-bells announced guests from regional estates and those that the liveried coachmen had fetched from the train station. Servants bustled about preparing rooms, bedding, meals and winter clothing. Silver, crystal and porcelain were cleaned. Shouts of greetings and toasts of welcome were heard throughout the manor.

1937 BISPING HUNT. LEFT TO RIGHT:
ADAM, UNKNOWN, JAS, UNKNOWN, PIOTR, KRZYSZTOF, TERENIA

Cold winter days were short. From early morning the house crackled pleasantly with ceramic furnaces radiating their pleasing warmth throughout. All sizes of alcohol lamps were cleaned, filled and lit in the credenza. Upon early twilight they were distributed throughout the house, illuminating it with clean, sun-like light.

On Christmas Eve a forester brought in a young fir tree sufficiently tall to reach the three-meter high ceiling. The younger children, with the help of their governesses, dressed the tree with decorations they had prepared during the previous weeks. Special small candles were clipped securely to the branches. Since the decorations were made of colored paper and straw, each candle had to be placed carefully to not start a fire when lit. Marynia placed gifts under the tree for the children, the servants, the children's nannies and governesses, and various administrators, as well as for the numerous guests.

Early morning Christmas Eve, the men went off hunting. Jan would plan this hunt with the foresters for months; it was the premiere hunt of the year. The foresters hired and instructed some fifty local boys, "beaters," who would drive the game. Work sleds, insulated with straw, were filled with the hunters, their firearms—and occasional sweethearts "for good luck!" Upon leaving the manor the hunters toasted one another with a hearty swig of vodka from leather-lined flasks. Cold winter air was filled with the steam of horses' breath. Crossing fields, they entered the forest and headed for a forester's cabin. Pulling up at the cabin, all amassed to draw lots for pre-established firing positions along the fire-lane, then took their positions to await the game.

With the blare of the forester's horn, the beaters moved their line toward the hunters. Thrashing the woods, they made as much noise as they could to flush game from resting places toward the hunters. The hunters stood in their assigned positions and waited eagerly for any approaching game. The hunters could shoot at any game that approached, but with the second blare of the horn, hunters ceased firing as the boys beating the brush drew near. The hunters then waited until the frantic game crossed the fire lane.

It was then safe to turn around and commence shooting on the other side of the fire lane without fear of hitting anyone. The boys picked up any game hit between them and the hunter's line. After they reached the lane, they waited for the last shot and the sound of the horn that signaled another cease-fire. All the kill was collected and hung on racks that had been installed on the sleds. Then the appraisal of each hunter's luck, success, and skill was ascertained in boisterous camaraderie. The occasional disagreement ensued as to which hunter had claim to the kill on a particular animal. Though heartily discussed, arguments were usually short lived. The hunters went off to another fire-lane where the process was repeated.

As midday approached, the hunters returned to the forester's cabin where a bonfire roared. On it simmered a great kettle of meatless *bigos,* the favored hunter's stew, known to every Pole. They warmed themselves by the fire and fortified themselves with *bigos* and, perhaps, the contents of a flask that was passed about. Each hunter dared not have more than an occasional small swig. Earning the reputation as a dangerous fellow who got drunk while hunting would ostracize one from future invitations to hunts and the camaraderie it provided.

After another hunt or two in the forests, sleds were loaded with the game. A dozen or more hunters might in this way harvest a hundred or more hare, fox, deer and, in some forests, boar. Taking their sleighs, they encircled a large field for one final hunt. The hunters and boys would make a large circle. Upon hearing the blare of a horn they slowly walked toward the center. Hare would erupt from their holes and the hunters would round them up to the center. As the circle became smaller, the hare had nowhere to run and would stop in a group in the center of the circle. The hare were then allowed to escape the circle and the hunters would turn around, shooting the hares as they exited the circle of hunters.

Hundreds of kilograms of meat, already freezing in the cold winter air, were thus harvested, taken to the icehouse, hung and frozen solid. Meat would be distributed among the hunters, and some would be taken to Grodno and sold. Most was kept to be consumed on the estate.

Jan paid the boys who did the thrashing, and the forester for his extra work, and then the hunters headed back to the manor. Upon returning, the hunters retired to their rooms. There they would clean up. After taking a refreshing nap, everyone would dress elegantly for the evening's festivities and slowly gather in the salon.

Since early morning the kitchen had been busy preparing the twelve courses, representing the original twelve apostles, for the *Wilia* feast. On Christmas Eve, no meat was consumed. These twelve servings could include a variety of foods: soup of mushroom or fish, borsch,[5] various delicious hot and cold preparations of fish, poppy seed dumplings, vegetable preparations and pickles, fruit *golabki,*[6] *pierogi,*[7] poppy seed cake and dried fruit compote.

---

[5] *Borsch:* soup made from beets.
[6] *Golabki:* boiled then simmered cabbage leaves stuffed with rice, ham, sausage or fruit and smothered with sour cream.
[7] *Pierogi:* large ravioli-like boiled flour-based shells stuffed with vegetables, meat, sauerkraut or rice and cheese.

Brought to the salon by their governesses, the younger children were all dressed in white frilly dresses or jackets and pants. Used only for Christmas and Easter, a supply of these outfits was kept in all sizes so that the children always had access to one that fit, regardless of how they grew.

With everyone refreshed and eager for the evening's activities, the household gathered in the salon by the Christmas tree. The mood was jovial. Fine French wines were poured. Everyone participated in simultaneous conversations about the hunt, preparations for Christmas, school, the state of the nation, their individual estates and the goings-on of the extended family.

The atmosphere and these conversations grew in intensity until Jan and Marynia entered the salon carrying the *oplatek*.[8] They eagerly awaited the first star to show itself in the sky, which would signify the time for the festivities of *Wilia* to start. Jan approached his wife, his guests and his children, each in turn, breaking off and sharing a piece of the Christmas wafer. He broke off a small piece of the wafer for himself and ate it, sharing good tidings for the next year as appropriate with each person. They, in turn, would share their wafer with the others, until all had shared their best hopes and wishes. The congenial mood continued. Everyone sang carols together until Marynia invited all to be seated in the dining room for the *Wilia* meal. Prior to sitting down, Jan handed Adam a small bowl of grains to scatter outside as Jan prayed for continued good harvests.

The meatless meal was slowly served amid discussions of diverse and wide-ranging topics. Everyone, regardless of age, had something to add to the active conversation. Delectable, fine white and red French wines accompanied the meal. Even the children enjoyed wine, though theirs, depending on age, was mixed with a generous dose of water. The table was covered with a white tablecloth specially loomed with the "star and grapevine" pattern of the family crest at its center and rich ornamentation throughout. Beneath the tablecloth, straw had been scattered to remind everyone that Christ had been born in a stable. Each child and often the adults — perhaps with even greater interest — pulled out a piece of straw that was to foretell the length of their lives.

After all the servings had been eaten, Jan would pull out various exotic dried fruit and specialty liqueurs for the adults. Everyone shifted back to the salon. The children now had the opportunity to recite to their parents the poems they had been studying for weeks or months and to give the presents they had made. The staff, waiting eagerly in the credenza, was called in. Jan and Marynia presented gifts of money and vodka to the men and bolts of material

---

[8] *Oplatek:* Christmas wafer (similar to communion host).

to the women. The rest of the presents for the family and guests were then distributed. For the remainder of the evening, everyone enjoyed the gifts, talked, played games and sang songs.

Toward midnight, the weather outside was checked. If it was too cold they would stay in the manor and the priest would say Midnight Mass in the manor chapel inside the front door at the entry. Weather permitting, they all dressed warmly and walked across the frozen lake to the chapel for Mass. Christmas was celebrated with everyone singing together. Mass over, they returned to the manor. As it was late and quite cold, the children were watched to be sure that no one fell asleep and was left behind along the way. Safely back in the manor, they enjoyed a warm night's sleep.

Christmas morning was quiet and calm with each person rising as they wanted. There was no set time for breakfast. Everyone decided for themselves what they wished to have and when to have it. All the meat dishes were available now. By midday there were various relaxed activities and discussions in progress involving guests and family members. After lunch, a group of local children from nearby hamlets, often children of the staff, came to the manor with their teacher. They played out the Christmas story for the Lord of the manor and his guests. Jan's children, familiar with each part of the story, watched with eager anticipation that no errors were made during this favorite production. The play, to the delight of the children and pride of their teacher, was enthusiastically applauded. Jan generously rewarded the teacher, and the children, to their joy, were amply bestowed with candies.

The next days were filled with ice-skating, hockey, skiing, sleigh rides, as well as story-telling, card games, chess and playing with Christmas gifts. After dark, the governesses had time to themselves, as the children joined everyone for singing and more activities with the family and guests. The entire family ate dinner together—one of the few times that younger children joined the adults for dinner. After dinner their governesses and nannies put the young children to bed and the discussions and games continued, often until early morning hours. This time was enjoyed with various delicacies, wine, drinks and hot tea.

The New Year was likewise celebrated. Hot red wine with cloves and gingerbread was served. At midnight, everyone bid one another best wishes for the coming year. The ceremonial New Year Mass was attended the next morning with prayers for a good year.

On the sixth of January, the Feast of the Three Kings was celebrated. This celebration had a special appeal for the children. Adults joined the children in their dining room as the children were served *paczki.*[9] Three of the *paczki* had almonds inside, two white and one black. Those children lucky enough to get *paczki* with almonds were crowned. Whoever received the black almond had their face painted black to symbolize the black Magus. With this accomplished, everyone sang a carol to the Three Kings. All helped to take down the Christmas tree, thus marking the end of the Christmas season. Guests departed the next day and the older children left for school. Life returned to normal.

---

[9]*Paczki:* A favorite polish "doughnut," round, without a center hole, filled with a dense (Italian) plum jam.

CHAPTER 4

January and February were the coldest months, with temperatures reaching −40°. When it was so cold, the children were not allowed to venture outside. On warmer days, however, the children were bundled up in heavy fur coats, hats, gloves and fur-lined boots for some exercise and to enjoy the snow. They built snowmen, had snowball fights and slid down small hills on sleds.

Their parents would sometimes take them on rides in the big horse-drawn sleighs to enjoy winter scenes. Everyone would be well bundled in fur parkas. The sleigh had large sheepskin blankets to keep everyone warm. The horses enjoyed the exercise and being out of their stalls. Having been fed a good dose of rich grain, unhampered by the cold thanks to their heavy winter coats, they briskly pulled the sleigh through powdery snow. Jan drove the team, taking the family to favorite spots.

Riding across fields, the children gleefully pointed out hares jumping across the snow. One day Jan pulled the sleigh to a stop and told the children to watch. Walking over to a hole in the snow, he reached down into it, to the depth of his shoulder. To the delight of the children he pulled out a partridge and released it. Then Jan reached in and pulled out and released another, then another. In all he found fifteen partridges in the hole. The children were concerned about the birds being released out in the cold. Jan coaxed the team to pull the sleigh off to the side of the field. He told the children to quietly watch the spot where he had pulled out the birds. It was not long before one of the partridges flew up to the disturbed snow and came to sit by the hole for a few seconds. It then disappeared inside. Soon another showed up, until one by one, the entire flock had returned to their burrow. The children tried to see more burrows, but were unable to spot them. Asking Jan if it was the only such burrow, Jan said that they had passed several, but that it took a practiced eye to spot them.

They sleighed on into the forest. The snow-covered scene resembled a dream. Fir boughs were dragged down to the snow surface with the weight of snow. The sun glistened and made sharp contrasts of rich colors amongst the trees. Jan identified tracks of various animals and birds for the children. It became a point of pride for the children to be the first to correctly identify a new set of tracks. Occasionally, a deer or fox could be seen hiding in the trees. Jan liked to take the opportunity on these pleasant rides to observe the condition of the trees. In such cold conditions, they would sometimes crack open. Having planted this forest, he was sorry to lose trees close to the manor.

Jan was also concerned that his foresters kept out people who would cut down trees without authorization. Local women had permission to gather branches in exchange for picking and delivering berries to the manor during the summer. With the assistance of the men-folk, this "branch gathering" became outright harvesting of trees, which had to be controlled.

As the locals did not have much work from the estate during the dead of winter, they might decide to poach some game. Jan kept an eye out for this, since poaching out of season could easily endanger the wildlife when not checked. If a forester was staying in his cabin too much and not keeping an eye out for the forests and game in his care, Jan might pay a surprise visit with his observations as to what was happening. Once in a while the children might observe Jan talking quietly, but sternly, to a forester about his responsibilities.

During the winter the fields froze solid. The days were short. Work in the barnyard progressed. The carpenter and blacksmith were concerned with construction, maintenance and repair of various tools and equipment. Groups of men were sent out with the foresters to harvest timber for the mills or for firewood. Cordwood was brought to the woodshed by the kitchen where it was cut and stacked for use the next year after it had dried. Ice was cut out of the lake for the icehouse. Open holes allowed the opportunity for some fishing. Sometimes local young men were seen stripping off their clothes out on the ice. Jumping into the frigid water, they quickly emerged running to warmed hovels. For those that had a strong heart, this was an old Russian tradition for cleaning out the pores.

Jan's estates were licensed for three distilleries. The making of alcohol was a state monopoly, and required licenses that allowed production of a set quantity of alcohol. Owning several estates, Jan was able to obtain distillery licenses for three of them. He employed a chief distiller, Mr. Swistun, to run these distilleries. As the state kept reducing the production quantity allowed, each of the distilleries was capable of producing its licensed quantity in just two or three months. Mr. Swistun suggested to Jan, and then obtained state permission, to produce the alcohol for all three distilleries in one location. He then rotated production at all three. Thus he was able to economize by having only one distillery running each year, yet having the output of all three.

Potatoes were the main ingredient for making alcohol. Each of the estates planned its potato production based on which estate would produce alcohol that year. Jan's main estate, where his manor was situated, had one of these distilleries. It was located beyond the teamsters' houses, across the main road that went through the barnyard and beyond the farm implement barn. Its tall smokestack could be seen from far away. The main distilling stack was about seven meters high and almost two meters in diameter and made of several sections. It was heated with steam, generated by burning wood and peat.

Potatoes were washed in a tub with a stream of clean, cold water and then transferred to an enormous kettle. Steam was infused, turning the potatoes into a mash that was passed into fermentation vats and blended into grist. Adding fermented, crushed barley sprouts into the potato mash made the grist. Within the fermentation vats, the grist changed into sugar, which in turn, turned into alcohol in a matter of a few days. The boiling mass of grist, at its peak of alcohol content, was then pumped into the distilling stack. The grist was further heated in the stack. This produced alcohol steam that was cooled into 94% liquid alcohol, which was bottled and corked, with each bottle sealed and numbered. These bottles were later sent to another location, where the state put the alcohol through another distillation process for the making of vodka.

The distilleries had several by-products. Waste grist, after the alcohol had been removed, was turned into cakes mixed with chopped straw. These nutritious cakes were added to the cow's feed. Electricity was generated from waste steam after it heated the distillation stack. As the distillation process was done in the dead of winter, with the shortest days, electric light was available during distillation. The estates were not yet electrified and this provided a low cost alternative for lighting.

There were two disadvantages to this electrical source. The first was that it was only available for the short time that distillation was in process. The second was that the electricity was unreliable as the generator might at any time be pulled off-line depending on the distillery's needs. As Jan had three estates and alcohol was made at each estate only every third year, it did not provide regular electrification. Jan introduced alcohol lamps in the manor, which produced a clean white light with negligible smell or smoke. Kerosene was used throughout the rest of the estate.

Peasants in the villages and hamlets lived in small cabins—hovels —made in the log cabin style. The cabins had small, low doors and small windows with an inner and an outer pane. Spaces were filled with moss for insulation. Each cabin had an iron stove that provided both a place to cook and a source of heat. Often, behind the stove yet inside the room, a rock wall was built to protect against fire. As important, this wall would absorb heat from the stove. The other side of this warm rock was a particularly popular place for older people to sit, their aches soothed by the constant radiant heat.

Everything a peasant family owned would be in this small cabin. During cold weather, this might include any chickens or other domesticated birds, goats, piglets, or sheep that a family was fortunate enough to own. Amongst this chaos lived any member of the surviving older generation, unmarried brothers or sisters and usually several children. Life was simple. The same clothing was worn every day, sometimes year round, and was washed in the stream during warm spring weather.

The same basic food was eaten every day. The mainstay was potatoes and cabbage. Pigs provided much-needed fat, although their meat was principally a source of cash. Little meat was eaten, as it had too much value to be squandered by simply eating it. Lard was, however, saved and savored. Birds were used for eggs and feathers.

The number of feather quilts a family possessed denoted its wealth. Sheepskins were used for coats. Long dark winter days and nights were filled with making thread or yarn on spinning wheels. Later, the yarn was loomed into material. Wood was carved into needed implements or crafted into folk items. Seasonally, special things were made such as the intricate painting of eggshells for Easter.

The Easter season was preceded by Lent, with six weeks of fasting. Food supplies were usually short by this time of the winter. On rich estates more food was available, both due to availability and better conservation. Despite availability of food, even on these estates, families did not eat meat during lent. They ate one full meal a day. No festivities were arranged. There was no dancing. As the week before Easter approached, much attention was paid to preparing for the various upcoming church activities. Holy Mass was attended regularly.

The children who were studying in Poznan came home for the Easter holiday. 1929 was particularly cold and snowy. When the train carrying Niula and the children arrived in Grodno, they found everything snowed in. Jan had dispatched three heavy work sleighs for them. His most experienced teamsters drove two; the third was driven by his trusted chief coachman. They had no sooner arrived in Grodno than they quickly loaded the trunks into one sleigh. The children and Niula were placed in the other two sleighs. All were covered with warm furs and surrounded by heavy covers made of sewn sheepskins backed by a waterproof tarpaulin. In this way they set off for the forty-kilometer ride home in howling, bone-chilling wind. The horses were encased in frost from their breath and sweat that had frozen on them.

All the roads were completely covered over with drifting snow. As they traveled through the white-blanketed countryside, often they could not see where the road was, and allowed the horses free rein to find the way. Once in a while a strange black pile could be seen on the snow. Investigating one of these, they found that crows were sitting, one atop the other, trying to survive by sharing their modest warmth. The top layer of crows was already frozen to death, but had served to save some of the others insulated within the pile.

Several times a sleigh would be turned over on its side by a drift. When lucky, the children, packed in tightly with furs, would remain in the sleigh, but sometimes they would find themselves hurled into drifts. The coachman and teamsters would jump down to check the children, right the sleigh, pack the children once again with their furs and continue on.

The trip grew long and treacherous. The teamsters started to look concerned as the trip was taking longer than anticipated and the winter days were short. Unable to see familiar landmarks along the way in the whiteout conditions, they were afraid that they might be lost and traveling in circles. Everyone had heard of people dying in such circumstances. After several hours, one of the boys, frozen and tired, gave up, stating, "I've lost all hope." Since all the children were equally cold, his complaints met with little sympathy.

Sunset approached. The teamster's fear was becoming obvious. The coachman had stopped talking, intent only on his horses, the other sleighs and the snow in front of him. The fear of nightfall was underscored with the knowledge that starving timber wolves were out in packs of as many as fifty. Such a pack would not hesitate to attack the small caravan in the dark. Darkness started to descend on them. They were lost!

Out in the gloom of twilight the coachman suddenly recognized a peasant hut. It was close to the estate! With a powerful yell he pointed it out to the teamsters and cracked his whip. The fear that had only moments ago permeated the three sleighs was whisked away with the wind. The horses, although tired, picked up their pace as they recognized that they were coming closer to their stalls. Soon the manor was in sight where Jan and Marynia were anxiously watching through ice encrusted windows, awaiting the overdue sleighs. Everyone was happy to have the trip over. Servants helped Niula and the children remove their furs and gave them warm drinks to the chorus of excited, exhilarated renditions of the ride. The coachman and teamsters cared for the horses and joined relieved families in the midst of Easter preparations.

The kitchen staff had been working intensively for a week or more in preparation for the Easter repast. They were responsible for preparing food for the manor, for the administration, and for the parish pastor.

Experienced cooks used ancient recipes to prepare favorite delicacies: *babka,*[10] some of which were half a meter high, were baked in the huge oven; *mazurka,* flat chocolate cake covered with various nuts and dried fruit; tortes of various kinds; pickled vegetables; gelatins and pates from meats or fish; and whole pickled piglets, pheasants, hares and ducks. All were preserved within the coolness of the storehouse.

During the evening before Easter, a great table was placed at the end of the dining room. The table was decorated with small boxwood branches on top of an elaborately embroidered white tablecloth. Numerous cakes, meats, sausages and painted eggs were placed on it. There was enough food on this table for the family and guests to all be satisfied for several days. During the upcoming days the kitchen staff was given free time and did not cook.

Everyone fasted through the morning and awaited the arrival of the priest, Father Pietkiewicz, who came several kilometers from the *Wielkie* (Great) Ejsmonty Parish. Easter Mass was said amid festive singing in the chapel, led by Mr. Szemiot's wonderful deep voice. Many local people crowded the chapel for the celebration. They came not only from the estate but also from nearby villages and hamlets. After Mass, the priest blessed Easter foods bundled in scarves that had been brought by peasant women. Everyone then returned to their respective homes for the family Easter feast.

The priest accompanied Jan, Marynia, their family and guests back to the manor. He blessed the Easter table and then followed Jan on a quick tour of the house, blessing each room as they went. Jan led with the holy water and

---

[10]*Babka:* a cake rich with eggs and butter made especially for Easter.
[11]Aspergillum: brush used for sprinkling holy water.

the priest briskly followed, waving the aspergillum.[11] Marynia once overheard some of the younger children asking one another what Papa had done wrong. They had observed their father being hastily followed about the manor by the priest and thought that the priest was chasing Papa with what they thought was a switch.

While the blessing was taking place, Marynia was in the storehouse with her older daughters, distributing an assortment of meats, sausages, cakes and eggs to each administrator. Everyone then gathered in the salon.

Jan, taking a tray of peeled and sliced hard-boiled eggs, shared them with all those gathered and everyone wished one another a happy Easter. They then proceeded to the dining room. Unlike the rest of the year, there were no servants present to help. The table was set and meats cut. The only hot dish was borsch, which was drunk from cups. Each person took a plate, filling it with his or her choice of food.

Jan, a connoisseur of wines, made sure that there was an ample supply of good wines to be enjoyed. Children drank *kwas*. *Kwas* ("bitter") is a sweet but bitter, golden colored drink made from dried whole-meal black bread that is soaked in boiled water and then left for a few hours until cool. The liquid is then strained. Sugar, yeast and lemon juice are added to the liquid. After being allowed to sit for 24 hours, it is tightly corked and left in a cool place for three days. The contents, pressurized through fermentation, can explode, shooting the cork like champagne.

The meal was eaten slowly, over a long period, and especially enjoyed after the previous weeks of Lent. Everyone returned to the food table numerous times, tasting the many assorted dishes. The company was boisterous as everyone ate, discussed, argued, debated, told stories, and participated in indoor games, such as bridge and chess, that were played into the night.

Though everyone went to bed late Easter night, they were sure to be awakened early the next morning by the *dyngus* where boys, following old traditions, doused all the girls with water. Usually the boys tried to awake early, to catch the girls still sleeping. This erupted to a wholesale watering of everyone in sight and would continue throughout the day. Marynia disliked this custom! Concerned for the fine parquet floors in the manor's main rooms, she forbade these dousings. The traditional dousing, despite Marynia's objection, could not be stopped and continued in the children's wing and particularly outdoors.

After the deep cold of winter, spring was eagerly anticipated. During the first warm spells, ice on rivers would break, often with cannon-like booms. Thick blocks of ice shot into the air. Previously smooth surfaces of waterways were now blemished with ridges formed from irregular sheets of ice protruding at odd angles.

Occasionally, fish were caught in a sudden expulsion of ice and water. A young agricultural intern was once living on the estate. Out hunting, he shot what he thought was a hare among some brush. It turned out not to be a hare, but a sturgeon—more than two meters in length. It had been flung out of the water by one such explosion of water and ice. He brought it to the kitchen, dragging it along, holding the head over his shoulder. The kitchen, always happy to have some fresh fish, fed everyone with this one fish. It turned out that there was an added bonus from this sturgeon. She carried within her many kilograms of roe. Under Jan's direction, the roe was turned into caviar. Those with a taste for caviar enjoyed it enthusiastically.

CHAPTER 5

THE GREAT depression of 1929, felt around the world, also affected the great landowners in Europe. Jan's finances were in good standing. However, observing the severe impact the depression was having on others, he decided to reduce expenditures. One economic savings was to bring the children from the school in Poznan and to relocate their schooling to Grodno, the closest city to his estates. Once again, he rented a large apartment for them, bringing all the furnishings and other items from Poznan. Niula and one of the servants were also relocated. The boys went to Mickiewicza High School and the girls to Emilja Plater High School.

The children were very happy to be only a few hours bus ride away from home. The bus made it possible for them to go home whenever they wished. They could even make a one day visit that had previously been impossible with the long trip from Poznan.

The bus also enabled the sending of food to Grodno each week. Part of the shipment included a large can filled with fresh milk. In order to better keep it, the staff in Grodno boiled the milk to pasteurize it. The rich milk had a large amount of cream that the cook would skim for use in the kitchen. Adam, who loved this cream, would often help himself to it, to the consternation of the cook.

One day when the food and milk arrived from the estate, Adam spotted a pitcher of cream and stole toward it. His sister Ela saw and anticipated what he was going to do. She loved a good joke and saw the opportunity to get him. Ela sternly said, "I won't tell on you if you drink that cream, but you have to drink all of it." Thinking that he was going to get away with having the cream — and that his sister was being unusually cooperative that day — he agreed and took a big swig. He almost choked. Whenever the milk came to Grodno and was boiled, a thick, disgusting skin developed on top. It was this skin, that had been prepared for another use, that Adam now had to drink. Looking at his gloating sister, he knew there was no way out. Somehow, he managed to drink all of it!

Adam, in particular, enjoyed being able to go home on non-school days, as he, of all the children, loved the estate activities. Whenever at home, he rose early to go to see how work progressed in the fields, and enjoyed every opportunity to go hunting. He came to know the administrators, workers and their children and even each workhorse by name. He soon organized the workers' older children into teams and arranged various competitions with them. These competitions included bicycling, swimming, football (soccer) and various races.

One regular guest on the estate, a priest who taught religion in Bialystok, came to the estate each summer for his vacation. He was Father Mikolajan, but the children secretly called him *Pomidor* (Tomato), due to his ruddy complexion, round face and his eagerness to partake of finer foods. He was recruited by Adam to act as the umpire for the races. Adam requisitioned various items from family members and had Pomidor award these as prizes to the winners of various competitions.

While Adam loved the workings of the estates, it was Krzysztof, Jan's eldest son, who was heir to the estates. Adam was once asked what he wanted to do with his life. He said that he would love to run the estate. Hearing this, Jan and Marynia cautioned him that he must know that the estates were the inheritance of Krzysztof. Adam said, "I know that. Of course! Krzysztof will inherit the estates, but maybe he would hire me to help him run them. None of the children in the family loves and knows the estates as I do." Unfortunately neither Adam nor Krzysztof were to have the opportunity to explore such cooperation.

When he was a young man, Jan purchased one of the first automobiles in the region. He had a serious accident with this car. It overturned one day and he was covered with gasoline that ignited. Rescued by his companion, he was nevertheless severely burned. He lost the use of his right hand and was severely scarred over his upper right side, including some scarring around his right ear. Due to the loss of feeling in his right hand, he was unable to write, and so hired a secretary to assist him in his correspondence. He often prayed to Mary, the Mother of Jesus, to regain the use of his right hand, though doctors told him that he would never have use of it again.

JAN BISPING WHILE CHAMBERLAIN FOR POPE PIUS X, 1908

It was fashionable at that time to carry a cane. One day, after prayers, he reached out without thinking and grasped his cane with his right hand. Until now, he had been unable to hold his cane with that hand. Surprised, he visited his doctor who was unable to explain the sudden change. With the miraculously returned use of his hand, he was able to dismiss the secretary.

At age 24, Jan had married Ewa (Ewa Barbara Celina Maria Seweryna Olimpia Dusiacka Rudomino, 1876–1904). He soon lost her when she died, along with their stillborn child. He was broken-hearted. He requested that his brother, Kazimierz, take care of the estates for him. Knowing several languages and being a frequent traveler, Jan left for Italy where he became a Papal Chamberlain for Pope Leo XIII and later Pope Pius X. For the next several years he spent six months of each year thus serving the Pope, returning to his homeland each summer.

While in Italy, he was frequently invited to significant social events. Though Jan entertained entering the priesthood, he was considered a most eligible bachelor. He enjoyed the social interaction and, as was appropriate to his station, he became an active participant. His thoughts about entering the priesthood disconcerted his mother. There was a rumor that she requested the Pope to encourage him to re-marry and return to his rightful place in charge of the Majorat. One day Jan saw a beautiful young woman and whispered to a friend that, if he could marry a girl like that, he would give up any thought of becoming a priest. Much to his surprise, invited to celebrate Easter with the Polish community, he came face to face with her; they were introduced. She was a well-known Polish Princess, Marynia Zamoyski, widow of Prince Karol Radziwill. With her son Michal, she often stayed with her late husband's parents in Rome. She had regular private audiences with the Pope who was very sensitive to their tragic loss and enjoyed bouncing her child on his knee. As did many of the larger Polish families with means, she often spent the summer in Warsaw where she maintained an apartment, and the winter seasons in warmer climates.

Jan and Marynia had much in common. From the first meeting, as from the first sight of her, Jan thought that he would want to marry her. Jan soon became a regular guest at receptions Marynia held weekly at her grand Warsaw apartment. This relationship continued for several years before Jan asked Marynia for her hand in marriage. She accepted. Not wanting a grand wedding, they were married in Santa Croce Church, Florence on February 12, 1912. Their nuptials were registered in their parish in Rome, Santa Andrea

Della Fratre. Spending the rest of the season in Rome, they then returned together to Jan's estate, Massalany.

On their arrival at the estate they heard a story circulating in the community about their wedding. For several weeks prior to the wedding, the priest announced their wedding banns. In these announcements the complete names of the pair were given. Marynia had eighteen names: Maria Jozefa Zofia Izabela Rosa Franciszka Stanislawa Antonina Teresa Krystyna Karolina Ludwika Gryzella Stefania Michaelina Januara Dezydera Malgorzata. During mass, the often-tired peasant women might nod off a bit and not pay full attention as the priest read off the announcement in a monotone voice. As the priest read off Marynia's numerous names, some women were heard to recite "pray for us" after each name, confusing the announcement for a litany of saints.

Jan, now married, reassumed control of the estates. After only one year, the newly married couple met with tragedy. One afternoon, Jan was discussing business at a friend's estate. On their way to catch Jan's train to Warsaw, they were approached by two men who wanted to speak with his friend. Not wanting to miss the train, Jan took his leave. Later that evening Jan learned that his friend had been murdered. Notifying the police that they had been with the victim that afternoon, Jan described the two unknown men with whom he had left his friend.

Jan, much to his surprise, was subsequently accused and charged with the murder. Though initially arrested, the matter was to last many years during which time he was free on his own recognizance. During Poland's 1795 through 1915 partition, Poland was in Russian jurisdiction, and therefore it was a Russian court that initially found him guilty on the flimsy circumstantial evidence that he had been together with the victim. During the appeal, the First World War interrupted proceedings. Following the war, Poland was re-established as a nation. The matter was forgotten until an attorney discovered that the case was not fully resolved, and so it was reopened. At significant cost and with great difficulty, Jan secured the Russian court documents pertaining to the matter. The Polish court absolved him of any guilt, with the finding that there was no motive or proof of his guilt. Furthermore, the event occurred during the time that Jan had no use of his hand due to his earlier automobile accident and subsequent burns. The court acknowledged that it would have been impossible for Jan to have pulled the trigger of the gun that killed his friend.

Years later the family received information about a likely cause and guilty party for the murder. Jan's friend, the murder victim, owned a brick-works near Grodno. He had been approached to supply bricks for Russian fortifications for the defense against Germany, which were to be built nearby. In a meeting with a Russian general, a price was quoted. The general countered that the price could be raised if the bricks could be made without fully hardening them. Realizing that this was an attempt at sabotage, Jan's friend grabbed the general by the collar and ejected him out the door and down the stairs. Having thus dishonored the treasonous general, Jan's friend had signed his own death certificate. The murderer, years later, made a deathbed confession of his culpability.

During the years following his accusation, Jan and Marynia had several more children. Jan continued to run his estates. Busy with the estate and the children, and preoccupied with the distasteful legal matter, they did not venture far from the estate. Jan never returned to Italy again. Having resigned from further public service and social activities, he directed his energy to the care of his family and running the estates.

CHAPTER 6

WITH THE TREATY at Versailles in 1919, The Great World War — the war to end all wars — World War One came to an end. During this time the Russian Revolution started and the Czar of Russia, along with his entire family, was murdered. The Bolshevik revolutionaries, having succeeded at home, initiated their expansion to unify Europe under communist ideology. Jan's estates were continually being attacked and subverted by local Bolshevik gangs.

Learning one day that his estate was to come under imminent assault, he made the decision to flee. It was the worst possible time. Two of his children, Ela and Stas, were deathly ill with diphtheria. His wife was pregnant and due to deliver at any moment. There was nothing else to do. It was insane to stay any longer. Making arrangements for the two ill children to be cared for by one of the women of the manor, he loaded provisions in a wagon. With his three remaining children in the carriage with his wife, he joined the coachman at the boot to help steer the way to safety.

After a harsh, bumpy fifty-kilometer trip lasting a few days, they finally approached Bialystok city. The team was getting tired. They stopped to change teams. Jan went to inspect the horses and to talk to the coachman.

"How is she m'Lord?" asked the coachman, nodding toward the coach.

Allowing the trusted man to see his concern, Jan replied, "She is going to give birth soon." Seeing a wagon approach from the opposite direction, Jan motioned the young peasant driving it to stop and asked, "What is the situation in the city?"

The boy answered, "Not good, Sir. The city is devastated and full of refugees. I sold our potatoes, Sir, but there was no place to stay the night as I might normally. With all the people and disorder, the city has become dangerous." Jan asked if the boy knew of any place where they might stay. "As I said, everything is full." Seeing Jan's disappointment he hastened to add, "You may wish to stay in the old abandoned cabin down a way."

At that moment Jan was approached by the coachman, accompanied by the governess. They had been speaking in a hushed, urgent tone. "She is in labor, m'Lord. She will give birth soon," the coachman told Jan.

Looking at the coachman and the governess, Jan made a quick decision, saying, "Have this boy show you the cottage he spoke of and see if it will do."

Saddling one of the horses, the coachman helped the boy sit behind him and urged the tired horse to a trot toward the city. Over the next kilometer, they talked about the local situation. The city was apparently overrun with people from the east, telling terrifying stories at the hands of Bolsheviks. In Bialystok, hotels and any available rooms were all full, beyond capacity. The boy said that the cottage belonged to a friend of his father's and that no one had lived there for several years. He cautioned the coachman that, when he had passed the cottage earlier, he had noticed it was still in disrepair and empty. He had then thought to himself that the cottage must be in very poor condition not to be occupied under these difficult times.

The boy told the coachman to stop in front of a cabin. The coachman was happy to see a well cared for yard and smoke coming out of the chimney. Jumping off the horse, the boy said, "This is my uncle's home. He can help us." With that, he disappeared inside.

After a few minutes, an older man came out of the cabin and up to the coachman. As he approached, he threaded characteristic wooden pegs through loops of yarn, buttoning a warm heavy woolen coat. Removing his hat he said, "I hear your Lord needs a place for his wife to have a baby. The cottage this boy told you about is not suitable!"

The coachman got off his horse and shook the man's hand. "Can you suggest another place?"

The man, scratching his head, put his hat back on and looked about in the gray, snow-filled clouds. "There are no other places. Maybe he should try the city."

"Uncle," said the boy, "I just came from the city, and the place is totally overrun."

"Well, I'm sorry but I can't help you," said the man. Turning toward his cabin, he stopped, paused and then glanced back to the coachman. With a voice of understanding concern he said, "Let's go take a look at the old cottage and see what can be done."

Telling the boy to take care of the coachman's horse and to go in and get something hot from his aunt inside, the man set off saying, "It's this way." The coachman followed him for several minutes down a path covered by ice filled potholes. Finally the man passed through a broken gate and they entered a dark, cold, dilapidated cottage. The coachman reacted dejectedly. How could his Lord stay in this pigsty and the Lady birth a child in this filth? The man showed him a back room and seeing the coachman's disappointment he said, "The *piec* is broken, but my friend can fix it quickly and my wife and I can clean this up in a short time. If she is to have the baby now, there is no other place." The coachman reluctantly agreed and followed him to a nearby cottage. There, they arranged for the *piec* to be repaired. Returning to the man's home, they found the boy brushing the coachman's horse, obviously enjoying grooming such a fine animal.

Entering the cabin, they then talked with the man's wife. Having heard that the Lady was to deliver a child in the old cottage, she was already preparing, and started directing the man to join their children as they gathered supplies. She came up to the coachman and said confidently, "Don't worry, we will take care of everything. It won't be as luxurious as your Lord and Lady might be accustomed to, but it will be clean. I have helped our doctor with the birth of many children, noble and peasant; babies all come out the same way. I have already sent my son for the doctor."

With this, the coachman had the feeling that something might go well for the first time in some days. Thanking the man and the woman, he mounted the horse, helped the boy get on behind him once more and returned to report his findings and arrangements to Jan.

As the coachman approached the small caravan, he could see that they had set up a temporary camp to await his return. Marynia's capable servant girl was bending over a boiling pot atop a campfire. They had obviously made the best of an opportunity to rest and get something hot to drink. The teamster's son, whom Jan had asked to come along to drive the livestock, was watching the hobbled cows and horses as they contentedly munched on hay he had spread for them from the wagon. The teamster had a hammer out and was pounding on a wheel rim that had apparently loosened. As the sound of the hoofbeats of the coachman's horse reached the caravan, the girl looked up and called out to the coach. Jan came out of the coach and met the pair on the horse as they came to a stop. "We have everything arranged, and this boy must get home," the coachman said to Jan.

Jan reached into his pocket. Pulling out two coins, he held them out to the boy saying, "The teamster fed your horse some hay and I thank you for your time and help." Taking the coins as he thanked Jan, the boy mounted his wagon, giving his horse a whistle to head home.

Turning to the coachman Jan asked, "Well, what did you find?" As the coachman explained what he had found and arranged, Jan said, "It will have to do," and called out to the group, "We're off—we are taking the carriage and wagon ahead. Bring the livestock on down the road, a kilometer or so, until you see the carriage. Then set up camp." Anticipating this call, the teamster had his horses ready and hitched them to the wagon. As soon as Jan and the coachman were on the boot, the coachman snapped the whip, let out a whistle and, with a quick glance to see that the teamster was with them, drew the horses and carriage back onto the road. The teamster's son and the servant girl had already kicked out the fire, removed hobbles and were close behind, not wanting to be left too far behind in the cold and dark.

Deep in the frigid winter of 1919, a plain coarse wood wagon stopped before a dilapidated cottage. It was heavily laden with round-topped, leather-strapped trunks. An elegant carriage followed. Energetically bounding down upon the frozen dirt drive from the carriage's protective boot, where he had been seated beside the teamster, the anxious gentleman's words disappeared into a biting wind.

Swinging open the carriage door, he heard the passenger inside delicately ask, "Is this it?"

Not taking time for extensive explanation, he offered his hand and replied, "Yes, the locals are completing preparations for childbirth."

Taking his hand, she abandoned the carriage with difficulty. A magnificent fur coat enshrouded the fine features of her face and gently swiped a light dusting of fresh snow as they made their way to shelter. Three children, equally concealed in fur, alighted to follow her and scurried toward the low cottage closely followed by their governess.

They arrived as the door opened and a workman with tools in hand emerged from within. He simply stated to the gentleman, "The piec is fixed. We started a fire and it's starting to warm up inside."

The gentleman, his face instantly showing relief, expressed a heartfelt "Thank you!"

Thus our story began—the start of Terenia's life.

CHAPTER 7

Y FIRST MEMORIES were three years later, watching with great interest as Mama changed Ewa, her new baby. She stood at a large, heavy, light-colored, wooden changing chest, with shelves holding diapers and various clothes below and panels around the back and sides to protect the child. In the back a panel held powders, medicines, pins, etc. It stood in the baby's nursery situated between my parent's bedroom and the beginning of the children's wing.

I looked up as Mama took care of my sister high up on the changing chest, and mimicked her actions with my porcelain baby. My baby needed all the same care as did Ewa. She needed to be changed, fed, cleaned, dressed, played with and put to bed to rest, or for the night. She was a demanding baby and occupied all of my day, as did Ewa occupy Mama.

One day, my brother Jas, feeling jealous over my attention to my baby, hid her away. I searched single-mindedly, and finally found her. I took her to my mother to complain about Jas' maltreatment. Wanting to underscore the abuse he had perpetuated, I repeatedly struck the doll upon the ground. After a few moments of this cruel treatment, I realized in horror that the porcelain doll, with its beautiful face and fragile body, was destroyed.

The loss of my baby due to my tantrum, while vigorously demonstrating that my brother should not have touched her, was a great loss. Looking down at the broken porcelain in my hands, I realized that my "baby" was not a baby at all, but a porcelain doll that I had destroyed. The "baby" that I had cared for so tenderly, that I had now destroyed in a fit of anger at my brother, was no more. All that was left were broken pieces of porcelain, not my baby. Not my cherished baby. Only broken porcelain. I did not have a baby as Mama

LEFT TO RIGHT: ELA, MARYSIA, JAN HOLDING ADAM,
KRZYSZTOF, JAS, TERENIA, EWA, 1923

LEFT TO RIGHT: MARYSIA, KRZYSZTOF, ELA, JAS, TERENIA, EWA, ADAM, ANDRZEJ, AND PIOTR WITH NANNY, SUMMER 1925

had Ewa. All this time I had not been caring for a baby at all, but only playing with a porcelain doll. From that moment forward, I had no use for dolls.

Seeing my anguish at the loss of my doll that I had spent so many hours tenderly caring for, my parents soon gave me a new doll. Not realizing the transformation in my mind, they had tried to replace my baby, but I was not to be consoled with another porcelain doll. They were not able to understand that all I saw now was a doll—a thing of porcelain, not a baby—and I had no interest. They could not understand how I had changed and that I was no longer interested in make-believe with a make-believe baby.

No longer playing with dolls, I spent more time with my siblings within the children's wing. Each morning I would steal away and spend a few tender moments with Mama. She sat at an ice encrusted window, embroidering. I sat beside her and would ask her to draw pictures for me. She took a pencil and I would watch as she drew scenes we saw through the window: the dog house, the chapel, trees with enormous stork nests blowing in the frigid winds, the old folks home and workers with their horses or sleds. She sometimes drew my portrait. This sketchpad became my greatest treasure. I kept it carefully put away in my private chest, where it survived throughout my childhood.

When I was five years old the celebration of Andrzej's baptism was joined by the extended family. He was born on the 23rd of May 1924, with a normal delivery at home. As usual, Zosia, whom Mama had trained as a midwife in Warsaw, helped with the birth. My first indication that we would have another brother or sister in the household was with the arrival of Zosia. Later, we noticed that any time Zosia came to visit, soon afterward a new sibling appeared. With each birth, Papa came to us with the announcement, "Be happy, you have a new brother (or sister) whose name is...." This time it was Andrzej who was thus introduced to us.

Several weeks later in the summer, Grandfather (Mama's father, Andrzej Zamoyski), Uncle Franciszek (Mama's brother), and his cousin, Antek Brzozowski, came to visit. The parish priest came and we celebrated the baptism at the manor chapel in the main entry hall. I stood next to Grandfather. At one moment we were to cross ourselves with the sign of the cross. I was holding a prayer book in my right hand and since it was occupied, crossed myself with my left hand. At this moment, I chanced to look up at Grandfather and our eyes met. His look communicated, quite clearly, that I had made a mistake and that I was not to use my left hand while crossing myself. This experience stayed with me throughout my life.

Grandfather stood tall and erect. He, with his white beard, was very distinguished looking. Whenever I thought about Grandfather, whose name was

Andrzej, I thought that my brother Andrzej was named after him. Having heard much about Grandfather from Mama, I was very much in awe of him. He was well educated. A collector of historic documents, he was well versed in the history of Poland and its noble families and was always eager to talk about them. Mama was his oldest child. She valued time talking with him and grew to share his interest in history. As a young child I felt respect and admiration toward Grandfather. Uncle Franciszek, young, very tall and, I thought, the most pleasant and best looking uncle I had, was easy-going with a character very different from Grandfather. Unfortunately, this was to be the only time that I was to meet either of them.

When I was six years old, I had a great adventure. My parents went on a trip to Warsaw; I was able to accompany them. They were going to make purchases in preparation for Christmas. My excitement was only contained by the need to get ready. It seemed that we left before I was prepared for such an adventure.

The trip from Grodno to Warsaw was my first train ride. I had seen the train with its carriages and great bellowing steam engine in the station before. To actually ride on it was a new experience! We quietly climbed aboard with the help of a porter who took the bags and stowed them for us. To my astonishment, I watched as a pack of people attacked another wagon in an enthusiastic rush. Pointing this out to Papa, he explained that there were different classes of carriages. There were more people wanting to get on the other carriages, as they were less expensive. Since there were more people than seats, they were eager to be first to choose a seat.

Along the way we were served tea. I was curious to see the waiter lift a small table hinged below the window and set the tea upon it. Fascinated by the view flying by, I was pleased that we did not have to leave the window to drink our tea, but could continue to watch the riveting glimpses as we rode on. Occasional puffs of smoke and steam would pass by the window minimally obscuring forests, fields, villages and hamlets as we flashed by. We often passed lines of poles holding wires along the track. With interest I noted that the frequency with which we passed the poles changed as the train sped on. Soon I could anticipate stopping when the frequency with which we passed the poles would slow down.

After many hours we arrived at the Warsaw Central Station. It was crowded with masses of people briskly coming and going. I held onto Mama tightly. A porter, who was carrying our bags, led the way to a carriage. I was surprised to see a line of carriages waiting for us at the side of the station house. None of the drivers looked at all familiar and I imagined that Papa must have people waiting for him wherever he traveled. Closed within the carriage against the cold, I was able to watch the enormous buildings, the bustling streets with carriages, masses of people and buses with sparking wires atop them. I could not understand why everyone seemed to be in such a hurry. What could have happened? After what seemed to be a short trip, the carriage stopped before a large building and Mama said to me, "Here is my apartment. It is on the third floor." I looked up, bewildered, at the many layers of windows reaching high above me.

We filed into an entry and then all crowded into a tiny little room. I couldn't imagine why my parents had us in there, when suddenly, to a number of clicks and hums, the room started to shake. I was afraid and looked up, for reassurance, at my parents who appeared calm. Mama looked down at me, saw the uncertainty in my face, smiled and said, "This is an elevator. It will take us up to the third floor."

I had no idea what she was talking about. Before I could try to reason an explanation, the room stopped its shaking, although my stomach felt queasy. Papa opened the door and we seemed to be in another room. Now I was very puzzled. I looked over to where the door had been and now there was a window in its place. I looked out to the carriage, but it was gone! What would I do without my bags? Had the carriage left with our things? Walking over to the window and looking out to see where it could have gone, I suddenly realized that the road was far below! I jumped back in fright. Where were we?

"Come along, Terenia," Mama called from a doorway. I followed her into a beautiful room and she closed the door behind me.

We removed our coats and hung them in a large coat closet. Entering a salon, I went over and sat upon a beautiful, large, dark leather sofa. The room smelled wonderfully of leather and wool. There were two large overstuffed leather chairs opposite the sofa. Then I noticed the low table between the chairs. It was of dark wood. What fascinated me was that it had glass over its top that acted like a mirror reflecting the dark leather chairs and the paintings hung on the opposite walls.

I got up to look at the paintings, thinking about my sketchpad. I looked up at a painting depicting three wild-looking horses pulling a sleigh over the snow, driven by what looked like Papa. He was standing on the sleigh cracking a whip over the horses' heads. At that moment I realized that Mama was standing behind me, also looking at the painting. "Is that Papa?" I asked her, pointing at the painting.

"No," she said squatting down beside me still looking at it. "This is a very well known painting called *Trojka*.[12] Aren't the horses and driver wonderful? But that is not your Father." We examined the painting for some moments, together, in silence.

Just as I started to look at the other paintings, a woman entered and announced that our dinner was ready. "Ah, I am hungry and will eat with pleasure," Papa said rubbing his hands together.

Mama laughed, replying, "You sound just like your Brother Kazimierz." We ate a wonderful mushroom soup, *sznycel*,[13] potatoes and sauerkraut. This was followed by an assortment of small cakes.

"Try this one," Papa urged seeing that I couldn't make a decision from among the rich offerings. "It has *marcepan*[14] in it." I tried it. It reminded me of the chocolate candies we had sometimes, but this flavor filled me with delight. I ate it as slowly as I could to relish every tidbit. "Well?" Papa asked.

I turned to him with big eyes and answered, "Is everything in Warsaw this wonderful?," to which both of my parents heartily and good-naturedly laughed.

"You will enjoy your visit to Warsaw, I think," said Mama. "Come, now it is time for you to go to bed."

Papa lifted me up in his arms and I kissed him on both smiling cheeks. "Thank you, Papa, for bringing me with you to Warsaw," I said and he gave me a snug, firm hug.

"Sleep well, tomorrow will be a long day," he said. He set me down and I ran over to Mama's extended hand. She took me to a small bedroom that had in it a high, large bed. The fresh linen was turned down. We washed my hands in the bowl on the chest. I knelt on the rich, soft, Persian rug and said my nightly prayer. Thinking that I could not get to sleep, as I was too excited, I was surprised to wake up the next morning, not remembering having put my head on the pillow.

I awoke. My bed felt so comfortable and soft. It seemed that I must have awakened very early for I could not hear my brothers or sisters or the house staff. Opening my eyes, I realized that I was not in my room and the memories of the past day flooded to me. I stretched luxuriantly in the large bed, making sure that I did not get too close to the edge, for I remembered how high it was and did not want to fall out. The linen was so soft. Its edges were carefully and delicately embroidered. My room was dark, but I could see light

---

[12] *Trojka:* (Polish) a team of three horses.
[13] *Sznycel:* [schnitzel] a breaded cutlet of meat, typically pork.
[14] *Marcepan:* [marzipan, macaroon] almond paste.

coming from the doorjamb. Finding my robe on a chair next to the bed, I put it on and quietly opened the door. The window drapes were pulled open and the room was bathed in sunlight.

"Good morning, Miss Terenia," said the woman as she came from the kitchen. "I am just setting the table for you and your Mother's breakfast."

"Isn't Papa hungry?" I asked, just as Mama came into the room dressed in a brown jacket and skirt.

"Papa is already gone, Terenia," Mama told me. "We will eat now, you will dress and then we will go visit some of the family. Papa will join us at his Mother's apartment, where your Grandmother expects us for dinner."

For breakfast we had coffee with cream and small Kaiser rolls with jam and butter. Kaiser rolls were one of Papa's favorites, but I did not remember ever tasting such good ones at home. "We should bring some of these home with us for Papa," I thought. After breakfast Mama gave me a new dress to wear and told me to dress quickly. It had a very full skirt made of white and blue stripes, with a square neckline. Its puffy sleeves and neckline were finished with lace. The woman made a phone call to have a carriage sent round and we put on our furs. When the woman saw the carriage out front, Mama and I went out onto the landing.

Passing the elevator door, Mama said, "Let's go down the stairs." We approached an opening in the floor such as I had never seen before. In front of me were not the two or three steps we had at home, but steps that went on and on. I could see the expanse below through an open railing. Mama seemed to glide down these steps with ease, but I could not face such danger with the bravery Mama possessed. Hugging the wall, I decided that I could turn around and descend the stairs safely only by climbing down as I would a ladder. Thus I followed Mama. As I climbed down this way, I heard soft laughter erupt from below and Mama inquire as to the cause for the laughter.

"Look behind you," said a woman's playful voice, following which Mama's pleasant laugh joined the first.

"She has never seen a staircase like this before," explained Mama to the other woman. She was then beside me and grasped my hand. "Come, I will help you down the stairs." She said, "Hold the railing with your other hand." In this way I climbed down more stairs in a few minutes than I had previously descended during all of my life. It was amazing to see down the long flights and to look through windows at each landing to find the street getting closer and growing larger with each landing. At last we arrived at street level, where I recognized the entry door and the elevator that we had entered the day before. Now I realized that the small room was the "elevator" that had taken us up to what Mama had called the "third floor." Thus we had avoided these stairs. Despite the shaking of that elevator room and the queasy feeling it gave my stomach, I preferred it to the endless, hazardous stairs.

Leaving the building, Mama told the carriage driver where we wanted to go. He tipped his hat, opened the door for us and we climbed in. I looked around inside the carriage. It was not at all as nice as the one we used at home. I could see that it was well worn with use. The leather seats, although oiled, were cracked, and depressions could be seen where people had sat. The floor was swept, but nevertheless covered with mud or soil. Looking out, I could see the towering buildings on all sides and imagined that they also must have three floors and endless stairs, as did Mama's apartment house. Just as I had noticed them doing yesterday, people seemed to be rushing about, as though something urgent had occurred. We did not go far before the carriage came to a stop and the driver opened our door. Opening the drawstrings on a small purse, Mama passed coins to the driver as he unfolded a step stool which we used to disembark from the carriage. He tipped his hat once more and we entered a shop where a boy, dressed in a bright coat, knickers, woolen socks and hat, opened the door for us.

The high ceilinged room was well lit with electric lights, similar to those that we had at home that worked when the distillery operated. I thought that they must have a big distillery working here, as they had so many lights. Then I saw the clothes! Before we got to the center of the room, we passed more clothes than our entire family had, and we continued on. We entered room after room, each filled with enough clothing to give each of Papa's workers several sets of clothing and more. Even if all the people we saw on the streets were to come in, they could all dress in these clothes and surely they could not use them all. Mama would pause briefly at various racks, glancing at one article or another, but did not stop to examine anything carefully. Coming to a counter, she asked the man behind it to show her a silk scarf. Taking it from him, she looked it over with a smile on her face. Passing it back to him she asked the man to package it for her, as she continued along the counter.

In this fashion she selected several items, and after paying for them, she placed them in a light leather bag she had been carrying. After visiting several shops, the bag started to bulge. When we entered another building and ascended a wide sweeping marble staircase, I held Mama's hand firmly, but found that the going up was not nearly as bad as going down had been in Mama's building.

We visited my Aunt Maria "Teresa" Zamoyski whom I had met the previous Easter at our home. Mama and she talked and laughed together. Mother gave her one of the small packages she had purchased earlier, and I quietly accepted a glass of fruit juice and selected another of the wonderful marzipan pastries just like the one Papa had suggested I try last night. It appeared to be identical, with the same wonderful taste.

After a short visit we departed with warm hugs and kisses. My aunt complimented me and thanked me for sitting so quietly and politely while they talked. The trip down the stairs was not as easy as going up had been. Holding Mama's hand firmly with one hand, the banister with the other, I still found the descent to be much easier than my first experience.

After a long carriage drive, during which Mama pointed out many big buildings, churches, monuments and historic sights, we finally arrived at Grandmother's apartment. She, Helena Holynski Bisping, was very old. Her lady-in-waiting lived with her and took care of all her household needs. Mama told me that this woman was known for her knowledge of how to prepare thirty different delicious kinds of *kasza*.[15] She must, indeed, have been very good because, although I hated *kasza,* the dishes she prepared were good.

My grandmother was very energetic, not like most old people I had seen. Mama explained that Grandmother had been an army nurse during the World War. In 1919 she was a prime member of the organizing committee for the Polish Red Cross and then elected as Vice President. That same year, she traveled to Geneva and obtained accreditation by the International Red Cross and then to Paris where French aristocracy responded to her by granting significant funds supporting the Polish Red Cross. Grandmother had much to tell about her recent exciting trip to America where she talked to the American president[16] who promised her to help Poland. The trip entailed two long ship voyages, each of which took longer than her stay. She was very excited about what she had seen there; the tall buildings, the vibrant lifestyles and the wealth of the nation were impressive.

Grandmother was very happy to see me and treated me as an adult, not as a child. It was wonderful to be made to feel so grown up; that is, not being told to be quiet, or even to go and play with some toys. I had expected to find Grandmother's apartment to be very grand, but to my surprise it was not as nice as Mother's apartment. She had a radio playing all of the time. This surprised me as Papa only played his radio at certain times. I asked Grandmother why the radio was playing and she replied that it kept her company. I thought

---

[15] *Kasza:* (Polish) cereal, porridge; grain cut and prepared in various warm dishes.
[16] Calvin Coolidge (1872–1933), 30th U.S. president (1923–1929).

TERENIA'S GRANDMOTHER, HELENA HOLYNSKI BISPING,
ONE OF THE FOUNDERS OF POLISH RED CROSS

that it was very funny to have a radio as company, but sad to think that while we had so much activity at home, here in this huge city, she felt so alone.

It was not long before Papa came and we sat down to dinner. I was very happy when I saw Grandmother's woman serve us *kwas,* but to my disappointment the *kwas* was terrible! This was especially disappointing as I was very thirsty from all the walking around the busy stores and climbing all the stairs. Later, when I told Mama that Grandmother's *kwas* was so horrible, she explained that it was not *kwas* at all, but beer.

The next morning the sun shone and although there was some snow on the ground, there was no wind and it was warm outside. Papa said that today he would take us on a tour of the center of the city. I was very excited to have Papa show it to us. He started by explaining that the city was started in the thirteenth century when many people lived there along the Wisla River. They built fortifications to protect themselves from various marauders. Showing us a statue of a mermaid, a beautiful woman naked down to her waist but with scales from that point to the end of her tail, Papa told me that she had been the symbol of Warsaw from its early days.

We walked through the squares and shops by the Royal Castle. A statue of King Zygmunt III Waza adorned the pillar in front. In 1596 he established Warsaw as the third capital of Poland (after Gniezno and Krakow). I noticed that many shops and restaurants had interesting metal signs hung outside. From their profile I tried to guess what was inside. A sign in the shape of a rooster turned out to be a restaurant. A loaf of bread designated a baker and a boot a cobbler. We saw many churches, but most memorable was the Cathedral of the Holy Cross with its beautiful statue of Christ carrying the cross. There was so much to see, but I was happy when Papa told us it was time to go back. I was very tired and fell asleep instantly amid the comfortable, soft linen.

The next morning Papa left early again. "What are we going to do today, Mama?" I asked.

"We will do some more shopping," she replied. We ate a quick breakfast and departed. I was very proud of how I could go down the stairs without any problem now. I barely needed to hold Mama's hand, but held onto the banister firmly.

The first store was filled with fabric, beautiful lace, embroidery and threads, in all colors. Two women helped Mama choose many bolts of material, which she ordered to be sent to her apartment. They seemed very excited to be helping her. I thought about how happy the servant girls would be to receive the bolts on Christmas Eve. We went out after a long time and Mother asked if I would like to stop and have a treat. "Oh yes, Mama!" I was quick to reply.

We entered a beautiful, large building near a big intersection. It was seven levels high with ornate rockwork and many windows across its face. Many carriages traveled around a circle in the middle of the wide cross street before the building. I could not understand how they knew when to stop going around the circle and in which direction to head. We entered through large oak doors under an arch. Though the doors must have been quite heavy, Mama did not seem to have any trouble opening them for us. I asked Mama whose home this was. She replied that this was the Polonia Palace Hotel, built and owned by Konstantin Przezdziecki, a family friend. We entered, gave our coats to a woman just inside the door who paid Mama with a metal disc. I was very surprised that Mama was selling our coats and wondered what we would do when we left, as it was a little colder today. Inside, through a passageway to the right, there was a long desk. A man in uniform came up and asked if he could be of assistance. He must have been a general, for his uniform was impressive. Thanking him, she indicated that this was my first time in the hotel and she was showing me around.

We went back through the passage once more and turned right into an enormous dining room with a beautiful inlaid marble floor. Tall, two-level-high walls were richly painted and illuminated with many electric lights. There was a veranda on each end. Above us, as high as a tree would reach, was a glass ceiling. A man led us up a few stairs, past heavy drapes, to an alcove on one side of the room. We were seated at a small table. On the main floor, from which we had just come, were over a dozen such tables at which small groups of people sat. Several tables had one man seated, often reading a newspaper while drinking a cup of coffee.

One man was particularly peculiar. He had long, dark, straight hair in a ponytail! Looking at him, I suddenly noticed that the poor man must have been somehow inflicted as a child. His eyes were slanted, almost closed and very long. He also looked ill, as he was entirely yellow in color. Asking Mama if she had seen the strange man, she, without turning around, said, "He is a China-man, but Terenia, it is not polite to stare."

A waiter soon brought Mama some coffee and fruit juice for me. Then he brought a large tray covered with fabulous small cakes. I noticed the same marzipan cake, was about to ask for it, when I saw a chocolate covered cheesecake, my long time favorite. I chose that instead and Mama had a slice of a tall, multi-layered chocolate torte. We ate our dessert in silence, enjoying each bite. We each then had another drink and I asked Mama what she thought

ADVERTISEMENT FOR THE POLONIA PALACE HOTEL, WARSAW, 1927.
THIS ADVERTISEMENT APPEARED IN A HOTELIER'S AND
RESTAURANTEUR'S PROFESSIONAL PUBLICATION.
NOTE THE USE OF BOTH POLISH AND FRENCH;
FRENCH WAS THE COMMON LANGUAGE AMONG
EDUCATED EUROPEANS.

the rest of the family was doing back at home. "Will you have many things to tell about when we return?" she asked.

"Yes!" I enthusiastically replied, "Especially about all the stairs!" to which she laughed joyfully. She then said that we would return to the apartment and have a nap. That evening we were going to the theater and then later we would have to catch the train back home to our estate.

After I had taken a nap, Papa returned and we dressed for the evening. I did not understand what was being talked about during the play, but it was very funny to see my parents looking at each other and laughing hysterically. Papa had tears rolling down his cheeks. It was nice to see them so happy. We had to rush out before it was finished to catch our train home. The woman from Mama's apartment was directing porters on loading the many valises and trunks onto the train. We said our farewells and she invited me to return to Warsaw again soon. My bed was made on the train and I fell asleep before it left the station for home, Massalany.

CHAPTER 8

ONE DAY that next spring, a big commotion commenced. Several wagons pulled up to the house and unloaded many large trunks and crates. Mama, in particular, seemed to be extremely preoccupied with their arrival. It seemed that all the household staff went to work unpacking. We younger children stayed in our rooms within the children's wing as the hubbub whirled throughout the rest of the house. Although we were quite curious about the strange packages, our parents kept busy and put off any answers. This commotion stretched out for a number of days. It soon became monotonous to us. As young children we were involved in daily matters and were somewhat upset that our parents were so involved in dealing with the arrivals that they seemed to have forgotten about us. We were not allowed into the rest of the house during these days, stuck in our quarters. We missed spending time with Papa and Mama. Mama was not playing the piano that we enjoyed listening to so much. We even noticed that Papa was not going out to the fields as he normally did. Those wagonloads had created havoc in our lives and we were somewhat disgusted with it all.

After almost a week, Papa suddenly appeared in our dining room just as we were finishing our lunch. "Get cleaned up, wash your hands and come with me. I have something to show you." This was quite unusual. We scurried about and washed up, realizing that we would, at long last, learn what had been going on. The governess seemed to take particular care that we washed our hands thoroughly.

As we followed our father and walked through the house, we immediately noticed that everything had changed. We entered the small salon that had been so familiar. We had spent so many hours here, often watching as Mama

SALON OF MASSALANY MANOR

SALON OF MASSALANY MANOR

did her embroidery and made drawings in my book. The room had been transformed! From the ceiling hung a large, beautiful crystal chandelier. The many candles on it were lit, bringing the entire room alive, radiating with the many reflections and refraction off and through the leaded glass prisms. The wall to the large salon across from us was adorned with an enormous painting, which Papa told us depicted the return of Napoleon's army after its defeat in Russia. "It was painted by the well known Polish painter, Juliusz Kossak," he told us.

Papa told us that Kossak had painted this to memorialize my great-great-grandfather (Adam Bisping, 1782–1858) for his support of Napoleon. During those times, Poland was divided and subjugated, with this part we lived in under Russian control. In 1812, Napoleon offered to free Poland if it assisted in his campaign against the Russians. A Polish patriot, Adam privately raised, financed, trained and led an army division against the Russians under Napoleon.

It was hard to tear our eyes off this painting that demanded our sympathy for those tragic souls depicted within it. My great-great-grandfather sat upon his horse backed by his mounted division. An unending column of French troops dragged itself home, defeated, not so much by Russian troops as by the Russian winter. The troops, if they could still be called an army, staggered home, dying along the way, frozen in the ice and snow. Adam's division, familiar with these winter conditions, guarded the retreat of the Frenchmen unaccustomed to such harsh realities.

To the right of Kossak's painting, past the door to the grand salon, was a large dark leather overstuffed chair that was to be Papa's favorite place to sit from that time forward. I was to bring him many cups of coffee as he sat there reading his newspaper. The chair was sided with a small table upon which he kept a few books, newspapers and a pack of cigarettes. The chair was in the corner, kept warm by the *piec* next to it, which made up part of the side wall between this small salon and my parent's bedroom.

Opposite the painting, where a large window looked out upon the entrance lane, a large desk now rested under the window. Mama used this desk for the next several years as she kept charge of the estate's financial books. From where she sat she could look out the large windows, left toward the entrance lane, or ahead out to the front. That window looked upon the entrance to the house and across the lake to the chapel and other buildings. Through that window we watched many beautiful sunsets reflected in the still waters of our small lake.

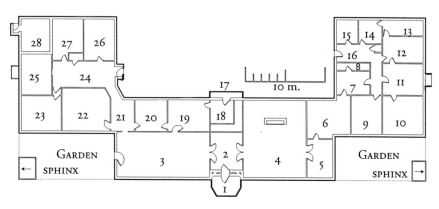

1 Veranda
2 Main Entry Hall
3 Dining Room
4 Grand Salon
5 Small Salon
6 Parent's Bedroom
7 Boudoir
8 Boudoir Bathroom
9 Baby/Children's Room
10 Children's Room
11 Children's Dining Room
12 Children's Room
13 Governess' Room
14 Servant Girls' Room

15 Wardrobe Room
16 Hall, Children's Wing
17 Rear Drive
18 Service Entry Hall
19 Credenza
20 Butler's Room
21 Anteroom
22 Library and Papa's Office
23 Records Room
24 Guest Wing Hall
25 "Pomidor's" Room
26 Blue Room
27 Rose Room
28 Student's Room

PLAN OF MASSALANY MANOR, CA. 1939

Papa next took us to the grand salon. Exquisite Persian rugs were laid to the left and right on the beautiful multicolored parquet floor. The parquet seemed to divide the room into two. On the left, the smaller northwestern side, which had two windows overlooking the entry drive and lake, stood a heavy, oak, tri-legged table resting on the rug with claw and ball feet. Two overstuffed chairs were beside the table. Between the windows was a mid-sized sofa. On the southeast side of the room was a large, oval, mahogany table surrounded by eight chairs. The table was covered with a Turkish tapestry, as was another mid-sized sofa on the far side. Illuminating the room was a large ornamental alcohol lamp that stood on the table. A large fireplace further divided this side of the room. Another great chandelier hung from the ceiling that enhanced the room with soft candlelight dancing from amongst the crystals. A three-part wooden ornamental screen filled the gap between the fireplace and the wall. Beyond the screen was Mama's grand piano. The fireplace itself was screened with a glass crystal panel onto which was etched the family crest. On the far right wall were two marble Louis XIV-style side tables. On them were a number of books and bronzes. Inset in this wall was a long sofa, within the area that we called the "arcade." It was here that we would sit to enjoy Mama playing the piano. Two windows allowed a northwest view of the back courtyard from Mama's piano and the arcade.

The walls of this grand salon hosted numerous paintings. Papa took us around the room and described a few of them. To the right of the doors, facing the small salon, was the painting *Branka* by the 19th century Monachium German painter, Jozef Brandt. It was purchased by the second Ordynat, Jan, Papa's uncle. It depicts a maiden tied to a pillar next to a Turkish tent. A woman at her feet, holds the maiden's legs in trepidation, as heathen Turkish soldiers throw dice to see which will claim this spoil of a battle. On the opposite wall was a Julain Falat watercolor depicting a man standing in a wagon driving three horses abreast in the traditional Russian way. It was also purchased from the artist in Krakow by Papa's uncle, my great-uncle, Jan Bisping.

To the left of the doors, facing the small salon was the life-sized painting depicting Papa's first wife, Ewa. She, along with their first child, Adam, died during delivery. Papa paused silently when he looked at the painting. After a long moment, we looked next at a painting of my great-grandmother, Leontyna, who was very beautiful. She had died at the age of thirty-seven of tuberculosis. Beside it was a small painting that Papa told us he had purchased in Italy from the artist Siemiradzki. It depicted an intense scene of a young woman tied to the back of a bull as Nero Claudius Caesar, Emperor of Rome, persecuted the Christians.

PAINTING OF EVA DUSIACKA RUDOMINO BISPING (1876–1904),
FIRST WIFE OF JAN BISPING

The scene was similar to an episode described in Sienkiewicz's book, *Quo Vadis,* for which Sienkiewicz received the Nobel Prize. Papa told us that Siemiradzki then painted a wall-sized duplication of the scene in Warsaw, which was widely acclaimed. A controversy erupted when Sienkiewicz claimed that his book inspired the painting that hung here in our grand salon. Siemiradzki argued that he had come up with the dramatic scene prior to the book being published. Siemiradzki won the debate based on this work that Papa was showing us.

"Suddenly a deafening noise of trumpets arose, and at this signal a grating opened opposite the imperial box, and into the arena rushed, amid the shouts of the people, an enormous German bull, bearing on his horns the naked body of a woman.

"Lygia! Lygia!" cried Vinitius.

Then he seized his hair near the temples, writhed like a man wounded by a spear, and in a hoarse voice cried out:

"I believe! I believe! Grant a miracle, O Christ!"

He was not aware that Petronius, at that moment, covered his head with a toga. He thought that death or agony had covered his eyes. He did not look. He did not see. A feeling of awful emptiness seized him. No thought remained in his head, only his lips repeated, as if in delirium: "I believe! I believe!"

Suddenly the amphitheatre was hushed. The Augustans rose in their seats as one man, for something uncommon had happened in the arena. The Lygian, humble and ready to die, seeing his princess on the horns of the wild beast, sprang up as if burned by fire, and bending forward, rushed toward the frenzied animal.

Cries of astonishment were heard on all sides. The Lygian overtook in a twinkling the raging bull, and seized him by the horns.

"Look!" cried Petronius, unveiling the head of Vinitius. Vinitius raised his face, pale as a sheet, and he looked at the arena with a glassy, vacant stare.

Everyone held his breath. In the amphitheatre a fly might have been heard. People could not believe their own eyes. Never before was seen anything like this.

The Lygian held the wild beast by the horns. His feet were buried in the sand to his ankles. His back was bent like a bow. His head was hidden between his shoulders. The muscles swelled on his arms so that the skin seemed to crack from the pressure, but he stopped the bull on the spot. The man and the brute remained so motionless that the spectators seemed to look at a picture representing a deed of Hercules or Theseus, or a group cut in stone. But in that apparent repose was evident the terrible exertion of two struggling forces. The bull as well as the man sank his feet deep into the sand, and his dark, shaggy body was so curved that it resembled a huge ball. Which would first be exhausted? Which first would yield? This was the question which at the moment was of greater importance to the spectators than their own fate, than that of Rome and its rule over the world. The Lygian, in their eyes, was a demi-god, worthy of admiration and statues. Caesar himself arose. He and Tigellinus, hearing of the strength of this man, had purposely prepared the spectacle, and laughing to each other, has said: "Let the slayer of Croto vanquish the bull chosen by us." But now they looked with amazement at the picture before them, hardly believing that it could be real. There were some of the spectators who had raised their arms and remained in this attitude. Sweat poured down the faces of others, as if they themselves were struggling with the animal. In the circus nothing was heard save the hiss of the flames in the lamps and the crackle of the torches. Words died in the throats of the spectators, but their hearts beat against their breasts as if to split them. It seemed to all that the struggle was lasting for ages.

But the man and the brute continued motionless in their terrible struggle. They seemed rooted in the earth.

Suddenly there reverberated through the arena a muffled roar, and then a shout arose from the spectators and then again silence fell. The people saw as in a dream that the monstrous head of the bull was twisting around in the iron grasp of the barbarian. The Lygian's face, neck and arms grew purple, his back curved still more. He was evidently rallying the rest of his superhuman strength. But he could not stand the strain much longer.

Gradually the groans of the bull grew hoarser and duller and more painful as they mingled with the whistling breath of the giant. The head of the brute was twisted more and more. A long, foaming tongue protruded from its muzzle. Next instant the crack of breaking bones reached the ears of the nearest spectators; then the beast sunk to the earth with a broken neck.

In a twinkling the giant slipped the cords from the horns of the bull, and, panting, raised the maiden in his arms. His face had paled, his hair was matted with sweat, his arms and shoulders were wet as though with

> *water. For a moment he stood as if he were scarce conscious, then he lifted*
> *his eyes and gazed around the amphitheatre.*
> *The immense audience had gone wild."*[17]

Eager to see what more was done, we all moved to the entrance hall. To the left was the main entrance. The double sets of large entrance doors had glass panels allowing light to flow within. Papa always kept these doors unlocked, thinking that keeping things locked just encouraged people to want to break in to see what was being protected. We often spent time after dinner outside on the rounded, covered veranda enjoying cool evenings overlooking the lake. To the far right of the entrance hall was a large closet which, when its doors were opened, exposed an altar within. Here the children were baptized and occasionally mass was celebrated. To the right and left of these doors were large oval mahogany tables. Guests would usually place hats or canes—which were very much in style—on the table to the right which afforded them the opportunity to check their appearance in the large silvered mirror hung on the wall behind. The tops of the tables could be lifted to expose a recess inside. A second table, on the left, was used to keep priest's vestments needed for the various ceremonies.

Ahead was another set of the large doors. All these large sets of doors were open, creating one large suite of the many large rooms. We moved ahead to the dining room. The great expandable table with its many chairs stood there, as it had all along, with the buffet and china closets. Now they were filled and covered with porcelain, silver and crystal. On a table, next to the wall before the door to the credenza, were two large silver samovars. Charcoal burned slowly in their inner container keeping tea hot. Mama never liked to use these samovars as the Russian tradition did not appeal to her.

Beyond the credenza door in the middle of the wall was a large, tall Gdansk buffet. Only Papa had a key to this buffet. He kept within it liqueurs, imported delicacies and spices. We would often see Papa have himself a small drink from the selection of bottles prior to dinner. As small children we rarely ate in this dining room. Occasionally we were admitted to be with the adults, but should one of us be very unreasonable and misbehave, Papa might set us up high upon his buffet until we calmed down.

The dining room walls were decorated with several family portraits from earlier generations. These were copies of the originals that hung at Uncle Ka-

---

[17]Henryk Sienkiewicz, *Quo Vadis*, translated from the Polish by S. A. Binion ca. 1897.

zimierz Bisping's estate. I rather disliked them, thinking that my uncle's originals were far better. At the far right wall was the door to a large hallway, or anteroom, with its tall closets that took up the entire wall from floor to ceiling. Here various small items needed for the estate were kept. It was where Papa met with individuals who had some minor business to discuss and where he would plan the activities of the next day with the estate steward.

From the dining room and into the credenza, a door to the left led to the butler's room. Ahead was a passage to the guest wing hallway through which to the left was Papa's library. Entering the library, we saw that the glassed shelves were now laden with rare and prized books. Glassed-in shelves topped closed cupboards. Papa withdrew from one of these low cupboards a rolled-up Juliusz Kossak painting of my great-great-grandfather Adam, depicting him hunting upon a horse with his dogs around him. Papa told us that the painting captured his great-grandfather's true character. He had loved hunting so much that to hunting he dedicated—and almost lost—what was left of his entire fortune after his unfruitful venture supporting Napoleon.

Papa showed us official documents and the family archives. The oldest of these documents, dated 1609 in Prague, confirmed the family's nobility and described its crest with the official seal of Emperor Rudolf II Habsburg. Another document was the act, dated February 23, 1635 with the seal of the Polish King Wladyslaw IV, granting the family Great Smolensk territories with Fort Starodubie, obligating the family's defense against Muscovites and Cossacks. Papa told us how these territories had been taken over by Russia. As the family wished to maintain its Polish identity and did not accept Russian citizenship, the family also lost the territories. Poland gave the family two small granges, wanting to recognize the family's losses, and gave assurance that if ever Poland should recover these territories that they would be returned to the family. Within the archives were my great-grandfather's memoirs about his active life.[18] Great-grandfather Jan was the second Ordynat. During his extensive travels he accumulated many valuable paintings, books and treasures that Papa was now showing us. Papa also showed us Jan's narrated journals of

---

[18]Great-grandfather Jan's memoirs, property of the Ordynat, were hand copied by Mama, with the authorization of Papa, as the Ordynat. She laboriously made two copies which were given to Papa's brother and sister, Uncle Kazimierz and Aunt Elzbieta "Lizia" Kossakowski, on their respective twenty-fifth wedding anniversaries. Jan's original and Kazimierz's copy were lost during World War II. Lizia passed her copy to my oldest brother, Krzysztof, after the war. He gave the copy to a person who was to duplicate them, but this person entrusted with their care stole them. Luckily, with much effort, Krzysztof was eventually able to track them down in an antiquarian where they were recovered. To assure that these documents would survive, he was able to make a few copies, which he distributed to his siblings and the original copy was returned to Aunt Lizia.

his travels, during which he had broad contact with distant family and many interesting people and places.

The journals kept by our Aunt Natalja, wife of General Kicki, were also here, a part of the family archives. She had been by her husband's side documenting the Polish November insurrection of 1830. Present with her husband, who was one of the chiefs in command that planned and carried out the insurrection, these documents were some of the best-kept chronicles of the insurrection. General Kicki died in battle and the insurrection failed. Natalja continued her journals well into the January insurrection of 1860.[19]

In the library's far right corner was a fireplace over which hung a large framed picture of Papa, dressed in his Chamberlain uniform as he served the Popes in Italy. On the mantle was a photograph of Mama's beloved cousin, Zita de Bourbon-Parma, wife of Emperor Karol I Habsburg of Austria, King of Hungary, who abdicated in 1918. When Papa showed us this photograph, Mama told us how it had saved the archives and the library during the German occupation at the time of the Great War. The chief German officer of the occupying Austrian forces came to the house. While in the library, he requested some "books to read." Mama, always efficiently keeping track of estate properties, asked him to sign for them, which he did with a sarcastic grin. Looking around, pointing out Zita's photograph, he asked who she was. It was explained to him that this was Mama's close cousin, the emperor's wife. The officer stiffened visibly. He was under the command of the emperor and now recognized whose family picture he was looking at and the potential peril he was exposed to. His attitude changed immediately and he departed in haste. The next day the officer returned the books, making sure that the return was noted in Mama's record, never again asking for more books.

Between the library windows overlooking the lake, on the left side of the room was a large chest over which were the portraits of the founders of the majorat. Under the second window was Papa's large desk, which was always covered with a mass of assorted papers that we were not allowed to touch. Beyond the desk was a chest where he kept his arms and ammunition. On the floor by the desk were bags of nuts and proof bottles from the distillery. The library was the only room in the house where the walls were not of plaster but finished with wood. Mama kept all the estate financial records here in this, the quietest room in the house.

---

[19] Natalja Kicki's journals, property of the Ordynat, were later prepared for publication in 1939. Just as they were to be released, the war came and the publication was destroyed. An unauthorized printing suddenly appeared, to the surprise of the family, released by the communists (PAX) in 1972. The unauthorized printing was incomplete as a portion, still undergoing final proofing, was held by the family.

Passing through two sets of doors (between which we would sometimes hide) we entered the entry hall of the guest wing. The guest wing was composed of four rooms, though one of them was accessible only from the outside. Different guests or older family members occupied these rooms periodically. One room we called "Pomidor's room," as Father Mikolajan was often a guest here. Hanging within this room was a large portrait of the first Ordynat, Aleksander. We all feared this portrait, for Aleksander's eyes followed us wherever we were within his sight. We later noticed that Aleksander's eyes did not seem to bother Pomidor, but thought that maybe Aleksander's eyes did not follow Pomidor as they did us.

Along the wall of the guest wing hallway was an enormous closet filled with winter fur coats. In two low chests were various heavy coverings used in carriages. Above these chests were large elk and moose antlers upon which coats and hats were hung. We went outside for the quick 25-meter walk across nicely raked gravel to the children's wing.

Entering the children's wing, we passed the small hand water pump on the right and the wardrobe room on the left where all the linen, tablecloths with their various crests, and miscellaneous clothing were stored. Here the dirty linen was tossed into chest-high, wide baskets. Every Wednesday the chief laundry woman brought in the clean linen. She checked a list to be sure that everything was accounted for and then distributed or stored each item. She then made a list of the dirty linen in the baskets, double checked the list and then took the dirty items to the laundry building situated on the entry drive.

The next room on the left, after the wardrobe room, was a servant girl's room. Ahead was the children's room. An interior door to the left led to the governess' room in the north corner of the manor. Between the servant girl's room and the children's room was a small door to a toilet. The hall turned to the right and on the right side wall was an entry to Mama's boudoir. The door to the children's dining room was in the center of this hall opposite the door to Mama's boudoir. Once inside the children's dining room, on the left was a door to the children's room. On the opposite side, was another large children's room in the southeast corner of the wing. This corner room also had a door into another children's room that could also be reached through a door at the end of the hall of the children's wing.

My parent's room was in the juncture between the children's wing and the manor's main section. To get from the children's wing to the main section without going outside, it was necessary to pass through Mama's boudoir, my parent's room, and then through the small salon into the large salon. The boudoir served a number of purposes. My parent's clothing was stored here and this is where they dressed. Each morning the cook would come here to discuss the menu for the day with Mama. Just past the boudoir was a full, large bathroom. It was the manor's best bathroom, with the only true tub in the house. In the bathroom was a large, heavy, metal plate on the floor which, when raised, allowed access to the wine cellar, the only basement area of the building. Here Papa stored fine champagnes, wines and liqueurs.

We passed through to the small salon, concluding our tour. After the children were served light tea and Mama and Papa coffee, Papa had the staff close the doors so that they would not disturb us. Mama started answering our questions about where all of these family heirlooms had come from.

CHAPTER 9

THROUGHOUT recorded history, Poland had been situated at the crossroads between north and south and east and west. The roads north and south, known as the "amber way" had been a source of commerce, and thus wealth, for Poland. Trade passed back and forth from the northern Scandinavian countries, crossed the Baltic Sea, passed through the amber trading centers near Gdansk, continued to the ancient, valuable salt mines near Krakow and progressed southward through south-central Europe to the Middle East and on to Persia with its spices, jewelry and exotics. Poland's main surface area is flat, rich agricultural and forestlands, providing foodstuffs and wood exported east and west. Its neighbors, particularly Germany and Russia, provided wealth through trade but also a constant threat. Poland's neighbors coveted her wealth and terrain. Innumerable attacks and invasions occurred throughout history. First one neighbor would attack, than another—and sometimes in multiples.

Prehistoric Slavic peoples, distinct from Germanic, southern or western European groups, lived in clans. Each clan was largely composed of an extended family headed by an elder, the patriarch. Slavic tradition upheld the significance of the family unit over the individual. Economic decisions, property ownership, and responsibility for family well-being rested with the patriarch. Every individual's opportunity started with his or her family's reputation and social standing. This provided strong social control and incentive to encourage maximum contributions, while keeping each member in line. An individual's contribution added to or reduced opportunity for all members and future generations of the family.

Poland is a proud nation with a rich history. "Poland" is derived from the word *pole,* meaning plain. The majority of Poland's expanse is made up of vast plains and forests traversed by slowly meandering rivers. Early legend tells of one successful clan led by Lech and his brothers, Czech and Rus. They thrived across the fertile plain and grew to the point where they decided to split up. Some people followed Czech south across the Tatry Mountains. Rus took another group east of the Bug River, forming the Ruthenian peoples of Ukraine and eventually Russia. Lech remained on the central plains and built his "Eagle's Nest" at Gniezno, between the Odra and Vistula rivers. This legend is validated by migration studies for the region early in the first millennium CE.

Clans needed to be ever vigilant. Though Poland as a country was yet to be defined, defense was frequently necessary to repel invaders who, through the centuries, descended from every direction. Individuals who distinguished themselves in battle grew in importance and prominence, and had conferred upon them the rights as noble knights, or *Szlachta.* They were frequently awarded land grants. The most successful families formed an aristocracy that led the emerging nation. Other members of the clans were happy to coexist behind the defensive shield the *Szlachta* provided. This natural social evolution split a common people into a noble class and a peasant class. With time, clergy, tradesmen, business people (burghers) and immigrants added to the social mix. Included were many Jews who were welcomed in Poland—in contrast to the persecution and rejection they experienced in much of Western Europe. Populations grew.[20] Peasants spent their lives close to home and field. Burghers conducted business in central villages and cities. Nobles maintained agrarian estates. Immigrants, as always, fit in where they could.

Aristocratic families from various clans were familiar with one another, interacting frequently. Though widely dispersed, they were bound together through intermarriage and the camaraderie of battles fought together against common enemies. Aristocratic families grew to have closer interests and interacted more with one another than with local populations.

Knights needed to be vigilant, and traveled frequently and fought battles far afield. Only knights were privileged to bear arms; the sword is a sign of nobility. Successful knights dominated larger and larger tracts of land and led the wealthiest noble families. Noble privilege extended to the family.

---

[20]Poland had 1.25 million inhabitants in the year 1000 CE, 2 million in 1350, 3–4 million in 1500, 11 million in 1650, 14 million in 1772, 34.2 million in 1937, 23.9 million in 1946, and 39 million people in the year 1999 CE.

Invaders grew in strength and posed an ever-greater threat. Many, particularly those from Turkey, came to battle in large camps. These camps included the invading family, servants, slaves, personal wealth, accumulations amassed from conquered lands, and rich regalia. Polish knights frequently went to battle accompanied by a page (usually a boy from another noble family) and perhaps others under his command. When successful in battle, a knight sent his staff to accumulate the wealth found abandoned in the invader's camp. They took these riches home as spoils of war. Upon returning home, in addition to having collected great wealth, knights were honored with great prestige and extensive landed estates for their success and heroism in battle.

Land bequeathed to, acquired or administered by nobles usually contained, among other things, villages of workers—peasants. Peasants were not owned by the landlords as slaves, but did rely on the lord's protection and justice. This dependence frequently was a practical subjugation, or form of serfdom. Peasant's families, in addition to tending their own plots of land, were required to spend three or four days a week working for the lord, a form of labor tax. A landlord might hire individuals (peasants or nobles) for pay, to work in a noble manor, on an estate, or on other properties or projects the noble might have. As in any agrarian society, common successes begat a better life. As there were few outside resources or opportunities, lack of success in agriculture brought on misery if not starvation.

During the time this social system was beginning to be established, peasants unwilling to go into battle (or not permitted to bear arms) accepted their limited position. Concerned with their immediate lives, their daily bread, they had little interest in national or international affairs that, to them, were distant and unimportant. Later, as this system became institutionalized, there was little opportunity for the individual to change their status. Noble families considered that they had earned their elevated position through many generations of deed and sacrifice. Noble privilege was accorded one's deserving friends and relations and not commonly shared with those who were uneducated, inexperienced and unable to demonstrate a family tradition of higher service.

Noble families defined Poland as a nation. Everyone with noble status, irrespective of wealth, had equal legal status. They created and served in the government, provided for the nation's defense, traveled widely and established high society. Some became deputies in the senate or *Sejm*. In later years they elected kings to rule the country, though with power limited and shared with nobility. Over centuries Poland developed a parliamentary republic of the nobility—an early form of national democracy. In Poland, a noble enjoyed rights unlike most European counterparts. Polish nobles were free from arbitrary arrest, and held ownership of land that could not be taken away.

The beginnings of Polish rule are lost in antiquity. Legends tell of several early members of the Piast dynasty, the first Polish rulers. The first historically documented Piast was Mieszko I (ca. 922–992). In the year 962 he converted to Christianity, subject to the spiritual authority of the Pope of Rome. This marked the start of Poland as a defined nation rather than an area or people. From that time, Catholicism dominated Polish culture. This in part explains Polish social, economic and political preferences and tendencies. Noble families continued to support the Church with their wealth, paid for the construction of churches, provided its educated sons as priests and encouraged participation by peasants. While this marriage between Church and Nobility served Poland well through the second millennium, its acceptance of Christianity subject to the spiritual authority of the Pope of Rome was not without problems. Most countries to the east accepted the Eastern teachings, those of the Christian Byzantine or Orthodox Church of Constantinople. Tensions among respective churches and their traditions created continuing strife among Poland and its neighbors.

A noble family's history was widely known and constantly evaluated in Poland. Proudly displayed crests, awarded to prestigious and worthy families, were the symbol of one's family's prominence. Older families, from the start of Polish history, with longer and greater traditions of honor, were held in the highest esteem. Their crests demanded respect. During pagan times, family names—"Christian" names—were unknown. Given names were more often descriptive in nature resulting from some physical characteristic, life event or personality trait. Once Christianity was introduced, many given names evolved into family names.

The Church supported and legitimized the status of Nobility. Family branches were identified by land holdings—estates.[21] As a family grew, brothers, then cousins of the same name sometimes formed new branches with separate identification and histories. The patriarch, with the responsibility not to leave family members to the wolves,[22] made provisions for each descendant. The oldest son might inherit the family's principal estate. A second son frequently became a priest. Additional sons might be given portions

---

[21]Estates, as in land holdings, should not be confused with social estates, the structures of society. For example, during the Jagielonian dynasty (1396–1572), five separate and exclusive estates existed: clergy, nobility, burghers, Jews, and the peasantry.

[22]In Poland the term "left to the wolves" was not just a saying, but also a real peril. Anyone wandering the wilds alone might well become victim of fierce timber wolves that prowled this domain.

of the family estate, smaller landed estates, work managing another noble's estate, become soldiers, or serve in the government. Daughters were married successfully within their social station and might also come into landed estates, their lives secured with rich dowries. Successful marriages raised a family's social standing, perhaps elevating a noble to royalty. The patriarch also had an interest in the welfare of non-family members in the area. He might set up schools, hospitals or other institutions for the welfare of the local populace.

Women were always a powerful force in Polish noble families. They were raised and educated to be loving, supportive wives; mistresses of the household with all its staff, social functions and fiscal control, and expected to hold their own in spirited conversation on varied topics. They were frequently estate owners in their own right, which required knowledgeable management skills. They had to hold and uphold the respect of the many workers, most of whom served the estate generation followed upon generation. Perhaps most demanding, women had to retain their social positions within noble society. They often were the bulwark upholding family roots and noble traditions. Boys were commonly raised totally under the mother's influence up to the age of seven, when their "hair was cut" and they moved to the realm of the man's world. Girls were given great freedom and latitude up to the time that they took on the responsibility of marriage. Women were expected to take control of estates at a moment's notice while husbands and sons went to war. Finally, women had to be prepared to be widows.

Though all nobles were theoretically equal brothers, there existed within nobility differentiating levels. Poland's noble class was a much larger proportion to the population as a whole than in other parts of Europe. As a family grew more successful, it might enjoy more than one crest and several estates. Crests and estates might also be combined. A common example was when one brother died. The surviving brother would often marry the dead brother's widow and take over the dead brother's estate.

Polish nobility, "aristocracy," interacted frequently with nobility throughout Europe. It was common to marry royal personages from the rest of Europe. Royalty is the highest rung of nobility. The next rung includes those of the most ancient lineage who contributed significantly to the nation's history (including the authors' ancient and distinguished family, Gniewosz). The wealthiest and most powerful nobles were referred to as the "Great Magnates" and consisted of forty to fifty families who lived in palaces, maintained private armies and directed national affairs. Beneath the Great Magnates was the middle nobility including Terenia's (Bisping) family, which also has strong ties to royalty. They maintained the traditional agrarian life and often had a prominent role in government. At the lowest level of the noble class was the *drobna szlachta* or minor nobility, who represented almost half of the noble class. While retaining all the rights and privileges of the nobility, *drobna szlachta* usually owned parcels of land that they worked themselves. Their land had usually been conferred upon them in reward for service in battle. With time, limited holdings were split amongst a growing family, to the point where any one son and his family could not subsist on the agricultural production of their meager holdings.

As the first millennium waned, the great plains evolved into a nation. The Piast family ruled to the mid-fourteenth century when the Jagiellonian period started. During Jagiellonian rule, Poland enjoyed its greatest geographical expansion through alliances made with neighbors, particularly the vast territory of then Lithuania, which reached from the Baltic Sea east almost to present-day Moscow, and south almost to the Black Sea. Russia was just coming into existence. This is where the Bisping family lived, on reaches east of the Baltic Sea, having emigrated from Germany centuries earlier. Distinguishing themselves in battle in the service of the elected Polish King Stefan Batory (1533–1586), they received vast land tracts in the Starodubie district, midway between Smolensk and Kiev. Upon moving to their new estate, presenting themselves to court, their nobility was challenged. Nobility was eagerly sought out and it was not uncommon in these times of limited communications for individuals to represent themselves as nobles unjustly. On January 5th, 1609, a petition was made before Rudolph II of the Habsburg dynasty, head of the Holy Roman Empire, King of Hungary and Czechoslovakia, at the Imperial Court in the Hradczany Castle in Prague where Bisping nobility was confirmed.

The confirmation document describes in minute detail the design of the family coat of arms. The centuries old coat of arms depicts a shield, divided in half horizontally. The upper half displays three vines of grapes shown on a silver background. The lower half displays an eight-pointed silver star set on blue. These documents remain today in the Vienna State Archives. The origin of the crest comes from a battle against an army of unknown strength. One soldier, eager to prove his courage, volunteered to ascertain vital information. On a starlit night he crawled through enemy territory across fields and vineyards to observe the enemy encampment from a hilltop. He was able to estimate the total number of troops by counting the number of campfires. Having this information, his commander immediately gave the order to attack. Taken by surprise, the enemy was defeated. The brave soldier was made a noble and received land and riches as well as the coat of arms depicting grapevines and a star.

This was only one of many Bisping deeds of honor. Teofil Bisping served in a Lithuanian unit of the Polish army's expedition to Vienna. In 1683, Vienna was threatened by a powerful Turkish offensive. Battle after battle was lost to the Turkish horde. Vienna was besieged and it seemed that all hope was lost. Two hundred thousand hardened Turkish solders prepared to overrun and ransack seemingly doomed Vienna. Vienna was the last European stronghold. If Vienna fell there was no hope for Europe. With Europe under the savage boot and sharp hoof of the Turkish horde, Christianity was at risk. Europe faced Armageddon.

Aware of the grave fate awaiting Europe should Vienna fall, Polish King Jan III Sobieski, with 102 Noblemen, leading 76 thousand men, heeded Vienna's cry of desperation. Racing down through the Carpathian Mountains and across Moravia, the Allied Christian Armies including Polish, German and Austrian troops under King Sobieski's Supreme Command, dared attack the seemingly invincible Grand Vizier Kara Mustafa with his overwhelming forces. On that one day, 12 September in the year of Our Lord 1683, King Sobieski defeated the opposition and sent the following message to Rome: "VENI, VIDI, DEUS VINXIT" (I came, I saw, God conquered).

The hilltop Roman Catholic Church at Kahlenberg honors the brave, chivalrous victors who saved the city—and Christendom. In a side chapel you can see even today the Noble family crests of those who left the comfort and security of their homes, risking their lives, for the welfare of Vienna, Europe and Christendom. They were of the families Jablonowski, Sieniawski, Szembek, Los, Pietruski, Krynski, Dunin, Kulesza, Radziwill, Rotharyusz, Czarnecki, Romer, Zoltowski, Miaczynski, Oskierka, Wielhorski, Zakrzewski, Brohl-Plater, Skarbek, Urbanski, Bisping, Turkull, Kossakowski, Moraczynski, Zamoyski, Orzeszko, Lipski, Szawlowski, Kosciuszko, Lanckoronski, Bobola, Puszyna, Lubomirski, Grocholski, Rozwadowski, Ledochowski, Mycielski, Breza, Gorayski, Rey, Jelowicki, Potocki, Szeptycki, Fink, Starorypinski, Mokronoski, Morawski, Tucholka, Kulczycki, Cieszkowski, Radzyminski, Czapski, Wielopolski, Tyzenhauz, Suchodolski, Kolyszko, Rudzki, Mielzynski, Skirumunt, Przezdziecki, Matczynski, Malczewski, Rostoworowski, Morztyn, Tyszkiewicz, Szoldrski, Karski, Hiz, Niemcewicz, Pulaski, Rulikowski, Leski, Taczanowski, Pac, Mlocki, Korsak, Glogowski, Bogusz, Grabinski, Wilga, Galezowski, Raczynski, Sierakowski, Gniewosz, Lacki, Grabowski, Darowski, Buffall, Stadnicki, Galecki, Gawronski, Szadurski, Kunicki, Cielecki, Cienski, Soltan, and Potulicki.

July 1st, 1853, marked an event of particular importance for following generations of the Bisping family. The Bisping sisters, Alexandra and Jozefa, established a land trust—the Seigneury of Massalany. This fulfilled a promise they had made to a favorite nephew, Kamil Bisping. While on his deathbed he had asked them to care for his children upon his demise.

The Seigneury, in addition to extensive land holdings, included a sizable fortune. Only proceeds—not the principal, were available annually, setting the holdings in perpetuity. The head of the land trust, the estate of Massalany, was the Ordynat. The first Ordynat was Kamil's second son, Aleksander Bisping. The trust document was rare in two ways. The first was that the trust required great wealth and a tremendous effort to accomplish. Few were ever recorded. The second unusual factor was that the trust, under specific circumstance, could be passed to women in the family. If an Ordynat did not have any sons, his daughter stood to inherit the property, even if the Ordynat had a brother. There was a condition attached: if the daughter got married and had a son, the son would have to have the name Bisping added to his own.

Polish history was marked by political strategy and intrigue—as often from abroad as from within Poland. Loyalties were split. The initial experiment with democracy was a catastrophe due to the "liberum veto." The system worked for two hundred years. It was based on the brotherhood of nobility where selfless concern for the welfare of the nation and self-sacrifice was the norm. Finally, however, as the vote of any one noble would veto any legislation, oft-outside insurgents proved the system as overly optimistic.

During the same period, America was discovered. Nations emerged in the new lands. European economic and political attention was redirected to the new world, at a cost to Poland. Polish production, particularly timber and grain, lost markets to low cost, abundant supply from the new world. With weak leadership, Poland succumbed to her more powerful and influential neighbors: Germany, Russia and Prussia. During the period of partition, 1795 through 1919, Poland entirely ceased to exit as a country. It was a black period for patriotic citizens of Poland. Loyalties were divided as many succumbed to new realities. To avoid loss of properties and estates, citizenship had to be accepted in the abhorrent neighbor nation that now possessed a portion of the no-longer-existent Poland. In some instances it became a State crime to speak or teach the Polish language. Yet, generation after generation, Polish Nobility refused to give up their unique culture or to forget their Polish heritage. Their hardheaded perseverance was to be rewarded with the re-emergence of Poland, but at a tremendous cost—after World War I.

With the Russian revolution, after the Czar and his entire family were exe-cuted, communists expanded their anti-establishment activities westward. All nobles, particularly those with wealth living within the Russian sphere, were alerted to this threat. Wanting to protect the family archives and valuables, Jan and Marynia decided to take the precaution of sending them west, within central Poland, where they would not be at risk. Having good relations with a quiet, isolated convent, everything was sent there, trusting that their treasures would be secure. It was during these events that Terenia was born.

Following World War I, Poland regained its identity as a sovereign nation. It was during this period that Poland achieved its economic zenith. Good weather in Poland and poor weather in Western Europe contributed to the creation of great wealth in Poland. The landed estates belonging to nobility had bountiful harvests that found eager markets. Life on the estates was good for everyone, including peasant, Jew and burgher, but particularly for Nobil-ity. It was seven years after the World War, when Poland was restored and life was normalized, that Jan and Marynia were able to bring back all the things from the secure convent to fill the manor.

CHAPTER 10

SPREADING my arms, I was lifted upward toward the crystals. They sang a pleasant folk tune to me in hushed voices as I flew amongst the prism-inspired colors. Brushing my shoulder against one of them I opened my eyes in surprise to see my governess, Miss Wanda. She was bending over me and I heard her say softly, "Get up Terenia, we have to prepare for a trip." Wide awake now, I saw sunlight glistening through the open window, sporadically interrupted by gently swaying tree branches. Miss Wanda continued her humming. Disappointed to have the pleasant dream interrupted, I asked her what was making her so cheerful. She replied, "The family is going to Krasnik.[23] Hurry now and get dressed in the clothing I have prepared for you." Dressing and eating quickly, Miss Wanda rushed me outside to where the family was already sitting in the loaded wagon.

Papa, holding the reins, called out to me, "You're the last, Terenia, hurry and jump on." I quickly jumped upon the *derka*[24] that covered the straw.

My brother Jas said, "Come sit with me, I saved you a place." I quickly found my seat and Papa called for the team to start out.

Jan turned to Krzysztof and asked him if he had remembered to bring the box of string and rotten meat. Krzysztof assured us that he had an ample supply for everybody. I knew immediately that this was meant for crawfishing as several of my siblings intoned in unison, "Is this a month containing the letter 'R'?" We all burst out laughing at the question. Fishing for crawfish was only permitted in the months containing the letter "R" in Polish. These months

---

[23]Krasnik: The name of an estate with a pleasant manor, surrounded by a beautiful park, which Papa purchased as a wedding gift for Mama. This farm did not belong to the majorat.
[24]*Derka:* a heavy coarse blanket, horse or saddlecloth.

were *czerwiec* (June), *sierpien* (August), and *wrzesien* (September). While other months contained the letter "r," they were too cold for crawfishing.

Once beyond the stables, Papa turned the wagon right, onto the bog-lined road toward Krasnik. After an hour or so we arrived and stopped in the shade of oak trees in the park by the Krasnik estate manor. Krasnik belonged to Mama, a gift Papa had purchased and given her that was independent of the Massalany estate. The estate administrator lived in the manor.

The administrator came out from within and talked with Papa who then followed him back inside. The rest of us were already off the wagon, spreading out a *derka* to sit upon while we had something to eat under the huge, ancient trees. After a while, Papa came out and called out to us, asking who would like to come to get a round of cheese. Always eager to see anything different, Krzysztof, Ela, Jas and I ran to catch up with Papa who was walking toward the barn with the cheese man. He was a local Jew who rented space at the farm and had started the small cheese business. His reputation for flavorful cheese was rapidly growing. He also provided a good market for local milk. Entering the barn, we could see numerous rounds of cheese of various dimensions ranging from the size of a cantaloupe to that of a large pumpkin. They were dark yellow in color. The man invited us to sample pieces, to choose which of the various ages we preferred. Selecting one small and one large round, Papa paid him and we returned to the wagon.

Mama had some food ready for Papa; for he had not eaten his "second breakfast." We children were climbing in the trees, the older ones egging one another on to see who could climb highest. The mighty oaks provided ample opportunity to show off our climbing skills. Just as Jas was reaching higher branches, Papa called out, "We're off!" Everything was thrown back into the wagon. We climbed in and Jas was just getting out of a tree as Papa cracked his whip. The horses pricked up their ears, raised their heads, shifted their weight forward and stepped out. The wagon circled around back in the direction from which we had come. Knowing that Jas was just about to get into the wagon, Papa good-naturedly urged the horses into a trot. Jas had to run quickly. He grabbed the end of the wagon rail swinging himself into the wagon just in time, to the amusement and laughter of everyone.

"It's good that you caught up with us, Jas." Papa said over his shoulder. "It would have been a shame if you had to walk in this heat and miss the swimming and fishing for crawfish."

Laughing at this, Jas retorted, "I could catch any wagon on this pockmarked old road. It's not as if you are riding an Arabian stallion at a gallop."

In half an hour, we reached midpoint between Krasnik and home. We stopped just beyond a small bridge that spanned the little river. "Boys on the left and girls on the right," Papa called out and we all jumped down to change into our bathing costumes.

We girls each wore our one-piece, blue and white horizontal striped, woolen suits that reached from our necks to our knees. I always envied the boys who could simply wear swimming trunks that reached from the waist to three-quarters of the way down to their knees. Regardless, all of us quickly ran and jumped into the water. Soon afterward Mama and Papa joined us.

The water was pleasantly cool in the hot summer weather. All of us could swim like fish but Papa would never get in over his neck. After frolicking in the refreshing water for some time, we got out to sit in the sun on the bank. We were all tanned like leather, but Papa was tanned only down to his collar. It was funny to look at him because the skin below his collar was as white as a bleached sheet. Putting on some clothing, as he feared burning his white skin, Papa told us about this little river.

It was a tributary of the Swislocz River that then flowed into the Niemen River, so much a part of Polish literature. It reached all the way to the Baltic Sea. He went on to explain that while here the river formed a large pool, in which many people enjoyed swimming as much as we did, just downstream it was small enough to jump over. While narrow, it had deep holes that extended down several meters. Then farther downstream the river spread out into bogs.

Krzysztof brought his box and we headed for a deep spot. Crawfish preferred the cool, deep waters. When we arrived at a likely place, Krzysztof put the box on the ground and opened it. We all groaned at the putrid smell of rotting meat and held our noses. Remarkably, Krzysztof seemed immune to the rank stench surging from the meat. He grasped a piece and firmly tied it with a length of cord. Preparing several such lines, he offered them to us, which we accepted with one hand extended as far from our bodies as possible, the other pinching our nostrils closed. Standing on a rock we were able to lower the cord deep into a pool. As the meat disappeared into the cool depths, the atrocious smell dissipated. Each of us waited to feel some movement on the cord, but with no results.

When Krzysztof pulled out his cord it was laden with a dozen or more hand-width sized, ferocious looking brown crawfish. He proudly held them up silently displaying his catch. He pinched each behind the claws, pulling them off the string one by one and closed the lid after dropping them into the water at the bottom of the pail. Exclaiming on his success and our lack, he intoned superiorly, "You just have to know how to do it!"

Badgering him to tell us his secret, he told us that we had to let out the cord carefully until we felt the meat touch bottom. Only then would the crawfish at the bottom of the pool start feeding on the rotten meat. Sometimes, he said, when at a particularly deep pool, a rock could be added to help the cord sink to the bottom. Pulling the cord up also had to be done slowly and carefully so that the crawfish, having eagerly attacked the meat, would not let go.

We kept only the larger ones. Smaller crawfish were put back in the water to grow for a future fishing expedition. Although none of us could match Krzysztof's success, we soon filled the pail. Proudly we headed home with our catch and the cheese. These crawfishing adventures became one of our most cherished outings away from home. We were always pleased to join a trip to Krasnik.

CHAPTER 11

ENTERING THE CHAPEL one summer Sunday morning, I noticed that it was almost empty. Papa seemed in a hurry to get to Mass this morning and Mama had noted that, hopefully, it would not rain before the service was over. Even the estate steward, Mr. Szemiot, was not there singing. I missed his rich baritone voice that usually filled the chapel. Mass started amidst a sense of apprehension. Just as the chalice was lifted during the blessing of the wine, the chapel was filled with an intense flash of lightning immediately followed by a deafening clap of thunder. Papa's head dropped to his chest. A heavy rain upon the chapel roof suddenly drowned out all other noise. Papa looked up and out a window. Mama looked at his face with concern and grasped her rosary more firmly. The chapel darkened with the sheets of rain that continued through communion and the rest of mass. Papa left immediately when Mass was over.

We collected at the open chapel doors. We could not even see the house across the lake for the drenching downpour descending from the heavens. The priest joined us at the door and said a prayer that the rains not cause too much damage to the harvest. After a while the rain subsided and then stopped. We had just started around the lake to the house, avoiding the brimming puddles, when the sun came out. A brilliant, double rainbow appeared. We walked home though clouds of steam as the hot sun started evaporating the rainwater. Papa was not there when we arrived.

"Well," Mama said, "at least we will benefit from mushrooms growing after this first rain of the summer. Tomorrow we will go picking."

That evening Papa returned from the fields. "It was not that bad. With everyone working late into the night yesterday and from first light this morning, we managed to get most of the crop under cover before the rain hit. The sun will dry the rest quickly. Maybe tomorrow you will all want to go mushroom picking," he said matching Mama's earlier statement.

We did just that. Around two o'clock, one of the stable boys, who worked under the coachman, brought a wagon around for us. It was the same kind of wagon we had used on the trip to Krasnik. Drawn by a pair of stable horses, the boy sat facing forward on the first seat. Each three-person-wide seat was made of *derka*-covered straw upon which some of us sat facing forward and some facing backward. The wagon had four oak wheels less than a meter in diameter. The front two wheels were attached to an axle that pivoted below the driver. A pole reached forward between the horses, to which the various tack and horse collars were attached. The floor was made of long wooden planks. Ladder-like rails were installed, leaning out on either side of the wagon, at about a thirty-degree angle. This type of wagon was usually used to haul materials rather than people. Planks were sometimes used in the place of the rails.

Mama, the five oldest children, and Mama's sister (Aunt Maria "Teresa" Zamoyski) who happened to be visiting from Warsaw at the time, all joined the boy in the wagon with our mushroom baskets. In half an hour we reached some of Papa's forests. These pine forests had been planted under Papa's direction more than twenty years earlier. Watched and cared for by a forester, the individually-counted trees, in their unwavering rows, created a cool dark environment under a tall canopy. Here the rich soil was littered with many fallen branches that provided a wonderful environment for some kinds of mushrooms.

We passed along the main forest road connecting the forester's house with regular fire lanes. Riding through these older forests, headed for younger stands where our favorite *rydze (lactarius deliciosus)* grew, the first mushrooms had appeared after the fresh summer rain. These we picked while they were young and tender. Most of what we picked would be pickled and held in the storehouse for the winter. Some would be fried in rich butter and served with our dinner. We salivated at the thought of this delicacy to be enjoyed that evening.

Each of us carried a basket made of light brown reeds that grew in the local bogs. Older folk frequently made and sold the baskets as a source of revenue. With basket handles in the crooks of our arms, we fanned out to locate an area rich with emerging mushrooms. The joyful cries of children could be heard through the trees upon their discovery of an abundant patch. When the baskets were filled, we all sat together in a warm open spot to collectively sort and clean our harvest. Removing the soil covered bottom of the stem and throwing away any infested with insects, the yield was cleaned before we started for the next spot.

The forests were planted in various types of trees. We proceeded next to a birch tree forest. Amongst these white barked trees grew the *kozlaki* and *borowiki* (boletus) mushroom varieties that were excellent when dried. We would often see strings of them hung in the storehouse. The *borowiki* grew particularly large and were very nourishing. Serving a big one, prepared as it normally was in heavy cream, was said to be comparable to serving a steak dinner. The *kozlaki* were smaller, growing on tall thin stems. Their heads were light brown on top and white underneath. The forests were filled with many varieties of mushrooms. Younger children would often pick any that they found.

Once, one of the children proudly presented a brilliant red mushroom with white spots on top. It grew impressively tall. Mama blanched when she saw it and immediately instructed the child to drop it. After cleaning the child's hands in a patch of moist moss, she assembled the children to look at the mushroom and advised them never to touch this variety, *amanita muscaria*.

Mama then told a horrifying, true story. "A Lord and his Lady returned to their manor, upon which the staff rushed out to them crying and flailing their arms. Asking what had happened, none of the staff could bring themselves to answer. The Lord, grabbing a servant woman, demanded an answer to which she finally replied, 'The dog died.'

Disappointed at the loss, he was puzzled by the extent of emotion over the death of a dog. He asked them how this happened. She replied that the dog had been served some mushrooms gathered the previous day. Still puzzled he asked, 'And what more?'

The servant woman then quietly replied, 'Your children also ate the mushrooms and they with some of the kitchen and serving staff were all taken to the hospital.'

'Where are they now and how are they?' he demanded!

Everyone suddenly hushed. In a quiet, barely audible voice, her head down, she replied, 'm'Lord, they are all dead!'"

The story taught us a poignant lesson. While the story was dreadful, it had been told splendidly. It underscored how the servant tried to avoid having to tell her master that his children had died by telling him his dog was poisoned. Looking at one another, appreciating the servant's subtlety, we all howled with laughter.

CHAPTER 12

TOWARD THE END of the summer of 1928, when I was nine years old, I anticipated leaving home for school with unease and melancholy. Loving life in the country, I could not imagine living in the city without horses, fields and forests. Having always avoided spending time studying, I did not know how I would deal with the constant demand to study at school, or how I would stand in comparison to other students. At least, I thought, Niula whom we all admired and loved would be there, and she would help and encourage me. She would be my supporter. In the days prior to departure for school, I packed all the treasures that I would leave at home. As I carefully placed each item in my chest, I hid the teardrops that fell on my picture book, toys and treasures. Closing the chest, I ran out to the stables.

Taking my favorite horse *Orzelek* ("Little Eagle"), I galloped through the forests and fields that I loved so much, saying my farewells as I went. Stopping by the village store, I purchased sugar cubes and shared them generously with my horse, envisioning this to be our last ride together. During the slow ride home, spotting several deer feeding at the edge of the forest, I thought of how lucky they were that they could just stay here and not have to go off to school and study. I tried to commit to memory each minute detail of what I passed, to remember all of this while I was at school. Returning to the stable, looking around to see that no one saw me, I put my arms around Orzelek's neck and kissed him a final good-bye.

Having thus said my farewells to all that I loved, I proudly did not show my sorrow when leaving home with Niula and the rest of my school-aged brothers and sisters. Putting a smile upon my face, so no one would suspect my true feelings, I said good-bye to my parents, noting their surprise at my lack of apprehension.

Boarding the train in Grodno and likewise later in Warsaw, I was impressed with Marysia's and Krzysztof's familiarity and skills with finding seats and dealing with the overcrowded train filled with students returning to school. As there were too few seats for all the passengers, Marysia and Krzysztof successfully elbowed their way in and occupied a compartment. Once inside, they closed the compartment door, did not allow anyone else in and secured it for us. They opened the window through which we passed our belongings. Once the turmoil caused by everyone trying to find a place calmed down, the rest of us assisted Niula up the high steps. With the agreed-upon signal we were admitted into the compartment and calmly occupied our seats for the long trip.

My first day at school! Marysia and Ela presented me to a nun for placement. The convent school was organized in three years of preparatory school followed by eight years of high school. I was placed in the final preparatory year. The next day school started in earnest. I quickly made friends and established good relations with my classmates and the nun, my teacher. I went to school happily and was always eager to participate. With Niula's help and direction, I was quickly able to master the material and made up any deficiencies. The year progressed well. Mid-year, the decision was made to change the school system. The following year, there were to be four preparatory years. Our class was to be divided in two, with the lower half creating a fourth preparatory class and the better students passing immediately to high school. Thanks to Niula's tutelage, I tested well and was to pass to high school with the next school year. My parents, Niula and I were all very pleased with these results.

Having spent the winter closed in behind walls, one sunny spring Sunday morning, Niula told us that she would take us to her favorite place around Poznan. Not far from the city was the forest at Puszczykowo. After Mass we went out for some exercise in the sunshine. We were very happy with this and eagerly boarded the train that took us there in a short while.

The forest was filled with spring fragrances and singing birds. The warm breeze reminded me of home, which I missed, though we had visited during Christmas and Easter vacations. I dreamed about how we would be returning there for the summer. Looking around the forest I saw the many lily-of-the-valley blooming around us. I thought of how often we had picked flowers for Mama. Asking Niula if we could pick some, she replied that these were wild and that we could pick all the flowers we wished. Tantalized by the freedom to pick this aromatic evidence of springtime, we all took to collecting them by the armload. Holding them carefully all the way back to our apartment, the train never smelled so good. Many passengers smiled at us, enjoying the fragrance and our happy expressions. At our apartment we filled many vases with the flowers and distributed them throughout the rooms. Each time we returned to the apartment over the next days we were greeted by the wonderful fragrance, which was to remain a lifelong delight.

One day a foreign yet familiar voice filled the apartment with a booming voice, "What is this wonderful fragrance?" It was Michal our oldest brother. We all ran to the entrance to greet him. Particularly happy to see my grown-up godfather, I asked him what had brought him from the University of Poznan that day. Michal was enrolled in the College of Law and Economics. He picked me up, placing me high on his shoulder, and asked if we would like to come and visit him next Sunday. Obtaining Niula's permission, we quickly agreed, excited for this first invitation to see how he lived.

That next Sunday, taking the opportunity to don nice dresses rather than the school uniforms we commonly wore, we took the trolley and walked up to the house where Michal rented his room. Greeted at the door by a Miss Sophie Chlapowski, she seemed to receive us particularly warmly and ushered us into her salon. She sent for Michal and introduced us to her niece, Aldona Chlapowski. Aldona asked that we call her "Dusia" as did her entire family.

Dusia invited us to the dining room where fabulous cakes and hot chocolate awaited us. Michal had, indeed, an excellent place to live, we thought to ourselves! Michal soon appeared and told us that when we finished, we were invited by his landlady and Dusia to play some games. For the next several hours we had a fantastic time hosted by Michal, his landlady and Dusia. The landlady was a tireless hostess. Dusia played with us unceasingly. She and Michal also seemed to get along very well. We learned much about Michal's studies and learned of Dusia's life and family. Her father was the chairman of the biggest oil company in Poland. She proudly explained how, though he came from a respected noble family, he had started as a lowly worker and had risen through the ranks to the top position. Familiar with all aspects of the company, he was popular with the company's many employees due to his extensive company experience. He had led the company as its chairman for a number of years.

We had a wonderful visit. On the way home we exclaimed to one another how well Michal's landlady and her pleasant niece Dusia had hosted us. We had noticed how Michal seemed particularly attracted to Dusia, and we later understood why we had been so well received when their engagement was announced soon afterward.

At last, the school year came to an end. I was pleased with a successful year but happy to return home to the family estate. That summer, the topic of endless discussion was Michal and Dusia's upcoming wedding. Controversy surrounded the couple's decision, as there was dissent from both families. Dusia's father considered that Michal, at twenty-two years of age, was too young. This was despite his having completed university studies and being the owner of two large estates, Oksa and Naglowice. He had inherited them upon the death of his father, Mama's first husband. Mama, in consultation with Michal's Uncle, Janusz Radziwill,[25] considered that Michal, a titled Prince, should not marry below his station and agreed that he was rather young to marry. In the end, Michal stated emphatically that the wedding would proceed. As they were of legal age and had made up their minds, no objection could overrule their decision. Everyone thus accepted his decision and the controversy evaporated.

Six months prior to the planned wedding date, Michal's grandmother became ill with pneumonia. The Holy Father, Pope Pius XI, hearing of her imminent demise, sent cardinals. The Knights of Malta had sack loads of straw laid on the street outside her house to lessen the noise so that she would not be disturbed. Despite the best of care, she succumbed only hours later. When her last will and testament was read, Michal inherited estates, large amounts of money and valuable property. Wedding plans continued. Mama and Papa decided that they would travel to the wedding with Adam, the oldest three children and Niula. I was very disappointed that I was not to attend the wedding as Michal was my Godfather and I had always felt close to him. Trunks were filled with fine dresses and clothing for the festivities and for the trip Mama and Papa planned to take around Poland following the wedding. Michal documented his marriage by writing:

"We fell desperately in love and in 1929, against the counsels of my family and misgiving from hers, on account of our youth, we celebrated our marriage on the 20th of July. The ceremony took place at Lwow and was attended by practically all the leading families of Poland and also the Bourbons, who came in force.

---

[25]Janusz Radziwill had two sons close to Michal's age, Edmund and Stanislas. Stanislas was to later marry Lee Bouvier, whose sister Jacqueline married John F. Kennedy (1917–1963), 35th U.S. President (1961–1963).

The post office in Lwow was inundated by telegrams from all parts of Europe, not the least being the benediction, by telegram, of the Holy Father, which was read out during the matrimonial service. The marriage was followed by an enormous luncheon for the 200 people in the Klub Obywatelski, the leading club in the city, after which we got into a motor-car presented to us by my father-in-law and departed for Naglowice."[26]

---

[26]*Michal Radziwill, One of the Radziwills* (Latimer Trend & Co. Ltd., Plymouth, 1971), p.80. The Holy Father referred to is Pope Pius XI.

CHAPTER 13

ATTENDED school in Poznan for four years during which there were a number of memorable occurrences. One of these started when we observed an unusual commotion at our cousin's home across the street. Our aunt and uncle and their six children spent winters in the city. We suddenly observed the unusual and urgent comings and goings of many people including doctors and a priest. When nurses started showing up, Niula decided to find out what was happening. She sent out a servant girl to talk to one of the servants at our cousin's apartment. Niula prepared for the worst, fearing that some dreaded disease had erupted and was wondering if she should start making plans to evacuate us. The servant girl returned with quite a tale. We were relieved to learn, first of all, that the problem had been resolved. The servant girl was laughing so hard that she could hardly tell us what had happened.

Apparently, a few days earlier, there had been a disagreement between our aunt and their governess. This governess, due to her overbearing ways, was disliked by all of our cousins. The fact of a disagreement did not come as a surprise. The governess had left in a huff. Nothing in particular was thought about it until two days later when it surfaced that none of the children had urinated since the governess' departure. Concerned that the governess had somehow done some devious mischief in misguided retribution upon the children, our aunt was quite worried. Not wanting to alarm the children nothing was said to them. Numerous tests were administered and they were carefully monitored. Still no flow ensued. Great concern had taken over the family and staff. The family doctor, not knowing what to do, suggested that an experienced nurse he knew from the children's hospital be brought in. She

ELA, 1923.

TERENIA, 1923.

came, listened to the story and said that she could try a few things. Summoning the children, she lined them up with a series of bedpans. Upon letting out a whistle, the children, in unison, proceeded to pee into the bedpans. Such had been the governess' iron rule over our cousins.

Niula was happy that there had not been any real problem and enjoyed laughing at the story with the rest of us. We all had a greater appreciation for how exceptional a governess Niula was. None of us had to pee at the sound of a whistle.

Poznan had a cavalry regiment that offered a riding school. One summer, my parents agreed to send me to the riding school, which I anticipated with great joy. On the first day at the riding school, an officer came out and introduced himself as my instructor. After learning that I could ride, he had me get up on his horse and instructed me to show him how I ride. Apparently I gave the horse a different signal than it was accustomed to, for it tore off across the arena kicking along the way! I hung on! Having ridden many different horses, I was able to ride it fairly well despite its unruly behavior. Niula watched in terror! Turning pale, she was worried that I might be injured, or even killed. The officer stood there watching, not moving and not saying anything. I managed to ride up to them and the officer proceeded to give me a lesson, to Niula's continued discomfort.

At the end of the lesson the officer complimented me on my riding. He turned to Niula and told her, to her further disquiet, that he would like to help me prepare to participate in the annual spring riding competition. I beamed all the way home, enchanted and enthralled. I couldn't understand, after many days passed, why we were not going to another lesson. Wanting to ride, I repeatedly asked Niula about the lessons. She explained that she needed my mother's permission for this kind of class. After some time, much to my surprise and disappointment, I received a letter within which Mama told me I was not going to take any more lessons. It was not until several years later that I learned how the decision had been made. Niula had been distressed seeing me tear across the arena on the unruly horse. Despite my joy, she told my mother that she would not take the responsibility for these lessons and asked Mama to write me a letter discontinuing the lessons.

We enjoyed Michal's occasional visits from the university. Unfortunately, his and Krzysztof's rivalry would often erupt into intense skirmishes. One time, during a heated argument, Michal pushed Krzysztof's head into the tub and soaked his head in cold water. Fearing the inevitable reprisal, Michal took off! Running out of our apartment into the building's common hallway, he descended the staircase three steps at a time toward the exit. Anticipating Michal's departure out of the building, Krzysztof quickly filled a pitcher with water and, standing on the veranda over the building's entry door, waited for Michal. When the door opened, Krzysztof let the water fly. Meanwhile, Michal had, per chance, met an elderly man upon reaching the entry door. Knowing his brother well, he politely opened the door allowing the elderly man to exit first.

As we got older, we held dances in our apartment. Pushing furniture to the walls, we would roll up the rugs. To the sound of the gramophone, we danced with friends and cousins who were invited. We instructed one another on what we knew about dancing the tango, fox trot, waltzes and various Polish national dances. The arrival of each guest was keenly anticipated and the inability of someone to come was lamented. As we had more of these dances, they were planned more and more carefully, and generated great anticipation. Various romances flamed and the occasional kiss was stolen when Niula was not in the room, but mainly, the entire group formed as a close union. Later, when we learned that we would no longer go to school in Poznan, it was these dances and the relationships forged that we would miss the most.

CHAPTER 14

AFTER YEARS of coaxing and cajoling Papa, Adam succeeded in obtaining his permission to establish a brood of pigeons at home. Adam quickly acquired several sets of carrier pigeons. Each morning he would spread peas on the park side of the manor for them to eat. He would then invite all of us to admire their beauty. Although at first they were quite tame, it did not take long for them to appreciate their freedom, upon which they became quite wild. To Adam's consternation, we soon started to notice that each generation was becoming further mixed with wild pigeons. Wanting to maintain his special breed, he read everything he could find on this problem.

The first matter at hand was to eliminate mixed-breed birds. How to do this was a puzzle, as catching them proved very difficult. Noticing that they had found a way into the attic and were living there, we children decided to attempt catching them there. We knew that Papa would not allow us to be up there for fear that we would fall through the unfinished floor, in reality just the ceiling of the room below. One day, when Papa was gone and Mama otherwise occupied, Adam and I braved everything to enter the attic. Hoping to catch the birds by their nests and egged on by our imagination that we may discover some treasures there, we sneaked in.

Adam stuck his head in first, but quickly withdrew. "Ugh!" he gasped. The attic, by this time blighted with the heat-magnified stench of bird droppings, was oppressive. Adam said, "The air is unbreathable, we wouldn't survive even a few minutes in there."

I pressured him to continue by encouraging him. "Pinch your nose and get in." I pushed from below. He disappeared within. After a while, hearing nothing, I became concerned that he had somehow succumbed to the odorous gases.

As I started imagining trying to explain the loss of Adam in the attic to Papa, I was relieved to hear his nose-pinched muffled voice call to me from deep within the recess. "You can get used to it. Come in, it's very interesting in here." Not waiting, I entered. It stunk terribly, even with my nose pinched. It was dark but I could see Adam. Carefully watching where I placed each step, I headed toward him as my eyes slowly became accustomed to the darkness.

Many nests were scattered about in various nooks and crannies. As I approached an occupied nest, the pigeon suddenly took flight and flew out a vent hole to the accompaniment of a cloud of dust and feathers. Startled, I shrank back, but then advanced toward Adam again, encouraged on by curiosity. Adam was collecting eggs in the basket he had brought with him. He caught a few of the birds and tied them with the cord that had been in the basket. Most were escaping out the vents. After catching a few birds, when the rest flew out, we started to look around.

Much to my surprise I saw the changing chest Mama had used with baby Ewa many years previously. My first clear memory as a child flooded back to me upon seeing the chest. This was quite a find! For years I had told Mama my memories about this chest. She always maintained that it was impossible for me to remember such details at that young age. This discovery was in itself ample reward for entering the inhospitable and forbidden attic. We found a few other furniture relics, but nothing of any great interest—no treasure. Having had enough of the asphyxiating air in the attic, we proceeded to the exit.

Climbing down, we encountered true fresh air. What a luxury! How wonderful it was to have clean, fresh air! It was worth suffering through the abysmal conditions in the attic just to experience this feeling of appreciation for the cool invigorating air.

Obliterating any evidence of our transgression, we went outside. Adam threw the eggs away into some bushes and carried the tied pigeons to the kitchen. Just as we were about to congratulate ourselves on a job well done, we stopped in our tracks. In front of us, pecking among the rocks, were many, many more of the undesirable crossbreeds. We had accomplished nothing.

Undeterred, Adam returned to his books and magazines. He was determined to find a solution for maintaining his purebred carrier pigeons. A solution appeared in one of his magazines. It suggested soaking the bird's feed in alcohol, enabling the owner to catch the birds drunk and unable to fly. Finding the distillery proof bottles by Papa's desk in the library, Adam took one, soaking that day's pea-feed with the alcohol. Scattering the alcohol-laden peas in the courtyard, we sat under the aged trees to watch. As always, the pigeons were not about to miss this easy meal and quickly gathered to pick the peas from among the rocks. Now, rather than picking up a few peas and flying away, the birds started to swagger about. More continued to arrive. Each arrival would eat then quickly succumb to the alcohol. They would spread their wings, but unable to fly they would amble about and then fall asleep in the warm sunshine.

The number of the crossbreeds appalled us. Only a few appeared to still maintain the characteristics of the original carrier pigeons. We quickly collected the crossbreed pigeons and delivered them to the kitchen. The kitchen staff exclaimed their displeasure at the additional work. Their displeasure was tempered only by happiness that they would no longer be targets of the well-fed birds flying above. The birds had necessitated covering trays with cloths to protect food from droppings. Following their experience with the alcohol-laden peas, pigeons that we did not gather for the kitchen, upon sobering up, did not return to their nests but flew off. In later years, we were interested to note, sometimes we could still see traces of Adam's breed in wild pigeons.

Adam learned many lessons from his carrier pigeon experience. The most interesting lesson Adam soon tested in other ways. Papa's stocks of distillery proofs were to be utilized again. Risking that Papa might not miss another bottle, he soaked a sausage in the bottle's contents and fed it to Lord, our favorite Irish setter. As expected, Lord ate the sausage with enthusiasm. Lord seemed very happy, jumped about in an animated way, smiling at us as only setters do. Krzysztof, who had joined us along with some of the other children, decided that we should dress Lord up in our clothing. Stripping off his shirt, Krzysztof dressed Lord in it. Lord, now under the influence of the alcohol, humored us with his unusual antics, but this was not enough. My brother Jas ran off and brought back a pair of pants, which were also put on Lord. Now in shirt and pants, too drunk and no longer able to jump about, but still smiling, Lord started to crawl toward us, asking for more sausage. We rolled on the ground in uncontrolled fits of laughter. Our laughter just excited Lord who, though incapable of functioning normally, seemed to enjoy his predicament just as much as we were. Finally, after one more piece of sausage, Lord could move no more and fell asleep for the afternoon. His snoring, while waving his paws about in the air, wearing the shirt and pants, kept us in stitches the rest of the day.

Adam was not finished. The next morning Papa's carriage was brought out for his ride around the fields. Adam, gesturing for the rest of us to come and see, soaked some sugar cubes with alcohol and fed them to the horses. The horses' reaction was immediate, and even frightening. They first started to beat the ground with their hooves. Soon they started trying to rear up on their hind legs but restrained by the tack were unable to. This started to scare us, as it was becoming dangerous. The horses neighed loudly and profusely.

Just then, Papa came out the door and strode toward his carriage. We backed away and hid behind some trees. Papa stopped in his tracks. He looked at the horses' strange antics with a puzzled expression. Having noticed our withdrawal, Papa called us to explain what we were up to. Seeing us trying to maintain innocent expressions convinced him of our guilt. Calmly but sternly, he instructed us to tell him what we were up to. Adam, pulling out the rest of the sugar cubes, though keeping the bottle hidden in his pants, explained why the horses were behaving this way. Papa said, "So that's where the bottles disappeared to! Don't ever do that again! Take the horses back to the stable. Tell the groom to give them a good drink of water and that I will not go out to the fields today." We were relieved to see Papa turn around and go back into the house, although I noticed him trying to keep a smile from covering his face. Having gotten off so lightly, Adam decided that at this point he would not try any more of his experiments.

CHAPTER 15

"COME, CHILDREN, there is a storm brewing!" said our ever-watchful nanny Miss Wanda. Looking up in the sky, we could see that it was a strange steel-blue color. Threatening looking clouds approached. A strong breeze was building. One approaching cloud in particular looked as though it might contain accursed hail; it had been known to reach the size of walnuts. Such hail, though usually pelting only a limited area, resulted in much damage and could be quite painful. We started to collect our things when a particularly strong gust tore through the trees. "Leave your things, we are going now!" cried Miss Wanda. She looked up into the swaying trees with a look of fright upon her face. Taking the hands of the smallest children, we then saw Miss Wanda running for the first time ever. We followed her, all of us running down the central lane through the park to the manor. By this time we were being pelted with leaves, branches and other flying debris. We crossed the courtyard and screamed in unison as another strong gust pushed us up to the house and through the door. The gust, having pushed us through the door, would not allow us to close it. Several of us heaved against it. Finally it latched.

Miss Wanda counted us to assure herself that all were accounted for. Gathering up Ewa, who was crying, she hushed her saying that we were at home now and everything would be all right. Just then, my brother Jas came running back from the children's wing hall calling to us, "Come See!" Adrenaline flowing, we followed him, wide-eyed, through our dining room to the corner bedroom where we could see the park and entry drive through one window and out across the lake through the other. Trees were swaying wildly in the wind. Branches were flying everywhere.

Everyone had apparently already taken shelter as no one could be seen along any of the lanes or paths. Usual activity had ceased. The sky now turned black! Our rooms darkened. Expecting the usual lightning bolts to strike, as in normal storms, we were surprised that we could only see flashes of light underlining clouds that boiled in the angry sky. "Look!" cried Adam pointing across the lake. There, across the lake, just to the right of the hospital (the hospice), one of the grand, old, enormous, poplar trees crashed to the ground. As we all crowded to the window, another of them, with its dozen large stork nests twisted in the wind, uprooted and crashed to the ground and partially into the lake. To our collective outcry it spewed a horizontal cloud of debris across the road. The debris continued in a furious cloud across the lake, momentarily obscuring the fisher's house. I wondered what would become of the poor storks, just as another, and then another of the mighty poplars twisted and fell in pandemonium.

Mama came into the room just as we heard a large branch crash against the wall. She said, "The house is all closed up. Thank God that all of you are all right! I saw Papa ride out to the fields earlier, we must all pray for him." Immediately we all recited *In Your Care*, the prayer to the Blessed Virgin Mary for deliverance from any circumstance of danger.

We place ourselves in your care
oh holy mother of God.
Listen to our prayer
in this time of need.
Protect us from harm,
illness and peril.
Defend us oh blessed,
and anointed one.
Our lady,
our tireless defender,
who pleads in our stead,
who restores our joy.
Unite us with your Son and
place us under his protection.
Pray for us O holy mother of God,
that we be found deserving
of the promises
of our Lord Jesus Christ. Amen

Mama, Miss Wanda and we, the children, all anxiously watched the storm as it progressed. All of us excitedly and urgently exclaimed on our various observations, pointing to some event as it occurred, talking over one another. On all our minds was Papa's safety. The unanticipated storm was wreaking great damage. Very frightened, we would have been in absolute terror were we not together in the safety of the massive manor. Suddenly, the majestic spruce tree between the entrance and courtyard lanes, within which we had played so many times, twisted and then thundered down, its enormous root ball pulled out of the ground.

Amazingly, soon after the spruce fell, the wind quickly dissipated. Then, the clouds passed by, clearing the sky and within minutes the sun came out. Somewhat in a daze from the rapid change in events, we all went out to see what carnage resulted in this brief but intense storm. We could see various individuals emerging from where they had taken shelter. The gardener soon came from beyond the downed spruce. He told Mama that while the spruce was an obvious loss, he had already quickly examined a number of smaller trees on his way over; he thought that some of them could be uprighted and saved. As he went on to look after the greenhouse adjoining his house, Papa rode up to our exclamations and prayers of thanksgiving for his safe deliverance! Handing the reins to the butler, who had come out when he heard Papa approach, Papa gave Mama a hug and kissed her on both cheeks. We crowded around him as Mama told him that we were all unharmed. She asked how he had weathered the storm.

"It was incredible!" he replied. "I was out in the fields riding down the lane from the forest when the winds struck. Along a field the sheep were huddled together. Then a mighty gust hit me." Papa continued, "Suddenly, I found myself on the other side of the sheep, out in the middle of the field. I don't even know, or understand, how I was carried there with my little carriage, horses and all! The horses were so terrified, that for a while they would not move. Finally, I had to get off and stroke the horses' heads to calm them. Just then, the winds lessened and I was able to get the team moving again. I came here immediately."

Deciding to take a look around the estate to examine what damage the storm had caused, Papa, Mama and we older children went out around the children's wing of the manor. We walked into the tree-lined park. Beyond the lane on our left was the barnyard. There appeared to be no consequential damage in the park or with the tennis court that paralleled the left lane. The courts were covered with leaves and branches. Deciding to pass the left and middle lanes, we took the right hand lane toward the monument to the

**MONUMENT TO ALEKSANDER BISPING (1844–1867),
FIRST ORDYNAT OF MASSALANY**

first Ordynat. As we started down the two-meter wide, fifty-meter long lane, on our left was the monument to our great-aunts that had set up the majorat—the Massalany Estate. Clearing branches as we went, we arrived at the monument to great-uncle Aleksander (the first Ordynat) near remnants of an old entrance gate. For many years now it consisted only of two white brick pillars on either side of the lane. Under us flowed the creek that refreshed the large pond, or more aptly, the small reservoir, dug by Turkish war prisoners, employed by the estate many years previously.

The prisoners were from the Turkish-Russian war of 1875. Thirty of these prisoners were dispersed to the estate by the Russian government. Poor and hungry, dressed in rags and unemployed, they sang their prayers at the lakeshore. Our great-uncle Jan (the second Ordynat) wanting to both help them and keep them occupied, employed them to dig a large pond, which perhaps saved them from starvation. It was to be on one side of the old gate with a culvert built under the road allowing the stream to flow to the pond. The soil dug from the pond was piled in the center creating an island upon which we often played.

From the lane we proceeded onto the main entry drive and walked toward the main gate. Beyond the gate was the road that ran between two villages: Olekszyce and Massalany. Just past the pond, we turned left onto the alternate road that connected to the barnyard. There on our right was a mission cross surrounded by its small moat. Always crossing ourselves whenever passing this cross, we did so today with added fervor. On the other side of the road overlooking the pond, was a life-sized statue of Saint Mary, Mother of Jesus, upon an ornamental cement pedestal. Each May, locals, whom we would often see praying there, richly adorned this shrine with many colorful fresh flowers and flower arrangements—some wild flowers, others from carefully cultivated private gardens.

Looking back across the entry drive, we could see the remains of an embankment stretching out far beyond us. This was an old rampart. It was built upon the boundary between two feuding brothers from whom one of our great-aunts bought the two estates early in the 19th century, from which the majorat was partially composed. The feuding brothers would shoot at each other across this rampart.

Walking back toward the manor, just prior to the old entrance, we passed a large, heavy rock-hewn cross on our left. It was said to be a memorial to an old Polish combatant. Not much was said publicly about this; it was feared that the Russians would demolish it. Halfway to the manor, continuing on the entry drive, between the lake and us was the gardener's house. On one side of the building was the greenhouse and on the other side was the laundry with the laundry woman's quarters.

The gardener maintained the greenhouse, or "orangerie" as it was known. He grew various tropical shrubs and flowers there. All winter the manor was decorated with flowers from this orangerie, especially cyclamen, which he successfully propagated and was particularly proud of. Everyone liked the gardener, for not only did he have a pleasant character, but also his many skills were appreciated. He employed many of the local boys who, with his tutelage, later went on to be prized gardeners for many other estates.

Ten meters beyond the laundry was a well-maintained lawn extending down to the lake. This lawn surrounded the original house of the estate. It was now used as a guesthouse or as lodging for some estate clerk. One of the especially memorable lodgers of this house was the very old stores-keeper, Mrs. Strzalkowski, who had worked on the estate for a long time and had served my grandmother, Helena Holynski. One of my earlier memories was visiting her with Mama. This was particularly memorable because she made exceptional candies and stuffed fruits, fruit cheese and other confectioneries that she served us. Unfortunately, many of the delicious recipes that she used were never written down and were lost upon her death.

Passing the manor, we saw that its gardens, on either side of the main structure before each wing, appeared to have survived the storm relatively unscathed. Each of these decorative gardens was enclosed with an ornate black-iron, meter-high fence. The outside corner of each had a pedestal upon which lay a large sphinx. A path, decorated with flowers and shrubs, crossed through the lawn from the lake to the manor. Each summer, ornamental plants from the orangerie were placed in large ceramic vases on either side of the veranda under the windows of the main structure.

The stables stood before us. The road along the lake was lined with chestnut trees, which seemed to have survived the winds without excessive damage. As we continued our inspection tour past the manor, the kitchen with its woodshed and smokehouse was on our right. The cook, Katarzyna, was zealously directing the kitchen girls to clear the lawn, roadway and paths of branches that littered throughout the area. Uninterrupted aromatic smoke gently curled out of the smokehouse, promising savory sausages. We passed the St. Jan Nepomucen monument. A culvert fed water under the monument and road to the sluice gate regulating water flow to a pond behind the monument. Adding or removing planks controlled the water level. This was a favored place. We would often stand here to watch as pike jumped over the sluice to get into the pond.

Continuing to the stables before us, we were greeted by the coachman encircled by his numerous children. "We suffered no significant damage m'Lord, m'Lady and young Lords and Ladies," he said addressing our group. His children, our ages, gathered around us as the coachman further addressed Mama and Papa. We excitedly shared our experiences.

Adam asked, "Did you see how easily the wind knocked down all the poplar trees?"

"Not all!" replied Jozek, the coachman's oldest child. He worked for the gardener and everyone seemed to like him, though the gardener and I were not as enamored with him and agreed that he was a poor influence on the local boys. As we continued, Jozek said, "Look, one of the poplars next to the hospice and another beside the stable survived."

Worried about the storks, I said, "Well, with these two poplars standing, some young storks might also survive."

The coachman heard my comment and, with a smile on his face, said, "I hope some of the storks survive to return again next year, that they may bring the manor more children."

"They may bring you more children also," we laughed. He grinned and nodded in agreement.

"And maybe not!" Jozek said in a menacing tone. None of us, at the time, understood this comment and the strange expression on his face, but with all the excitement no one questioned him and we all let it pass. We would only learn the significance of his strange statement after the start of war.

Hurrying to catch up to Mama and Papa we passed the road to Krasnik, made a sign of the cross as we passed the mission cross and went by the fisher's house. Mama and Ewa went into the hospice to check on how the old folk had weathered the storm and if they needed anything. The rest of us crossed the road to Piaski and went to the chapel.

Our great-aunts had the chapel built at the same time as the manor. Papa unlocked the door with the large key; we entered and followed Papa through the large, heavy wooden doors with their iron ties. We saw that a branch protruded through a window. Some glass was strewn about. Apart from this minor damage everything seemed unscathed. Dipping our fingers into the holy water by the door, we crossed ourselves and, trying not to walk on the glass, we walked over to our family pews on the right side before the altar. We all knelt down and said a short silent prayer. Mama and Ewa joined us. In a hushed voice Papa, nodding in the direction of the sanctuary lamp, said to Mama, "The lamp is still burning." I noticed that indeed, the perpetual candle was burning despite the draft coming through the broken window.

The chapel was about ten meters wide and twenty meters long, from the door to the wall behind the altar. Behind the altar was a wall beyond which was the small sacristy. In front of the right side of this wall was a heavy, dark, wooden chair with a lattice wood screen. The priest would always sit on the chair before Mass. He listened to the confessions of individuals, one by one, as they knelt before the screen. Often, while waiting their turn, a line would form before our pews. The whitewashed walls had tall, narrow windows on either side. Stations of the cross were around the chapel under these windows. In the rear was a steep staircase to a narrow choir loft spanning the back of the chapel with its small organ. Locking the door again on our departure from the chapel, Papa said, "The Lord Jesus has watched over us!"

CHAPTER 16

ALL OF 1932 marked many changes for the family. Michal and his wife Dusia were living on Michal's estate, Naglowice, near Kielce. My sister Marysia, having finished high school, decided to stay home and help Mama with the youngest children. Niula brought Stasia, one of the servant girls from Poznan, to the new apartment on Lionski Street in Grodno. Krzysztof and Jas went to the Stefan Batory High School for boys and Adam and Ewa went to the Nazaretanki preschool. I went to Emilja Plater Girls High School on Domikanski Street. Ela was initially sent to a private school, the Gimnazjum Imienia Swietej Tereski. The three Szczuka sisters in Rabka, near Krakow, organized it. It was thought that Ela, who was always more on the fragile side, would benefit from the healthy mountain air. The Szczuka School was attended by girls from high society and had high educational standards. Andrzej, Piotr, Jozek and Kryla remained at home.

When my parents suggested that I join Ela in Rabka, I protested. Knowing that I studied well and that I wished to participate in activities not available in Rabka, they acquiesced, sending Ewa and me to school in Grodno. While in school we lived in the Lionski Street apartment. The furnishings from Poznan arrived there ahead of us. This apartment proved to be a tight fit. We were pleased when, the next year, my parents liquidated Mama's apartment in Warsaw and rented a second, adjoining apartment in Grodno. With a common entry, Mama's furnishings were placed in the adjoining apartment. My parents stayed there on their frequent visits to Grodno. Ewa then joined Ela in Rabka and I was allowed to live in a room within the second, my parent's apartment, which significantly lessened the crowding in the first apartment. Here I benefited from the bedroom furniture that was so memorable to me

BACK: KRZYSZTOF
MIDDLE, LEFT TO RIGHT: ELA, EWA, JAS, TERENIA
FRONT: MARYSIA
POZNAN, 1932

from my first trip to Warsaw as a small child. I was not permitted to utilize my parent's salon, dining room or bedroom, but enjoyed my relatively elevated status and independence, along with the smell of leather furniture I remembered so fondly.

Lionski Street led onto Orzeszkowa Street, the namesake of the popular female author who wrote about this region, its legends and people. Every day I passed the house where she had once lived and written. Nearby was an old Orthodox church with its tall bell tower. We were fascinated to discover that only one man pulled all the various ropes that rang the many bells. He would attach specific ropes to his arms and legs and then, remarkably, "danced" the appropriate tune, which we all became accustomed to. Occasionally we would hear a misapplied note. Once, passing the bell tower, we noticed that a group of mischievous boys stood outside. As the bell ringer started his dance, one boy pulled out a slingshot. Targeting the poor man, whom we could see from below, they let fly with a pebble that struck the bell ringer. He flinched, pulling a rope improperly, resulting in the wrong note. We ran away lest we be accused of participating in some Orthodox sacrilege. Now we understood why the tunes sometimes seemed irregular.

We arrived home, breathless, just in time to hear Papa's distinctive one-horse carriage arrive below. Having heard the false note as he had turned the corner onto Lionski Street, Papa saw us looking up and then run away. Suspicious of our activities, he came up and confronted us. We hurriedly explained our innocence. Papa indicated that he was relieved that we were innocent of wreaking havoc against another church. Good-naturally, with a smile upon his face, he added that we could not have effectively contrived such a well-correlated story in the short time since his arrival on the scene. We did not tell Papa that his preference for his special carriage, with its distinctive sound, had often given us ample notice of his impending arrival. Though innocent this time, we were well aware of the advantage of advance notice to his arrival.

I immediately liked the school in Grodno, made many close friends there and increased my extra-curricular activities, particularly scouting. The nuns in Poznan had never fully accepted scouting, which we introduced there. In Grodno, scouting was well established and organized. The school fully supported it and was not threatened by the freedom scouting offered its students. Indeed there were close ties between school and scouting. Both supported individual incentive, initiative and responsibility. Scouting bolstered Polish patriotism and individual leadership.

In a short time I was elected Patrol Leader. My love for nature aided in preparation and implementation of trips and camp-outs around Grodno. I loved singing scout and patriotic songs around late night campfires and the communal lifestyle. We organized numerous celebrations supporting national heroes and days of patriotic remembrance. Participating in numerous parades, our troop was highly acclaimed for making a good presentation: proudly carrying our flags, being well outfitted and marching smartly. We learned how to best help the needy.

My leadership and active involvement helped raise my candidacy when the school needed to pick a person to run the school store. My responsibility, after a month of instruction and oversight, was to procure and then sell all school materials, other than textbooks, to the 500 students. Students were required to purchase all such supplies from the store. I had to make wise purchases from suppliers, price everything carefully, conduct sales and make a full daily and monthly accounting for all finances and supplies. I felt highly complimented by having been given such independent authority and responsibility and having accorded such trust. It did not come to my head at the time that I was a good risk. Had there been any shortage, Papa would have made up the difference.

When I was a little older, girls from many schools were organized in the PWK, the Women's Army Training Corps. This corps prepared us for the eventuality of war by teaching relevant classes: proper use of gas masks, first aid, marching drills, how to shoot rifles, and military structure. We also taught children and adults: to read, patriotic history, and crafts as a means of being productive while providing an alternative source of income. The training was conducted and completed very seriously. One main attraction for me was the fellowship of campfires.

I had the advantage that the local head of the PWK, Miss Krystyna Reut, lived in our same building on Lionski Street. I liked her very much and felt that the feeling was mutual, though she was much older than I. One day, just as some of us had been complaining that we did not have a center for our activities, she invited me to inspect a potential facility. Happily joining her, I was taken by surprise that we were to be given the use of author Orzeszkowa's house.

Ceremoniously obtaining the key from city officials, we entered the building filled with expectation of what we would accomplish there. Our expectant attitude was checked immediately as our eyes grew accustomed to the gloom inside. The building had obviously not been used or kept in repair for an extended time. Mice, which had ruled these confines for unknown months, scurried about at our intrusion. Walking through, we were entangled in spider webs. The stench of abandonment was oppressive. Quickly walking through, we silently stopped in the center of the room and looked about. It was getting late. We both recognized the tremendous amount of work that would be required. Almost as if by a signal we decided in unison that we would take this run down structure and make it the home for our organization.

At the organizational meeting that took place at school the next day, we identified each person's skills and capabilities to contribute and made a plan to clean, refurbish and decorate the building. The next afternoon, after school, Orzeszkowa's home was attacked on all fronts. I started working there during all available after school hours. Soon, rather than getting home for our one p.m. lunch, I started arriving late, even for dinner, sometimes late in the evening. Stasia, knowing me well from our days in Poznan, started holding over my lunch. I ate it ravenously, at whatever hour I returned home, some times even in conjunction with dinner, to satisfy my colossal appetite. One day, Niula approached me about my schedule, though it was known that I was always deeply involved in various activities and organizations. When I told her about our work at Orzeszkowa's home and that I was returning with Miss Reut when it was dark, she was appeased. Not wanting to sacrifice any time away from our work, I learned to complete homework during and between classes.

Progress was impressive. After three months, we had converted the inside of Orzeszkowa's home from a dank, forsaken space to a useful, inviting center for our activities. When work at the center was completed, we started singing songs by the glow of its fireplace. Miss Reut and others would often tell us stories about various camps they had attended. I soon started yearning to participate at one of these camps.

A family misfortune started in the summer of 1933. My sister Marysia fell in love with Papa's apprentice, Pawel Orlowski, who lived in the guest wing room with its independent entrance. Against Mama's and Papa's counsel, Marysia (age 21) and Pawel (age 22) could not be dissuaded and were married in Ciechocinek on the 23rd of December 1933. Mama and Papa attended the Catholic wedding Mass. Papa said that he would, for now, continue to give Marysia an allowance despite the family's disapproval of the union.

I had noticed a budding romance the previous summer, but knew nothing of their plans and only learned of the wedding after Christmas. That previous summer turned out to be the last time I would ever see Marysia, my oldest sister. I learned later that Pawel had worked in a plywood plant in Mosty. We heard that they had two children, Ryszard in 1935 and Andrzej in 1937. Through all these years Papa continued to send Marysia an allowance. Pawel was drafted into the Polish army in 1939. The last contact the family had with them was during the German offensive against Russia when Krzysztof, trying to get back to the estate, met Pawel in Grodno. Pawel was trying at that time to locate Marysia and the children. They had lost touch with one another during those turbulent years. During the war we learned that Marysia was shot and killed in 1943, whether by the Germans, or the "AK"[27] is unclear.

My last year at school in Grodno, the 1934–1935 school year, was marked by the death of Jozef Pilsudski (1867–1935), a Polish revolutionary, independence fighter and national hero, who became a dictator of resurrected Poland. Born at Zulow (near present-day Vilnius, Lithuania) on December 5, 1867, Pilsudski was educated at the University of Krakow. During his student years he became sympathetic to the Socialist movement, which advocated the independence of Poland from Russian rule.

Arrested in 1887 on a charge of conspiring to assassinate Emperor Aleksander III of Russia, although innocent, Pilsudski was sentenced to five years of penal servitude in Siberia. Released in 1892, he became a leader of the Polish Socialist party. In 1894 he began to publish a secret party newspaper, *The Worker*. Pilsudski later organized a secret private army of about 10,000 Poles to fight for the freedom of Poland. When World War I broke out, he offered his forces to the Austrians to fight the Russians.

Late in 1916, the Central Powers proclaimed an independent Polish kingdom and formed a council of state, with Pilsudski as a member. When he refused, however, to order his troops to support the Central Powers against the Allies, the Germans imprisoned Pilsudski.

He returned to Warsaw following release in November 1918. A national hero, he proclaimed Poland an independent republic. He was immediately accepted as head of state and commander in chief of the Polish army; as such, he supervised the disarming of the remaining occupation armies of the Central Powers and all Polish military commanders placed themselves under his command.

As his aim was the restoration of the territories belonging to Poland at the time of the partition in 1772, Pilsudski came into conflict with the new Czechoslovak and Lithuanian states and with the Bolshevik regime in the newly established Soviet Union. During the Russo-Polish War of 1920, Pilsudski, who was made marshal of Poland, successfully defended Warsaw

---

[27]AK: Armia Krajowa, "National Army," The underground organization that opposed the invading German army.

against invading Soviet armies. He resigned as chief of state in December 1922.

On May 12, 1926, however, disappointed in the performance of the parliamentary system, he led a military revolt that overthrew the government. Thereafter, until his death, he was the virtual dictator of Poland; he was uninterruptedly the minister of war and commander in chief of the army and twice during this time, from 1926 to 1928 and again in 1930, he was premier of Poland.

He died in Warsaw on May 12, 1935. His death was regarded with great sorrow by the entire nation, even by those who opposed his autocratic rule. Pilsudski was recognized as having ruled Poland through difficult times providing it with stability and prosperity, though with considerable opposition.

I learned of his death, as did many others, while in school. Each school sent a delegation to his funeral. One of my last activities at my school in Grodno was when I, along with another student and a teacher, was sent to Warsaw to represent Emilja Plater High School. Although my parents had criticized some of Pilsudski's mode of operation, I was grateful that they allowed me to attend the funeral. I was very proud to be chosen by the school for this honor although there was little time for preparation.

We departed the next morning and were hosted by various schools in Warsaw. Pilsudski's sarcophagus was laid on a catafalque,[28] before which a long line of mourners slowly passed by. We stood in this line for many hours together with, it seemed, all of Poland. The sense of a great national loss was overwhelming. Everyone was crying as mounds of flowers were placed around the sarcophagus. The entire time, an honor guard stood by. The line continued through the day and night until the next day when the funeral procession was held.

The funeral procession was unforgettable! We stood on a street that was lined with soldiers, shoulder to shoulder, not allowing anyone onto the roadway where the procession was to pass. As Pilsudski's procession advanced toward where we stood, the crowd behind us surged forward, wanting to view the casket that was upon a caisson drawn by teams of fine black thoroughbreds. The crowd pushed forward against us and we were pressed into the line of soldiers. With the soldier's line about to be breached, mounted police that had been patrolling the line, backed the soldiers facing the crowd. The crowd, nonetheless, continued to surge forward. Soldiers held us back, but the massed crowd pushed us forward into the line of soldiers, further forward

---

[28]Catafalque: draped platform supporting the coffin during a funeral or lying-in-state.

and into the street. As the line started to breach, the battle trained mounted police horses were made to rear up onto their hind legs! Standing there, threateningly, sharp hoofs opposed the surging mass.

Alarmed, frightened front lines of people pushed back for fear of being struck by the rearing horses. With people now surging back from the front and others from the back pushing forward, the body of the crowd was crushed. People started screaming out, fearing, as I did, being suffocated or trampled. Looking up at the hooves of the magnificent, threatening horses, whose hooves could come down on me at any time, many thoughts crossed my mind. Pilsudski, momentarily, was the least of importance. Being pushed in on from all sides I could not breathe. I feared getting separated from my teacher. I was unfamiliar with Warsaw and if we separated I would never manage to find her in these crowds. I realized, in a moment of alarm, that I had no idea even where we were staying, having simply followed our teacher there last night. Terror was encroaching not only myself but also the crowd that was now threatened from all sides. Then, as suddenly as it had started, the pressure of the crowd dissipated. Pilsudski's hearse had passed. We read in the evening paper that the over-exuberant crowds had crushed several people to death.

CHAPTER 17

THE SUMMER when I was fifteen years old proved to be a very busy and intense one, full of rich experiences. Mama and Papa agreed to the plans I proposed for attending summer camps organized by both Scouting and the PWK. I spent the few weeks at home prior to my departure in intense preparation. My plan was to go directly from one camp to the other. I therefore had to be prepared and take along everything for both camps when I first departed.

I first packed everything for scout camp in a suitcase. I then packed a knapsack for the first camp — with the PWK. Preparation was made very carefully. Each item's necessity and use was thought through numerous times. I first assembled the various uniforms that I would need and placed them on their respective piles. Next came shoes. I would need sturdy shoes for my upcoming extensive travels and for walking through the mountains while undergoing PWK training. Scout camp required another pair of shoes that would be in good condition, as we would be scrutinized at various events, including the visit of the President of Poland. Then came underwear. I tried to minimize these while sure to have an adequate supply. Next were all my toiletry items. I picked each item carefully to minimize bulk and weight, but to be sure that I had all I would need. Then I took a light raincoat and all the outdoor equipment such as whistle, compass, rope and a mess kit. Finally I organized maps, instructions, documents and money.

I was quite preoccupied with the fact that I was to travel by train alone for the first time, to places I had never been previously, with numerous changes at unknown train stations. I planned to travel to the closest station nearest the camps, but was unsure how I would reach the camps themselves. I did not share my apprehension with anyone lest they see that I was afraid and at the last moment stop me from going.

On the first of July, I left home by bus to Grodno. In Grodno I took the train to Warsaw, then changed to Katowice and then to Wisla Glebce. There I took the bus to camp. During the entire trip I was constantly concerned that I would miss a stop or get off in the wrong place, and therefore I did not sleep during the long trip or layovers. Uneventfully, after various trains and layovers, I was relieved to be on the bus to camp. I was able to relax and enjoy the scenery. We were in the mountains at the origin of the mighty Wisla River, so familiar from my studies of Polish history and geography.

Arriving at Camp Istebna, I quickly met with my friends from school. They noticed my extra suitcase but did not criticize me, even rather admired and envied my luck and enterprise of going directly to the second camp, an international jamboree. Large army tents were erected for us and I was able to place my things in one—my home for the next two weeks. Hungry, we went to the field mess. I wolfed down a considerable portion of food prepared for us, there in the invigorating mountain air.

Over the next days we spent the time actively participating in drills, marches, trips into the mountains and evening campfires. The food was simple and satisfying, though not luxurious. I simply felt that as long as I was not hungry, I was okay. I learned how to maneuver in the mountains and became proficient in utilizing my compass for orienteering. I learned many new songs and heard much about this region and stories about other camps. Time flew by.

Three times I was given the responsibility as one of the night guards at the camp entrance, including my last night there. Advising the camp commander that I had to depart one day prior to the end of camp in order to reach the scout jamboree, I was given permission to leave early while still receiving full participation recognition. Secretly I was pleased to miss the confusion of liquidating camp that would occupy the last day.

Thinking that I would catch the first morning bus upon completing my final night guard duty, I said good-bye and went searching for the bus. There was no bus until too late in the afternoon. Not wanting to miss my train, I took off on foot for the eight-kilometer trek into town with my knapsack and suitcase. Thinking about my many wonderful adventures of the previous weeks, I arrived in town without noticing the length of the walk or the unwieldy weight of my bags. I had just enough time to get something to eat at the station when my train arrived.

Sitting in the train, having eaten, I suddenly realized how tired I was after camp, night duty and the long walk into town. I fell into a deep sleep. A sud-

den change in the train's movements awoke me and I learned that we had arrived in Katowice. Making the quick change to the train to Warsaw, I felt refreshed and looked forward, this time, to watching the scenery along the way.
To my surprise I awoke in the dark, not remembering having fallen asleep,
and suddenly feared that I might have passed Warsaw! Learning that we still
had some time before arriving, I checked each station we passed, trying not
to fall asleep again as my head kept falling to my chest. Arriving in Warsaw in
the morning, I learned that I need not have been fearful of passing Warsaw as
it was the train's last stop.

The scout jamboree was on the outskirts of Warsaw. Upon inquiring, I was
told to hurry to catch the train to Spala. It was crowded with people on their
way to the jamboree. I got on the train with no difficulty and soon arrived.
There, great crowds milled about. As this was a gathering of scouts from the
entire world, every language could be heard. I had no idea where to go, how
to find my troop, or even in which direction to head. Going to the headquar-
ters, I was relieved to find that they had maps locating each building, identi-
fying each road and indicating where every troop was. Having no idea of the
scale of this jamboree, or the extent of the camp, I was fascinated to look the
map over. The center of the camp had an enormous campfire bowl. Outside
of this was a ring of campfire bowls for smaller events by individual or multiple troops. I located on a map where my troop was and headed there.

Upon arriving at the designated location, I met two young girls from my
troop. The rest had been delayed somehow. The two girls had a tent and
asked if I would care to join them. They were happy to have an older familiar
face with them and I was happy to be in a tent. One of them was to be our
jamboree correspondent, and she had a first-rate camera.

As I got settled in the tent it started to rain. It was to rain unceasingly for
the entire two weeks! The raincoat that I had taken was very appreciated.
Many times I lent it to our "correspondent." She used it to protect herself
and her camera from the liquid elements during her many hours working
throughout the camp.

Soon after it started raining, the girls asked me if I would make them dinner, as they had to go somewhere, but were hungry and wanted to eat first.
This posed quite a quandary, as I did not know how to cook. All of my life
kitchen staff or servants had prepared my meals and I was seldom in a kitchen
at all. Owning up to the fact that I did not know how to cook, the second
girl said that she would help me. I made my first meal ever that first day of
camp — meat cutlets and potatoes. Finally, toward evening the rest of our
troop arrived and we were able to get our camp quickly set up.

The next morning we were given the jamboree schedule and our duties. Each troop was assigned one day to provide two gate guards. I was given this duty for our troop along with another friend. We were given very specific instructions concerning these duties. *No one* was to be allowed entrance without a password. There were different passwords for scouts and for guests. In case of any problem at the gate, the jamboree office was to be immediately notified.

Each troop prepared some kind of skit or song for the smaller campfires. We learned that there would be an inspection of our camp, with every troop competing for how best they could present their campsite. Inspecting various camps of troops from around the world, with my tent mate, the correspondent, I was amazed to see what some had done. Very elaborate, imaginative and artistic set-ups were made by the many boys and girls represented.

There were to be two main campfires, which everyone would attend together, at the big campfire bowl in the center of the camp. One was to be held early in the schedule to open the jamboree, the second to close the jamboree. They were elaborate, fun filled ceremonies, organized by the main jamboree organizers. There were Polish patriotic, international and historic as well as modern scout presentations. Thousands of scouts were in attendance. In the quiet of the dark, amid a light rain, the heat of the enormous campfire and the fellowship of scouts from near and far warmed us all. These campfires lasted well into the night.

The President of Poland, Ignacy Moscicki, came to the camp. He arrived midday, with an entourage from the Polish government to tour the camp. He arrived at the gate when I was on guard duty. Asking him for the all-important password, he smiled back at me saying that he did not know what it was. Following explicit guard duty instructions, though I recognized him, I told the President that I could not allow him to pass. One of his entourage approached me and whispered, "This is the President!"

I replied determinedly, "I know, but I cannot allow him in without the password." The entourage started talking anxiously to one another. One of them rushed off to learn what the password was. Returning, he informed the President what it was. The President of Poland approached me again and with a smile on his face told me the correct password, at which I saluted him and opened the gate allowing him entry.

The President attended the closing campfire ceremony, where he made a speech. Welcoming all the scouts from around the world, he complimented the troops for their creative camp set-ups. He was impressed with the high caliber of youth represented at the jamboree and said that they would serve their respective nations well. With this, the jamboree came to a close. Soon afterward, everything seemed to end quickly. The next day we packed everything, still in an ever-present rain, and returned home.

CHAPTER 18

"YOU LOOK terrible! You're filthy and your hair is a mess! Your clothes are a disaster!" exclaimed Ela upon seeing me after the bus let me off before the manor. "The house is full of guests! You must clean up before anyone sees you!" Hurrying into Mama's boudoir, I took a long, luxurious, hot bath. It was such a pleasure after the limited facilities during my last month at the two camps. Dressing in some fresh clothes, not a uniform, I combed my hair and felt great — clean once again.

The family and our guests were off exploring the fishery Papa had started a year earlier. Going around the lake, I passed the fisher's house and went walking through to where the fish ponds were. Not seeing anyone close by, I ventured into what was once a bog, but was now a well-organized series of fishponds. On my left was the deep over-wintering pond. It was about thirty meters square and had been dug over five meters deep. In the fall, fish from the other ponds would be put here to survive the cold winter. The fisher worked all winter to keep this pond from being iced over. He chopped through and removed ice so that the fish would have sufficient oxygen within the water's depths. On my right and beyond on both sides of the raised road were many man-made ponds occupying several dozen acres.

Papa had built them in an interesting way. He instructed men to dig a large ditch in a ring, with the dirt thrown outward to create a dike, upon which a road passed. The ditches were a few meters deep with an island in the center. This area, including the island, would be flooded until the island was about half a meter under water. Water was passed through a series of channels from the lake in front of the manor. The ponds were stocked with carp, highly regarded particularly by the Jewish population, providing the manor with another source of income.

I heard a gunshot and headed for it, as I knew that it must be one of my brothers shooting the many birds that preyed on the fish. Sure enough, after another shot, I found the whole group surrounding Krzysztof and Jas. They held up a few ducks and a heron, which I knew would soon be delivered to the kitchen. Uncle Rainier, who occasionally visited from France, also sported a shotgun and had several ducks attached to his belt.

"Terenia!" The entire group greeted me: Mama and Papa, Krzysztof, Ela and Jas; Aunt Karolina "Karo" and Uncle Rainier de Bourbon (Mama's sister and her husband) with their two children, Carmen and Ferdinand; along with their teacher, Monsieur de Rouwille. I, in turn, greeted each. I kissed Mama and Papa on both checks. Then, I kissed Aunt Karo and Uncle Rainier on their hands and received a warm hug in return. Finally I greeted my brothers and sister.

When I kissed Ela, she looked me up and down saying, "Well, now you look presentable."

Overhearing the comment, Aunt Karo exclaimed, "She doesn't just look presentable, she looks positively radiant!" Having spent the last month in camps, out-of-doors and in the fresh air, I was deeply tanned, physically fit and had a big contented smile on my face. Freshly washed, with clean and well-brushed hair, I was the picture of health and happiness. Mama and Papa stood alongside with proud smiles, happy to see me back and enjoying the praise bestowed upon their daughter returned from her adventure.

Not able to stand by any longer, Papa said, "Well, Terenia, how were the camps?" At this I could not help but start telling, with great exuberance, of my adventures, starting with my meeting the President, which everyone listened to with great interest.

Uncle Rainier, addressing me in formal French said, "Well, Lady Terenia, you must now be finding yourself in the papers, being such an important person, having the discretion whether to allow the President entry. I hope that you, Lady Terenia, will allow me entry to your home." He said this with a serious flourish and a twinkle in his eye, causing us all to laugh. Uncle Rainier was our favorite uncle, but as we all knew, he was titled. He was S.A.R. Prince de Bourbon de deux Siciles.

I answered him smiling warmly, "Uncle, you never need a password to enter our home, you know that you are always welcome." With an exaggerated flourish I indicated the path home. With everyone agreeing heartily, we jovially walked back past the fisher's house.

On our way to the manor Uncle Rainier praised Papa for his successes with the fishery. He enviously remarked that we were lucky to have such rich hunting as a result of the fish, patting the ducks hanging at his side. As we passed, Papa continued to explain various facets of the fishery. Each pond had a platform where the fish were fed. Taking some feed from a bucket set by one such pond, Papa threw some lupus feed into the water. Immediately, a large school of small carp appeared.

"When will they grow large enough to sell?" asked Aunt Karo.

"In the fall of their second year they reach about two kilograms. At that time buyers from the city come with tankers and we sell to them. The water level of the ponds is lowered and we simply scoop the fish from the ditches into the tankers. Some we will save, winter over, and in the spring they spawn."

"Simple and ingenious," replied my Aunt.

We were passing the fisher's house as Papa continued his narration. "Constant oversight is needed and so I built this house and hired a fisher who lives and works here. He maintains the correct water levels, feeds the fish, keeps an eye out that no problems develop, and tries to keep the growing number of birds away. He also oversees the transfer and sale of the fish when they are the right size. Then he takes care of those that we keep over winter."

The next morning my cousin Carmen and I took some horses and went for a ride. We crossed some clover fields and entered the forest. She asked me many questions about my experiences in camp, saying that she never had such an opportunity. She told me about her teacher, Monsieur de Rouwille. He was the grandson of the engineer Lesseps, who had been in charge of building the Suez Canal.

Although de Rouwille was only a little older than we were, he tried to maintain a distance in his capacity as teacher. He insisted that we call him by his family name, not by his first name. Each morning he held classes with Carmen and Ferdinand, a responsibility that he took quite seriously. Carmen told me that she thought he was a wonderful teacher. After classes, we all enjoyed his company and had a good time sharing many wonderful days in a variety of activities during the month of their visit. We were sorry when the time came for them to return to France.

CHAPTER 19

URING THE mid-1930s Mama decided that she would like to try her hand at starting a fruit tree nursery. Her family had nursery experience, and she talked with them at length about how to get started. Papa consented to her utilizing the field to the left of the entrance lane, toward the main road. Making an agreement with the gardener, she obtained starts from her family, and various seeds for apple, pear, cherry, plum, peach and apricot trees. The agreement with the gardener was that he would earn a percentage from any income generated from the nurseries. This motivated him and he was eager to work on the project. One of the factors stressed by Mama was that her family's experience showed that the nursery should not have too rich a soil. If trees started life in poorer soil they would not be as shocked if subsequently transplanted into poor soil.

There were no other tree nurseries in the region. When in three years Mama's young saplings were offered locally, they were quickly snapped up. This started an ongoing interest in her trees, particularly as they seemed to grow well. Even the more obscure fruit such as apricots and peaches did well, although everyone had told Mama these would not grow in our region. The trees started producing large, high quality fruit. Fruit trees started to show up in front of peasant cottages. Papa would often give trees as presents, particularly to a young couple at their wedding, or at the birth of a child. Villages and hamlets started to bloom with fragrant fruit blossoms each spring. During the summer and into fall, children with happy smiles were often encountered enjoying various luscious fruits.

Theft of fruit from our old orchards had always been a problem, but now that the locals also had fruit trees, this problem was markedly decreased. Papa decided to line roads, along which workers traversed through fields, with fruit trees. Thus, thirsty or hungry workers could simply reach up along the way and refresh themselves.

Papa's brother, Kazimierz, purchased a good quantity of the trees. He set up a large orchard nearby on his estate, planning to grow fruit for the production of candies. Papa also planted a large orchard on the other side of the main entrance lane. The market for our trees soon outstripped supply.

When it was time to ship the saplings, all of our wagons were occupied and we had to hire wagons from around the area to help. Peasants, happy for a chance for an additional source of income, provided an ample supply of wagons. Mama started to think about buying a truck. Never forgetting his near tragic accident, where he was so severely burned, Papa opposed buying one of the gasoline driven contraptions and stated that he would never drive one. Krzysztof, who was very impatient to get up-to-date and eagerly anticipated the opportunity to drive a car, encouraged making the transition to more modern methods.

In spite of early success, apricot and peach trees did not catch on as did the other trees. People were concerned that these trees would not survive a hard winter. Many trees were left over toward the end of 1939. The gardener was prepared to dig them up out of the nursery and throw them away to make room for the more popular trees.

In 1939, as the war started, most of the older boys and young men were conscripted to military duty. The gardener was also drafted, leaving an exceptional crop, with no one to dig up the trees, or to pick fruit. The unwanted apricot and peach trees were particularly bountiful. Many people crossed our terrain at this time, trying to escape before the war front. At first, they moved eastward in front of the German army invading from the west, then westward before the Russians advancing from the east. Papa encouraged all of these unfortunate people to benefit from the bountiful, underutilized fruit, which they did thankfully. These were indeed dire times. People escaped with little or no warning or preparation, and often without provisions. Not only the fruit orchards, but also our gardens soon started feeding these refugees—but these events are getting ahead of the story.

Papa continued to expand development and economic activities of the estate, which I particularly noted throughout my teen years, starting in 1932 up to the pre-war days of 1939. It was funny to observe how proud he was to see the result of his interests, wherever he happened to be, while making his frequent tours of the holdings. It seemed that he wanted to be able to see his mark from any vantage point, standing anywhere on his estates. Many of the activities he undertook were intended to improve the welfare of the regional population.

Following an example out of Sweden, Papa organized the regional creamery cooperative, a form of enterprise previously unknown in this corner of the world. There were numerous discussions about the idea, but none were willing to be the first to start this unsure venture until Papa took the lead. A major component of wealth for peasant families was having a cow. This enabled their children to have ample milk, a mainstay for family health throughout the year. Additionally, these cows were bred each year with the hope of having a calf. When a calf grew and was subsequently sold, the family's income was significantly supplemented. A common scene was a cow or calf calmly grazing by the roadside, attended to by a child, or an older person, who held on to it by a rope lead. Each village or hamlet had its pastures for the cattle belonging to those families, under the care of a designated person. Folklore often surrounded these daily scenes. It was said that as the cattle meandered home, if a brown cow led the herd then it would rain, if a black one was at the lead, then the weather would be clear.

When Papa set up the creamery, families brought their milk to central points each morning and evening, where a centrifuge separated the milk from the cream. Our kitchen was one of the central points. The milk was then returned to the family. In this way families still had plenty of milk to feed their children. The cream was taken by wagon to the creamery in Indura, conveyed in large, metal milk cans. The creamery made butter that was shipped to Warsaw. Profits were tallied and each contributor was paid their percentage of creamery profits on a monthly basis. Everyone was very happy with this arrangement. A family could earn 30 or 40 Polish zloty a month from a cow's cream. This often doubled the family's income without significantly reducing the amount of milk available to the family.

The creamery proved to be successful, not only for the local peasant community, but also for us as we had our own herd of Dutch Jersey cows. The Jersey cows produced volumes of milk. When cream became the important ingredient, not just the amount of milk, Papa decided to sell his prized herd of black and white Jersey cows. He converted to the new line of red Polish cows. While producing less milk, the Polish cow's milk was high in fat content, producing more cream than the Jerseys. Having ample milk, after the centrifuge separated the cream, Papa shipped what excess milk could not be utilized on the estate, and sold it to the Jewish cheese maker at Krasnik. With the purchase of the new herd, Papa hired a specialist, Mr. Kucinski, who took care of them. The specialist maintained their health, ensured that they gave good milk and continuously tested it to be sure that the milk was safe. He also kept meticulous breeding records to maintain the strength and purity of the line.

One day Mama and Papa decided that the cows gave an opportunity for each of us girls to learn some lessons about economics. Papa gave Ela, Ewa, Kryla and me each a cow. Creamery proceeds from "our" cows were tallied. As individual members of the creamery cooperative, we were paid our share each month. There were, however, conditions attached. Papa said that we could not spend the money on day-to-day expenditures. We had to invest the money. Papa said that he would help us with investing. We could also propose ways to spend our money on major activities. When we reached the age of twenty-one, we would be free to do what we pleased with the money. In the meantime, we had to obtain his agreement on any expenditure. Each of us approached these finances in different ways.

Papa showed us how to deposit the money in the PKO.[29] We could also purchase stock. Papa would meet with us to discuss the relative advantages of various options. Ewa proved to be the best saver; her investments grew sizably. Ela slowly accumulated her stock savings, but spent the majority of her "creamery money" on travels and clothing. I spent my money each year on travels throughout Europe. Papa considered my travels a reasonable expenditure and supported such trips. I would buy train tickets and take 200 zloty in cash. This was the maximum amount of cash the Polish government permitted an individual to take out of the country. I don't remember what Kryla did with her money.

After World War Two, Ela, Ewa and I had a discussion about Papa and how he had set us up with our creamery income. Ewa, despite having lost everything (her savings disappeared during the war), continued to live conservatively. She always seemed to have ample funds. Ela had many pleasant memories from the experience. I gained a sense of comfort in international travels and felt as though I was a citizen of the world, though always a Polish patriot. I acquired a broad knowledge and appreciation from my travels and became acquainted with many individuals from our extensive family and friends of the family. I had spent my money on things that could not be taken away from me. Indeed, the knowledge and experience I had acquired helped me during the war. Papa's lessons in economics, through the income from our cows, benefited me greatly.

---

[29]PKO: Polska Kasa Oszoszczednosci, Polish Savings Bank.

As I write these thoughts sixty years later, people are amazed that I still venture afar into areas others fear to visit. They seem astonished that I am undaunted by lack of information about my route or destination, by less than first-rate conditions and accommodations or that meals might be meager. I continue to revel in each new experience.

There was no school near the family estate. We had nannies and governesses that took care of our primary education prior to being sent to school, but other local children did not have such advantages. Papa built a one-room schoolhouse, a few hundred meters west of the estate entry off the main road, for the children of estate workers and the families living nearby. Next to it he built a small home for the teacher. The school was for children ages seven to twelve. Papa paid the teacher's salary and for all the needs and upkeep of the school.

Soon after building the school, Papa built a large formal gate by the main road, where our main entry drive started. Next to it, he had a house built for the gatekeeper, Mr. Mielnik, in the characteristic style reminiscent of those found in the Polish mountains by Zakopane. From that time forward, individuals or vehicles wanting to enter the estate had first to be admitted by the gatekeeper. Papa installed a telephone between the small salon in the manor and the gate. When necessary, the gatekeeper telephoned the manor for instructions about a petitioner's request to enter. Obtaining instructions that a visitor was welcome, the gatekeeper took his large key, unlocked and opened the heavy iron gate, permitting entry. Building the gate and having a gatekeeper had the desired effect of reducing the constant traffic in front of the manor. People and wagon drivers who had become accustomed to taking short cuts on the driveway beside the manor now had to take the main road around as they travelled between hamlets.

CHAPTER 20

URING THE fall of 1935, Ela, Ewa and I went to school in Rabka, at the high school run by three sisters of the Szczuka family. In the previous year the Szczuka sisters had built a new, modern school building with financial assistance from students' parents. Mrs. Irena Szczuka was the school director. She hired a principal, Jadwiga Niedzwiedzka, who was responsible for the curriculum meeting State educational accreditation requirements. Zofia Szczuka was in charge of boarding. The third sister, Krystyna Szczuka, took care of the chapel and religiously related activities. Having lost a leg in an accident as a young girl, she had an artificial wooden prosthesis, which allowed us always to know when she approached.

The top floor, the fourth, was utilized for living and work quarters by service staff in charge of cleaning and laundry. Cooks and the women who cared for us during non-school hours were also quartered there. The next two floors down were where we lived, four to a room. Each room had a large widow, opened each night so we slept with ample fresh mountain air. Each student had a corner with her metal-framed bed. It had to be neatly made prior to class each day. Each also had a night table and a chair upon which we put our uniform dress every night. At the end of each hall were large common bathrooms that included six bathtubs, twelve showers and as many toilets and sinks. Each girl had a small numbered shelf where she kept her toothbrush, comb and hairbrush and maybe a few other small toiletries. The number on our shelf was the same number we used to label our clothing and personal belongings. I had been assigned the number "5." Dirty linen and clothing were deposited in the bathroom. The staff washed, cleaned and delivered them to our rooms.

Eight classrooms and a bathroom occupied the next floor down, the so-called first floor. Classrooms, as was the entire building, were well heated. Radiators operated from a large coal furnace in the basement. The classrooms had large windows that Miss Irena constantly opened, as she was always hot, explaining to us that the air was good for us. On cold winter days we would be chilled. When she left, we quickly closed the windows again. Next to the central staircase on the first floor was the principal's office.

Students each had their own assigned chair and desk within which we kept our books and personal supplies. Closeted shelves stood on one wall. They held reference books and materials as well as additional supplies. The front of each room was covered with a large blackboard under which hung a small shelf containing chalk and a sponge for cleaning the blackboard. In front of the blackboard the teacher had a desk and chair, though they seemed to be rarely in use, as our teachers generally wandered about our classes giving general or individual instruction. Each subject lasted just less than an hour, after which we had a short break. During breaks, teachers rotated to their next class. We had the opportunity to talk with students throughout the floor, make purchases in the store run by Miss Zofia, or take care of whatever other activities we were involved with.

The next level down, the *parter,* or ground floor, included Miss Irena's office, with its parlor, where all discussions with students, parents and visitors were held. One end of the floor had private quarters where the staff lived: the Szczuka sisters, their mother Mrs. Sroczynski (widowed again after her second marriage) and her sister Miss Szadurski, whom we all particularly liked partially due to her unimposing character. The other end of the building contained the kitchen and dining room that had long tables covered with white tablecloths, with individual wooden chairs on both sides. The main entrance opened into hallways; right to the dining room, left past Miss Irena's office and the infirmary and on to the Szczuka's private quarters. Stairs led up or down to the basement where we seldom ever ventured.

The school was quite successful. The Szczuka sisters put all their energy and interest into it and ran it well. They attracted excellent help and teachers who knew how to fulfill the many and varied needs of their charges. The school enrolled around a hundred girls in the fourth through the twelfth grades, ending with the difficult graduation examination required by universities.

The school had a family-like atmosphere. With only one hundred students, we all knew one another well. It was an exclusive, expensive school, primarily attended by girls from noble families, but also attended by girls from families of better-off business and administrative leaders. Many of the girls were related, often having met prior to attending the school. They expected to know one another throughout their lives. They had usually been raised with common ideologies, traditions and concepts for living. Their families were not only wealthy but highly educated, well traveled, had a diversity of experience, were multi-lingual, and connected to important families throughout Europe, if not the entire world. They wanted the same for their daughters. The girls were expected to know how to behave at court and at fine dinners, be appreciative of the arts, know how take care of themselves and a household, and potentially participate in the running of an estate. They were exposed to a wide range of sports and were expected to be active participants in them.

The school was not a convent. Ample opportunity was provided for the girls to meet and mingle with boys and young men, most often and in particular, with those from the nearby Benedictine boarding school for young men. Many celebrations, dances and concerts were organized cooperatively between the schools. The boys and young men were from comparable backgrounds. They were also often related to one another as well as to the girls. With time, many marriages resulted from the interaction among these young men and women.

I was not initially eager to attend the school run by the Szczuka sisters. One of the reasons was that the school was originally a school for delicate girls. This resulted in the school having some peculiarities. One in particular, which I strenuously objected to, was the requirement that the girls had to rest in their beds, or in hammocks out-of-doors, for two hours after lunch each day. The thought of having to endure this, I could not stand. Such repose might be fine for some inactive, fragile girls, but I had always been active and energetic. The thought of having to lie still in such a way during the middle of the day was unacceptable. I told my mother if I had to do this each day, I would soon tear the school apart. Prior to my arrival at the school, my sisters repeated and underscored my statements and my wild character to classmates and faculty. My mother obtained permission dispensing me from the cruel custom of two hours midday bed rest. I was allowed to be involved in active pursuits during these hours. The staff watched me closely to be sure that I did not get into too much mischief. Having this extra time allowed me to be involved in and to pursue activities in many school organizations and functions. I was elected to represent the student body in my third year at the school.

Six months after I arrived at the school, while in the store assisting Miss Zofia, she asked me if I was unhappy. Surprised by the question I replied that, to the contrary, I was amazed by how much I was enjoying the school and was curious why she asked this funny question. She then told me that

upon hearing about me from my mother and sisters, they had been somewhat apprehensive of my wild character. Since they were not observing such
behavior, they were concerned that I might be depressed. This conversation
opened a channel of communication between us that we enjoyed from that
time forward.

Toward the end of the first year, we were all animated by the news that a
few selected Polish students were invited by Balkan students to come and
become familiar with their nation. Each school was to choose three students
and one teacher for the trip. The prospect of going to Yugoslavia, Bulgaria,
Romania and Hungary was thrilling and many students were eager to be chosen. With only a month to prepare, my class was told that students from our
class would go, accompanied by Zofia Szczuka. I was one of the three! The
trip was to be in May. Now came the question. Would our parents approve
our going on the trip? Sitting down to write home for permission, I paused
to think how to ask. I prayed to the Holy Spirit for inspiration about how I
should write to move my parents that they embrace my participation in this
adventure. I inserted the pen tip onto the quill, dipped the tip into my inkpot
and held the blotter, in my left hand, nervously down on the sheet of paper. I
started, carefully, to write a neat and concise letter to Mama and Papa.

Rabka, April 23, 1936
Dear Mama and Papa,

*As I promised you when I left for Rabka, I have not brought upon you
any shame and have behaved myself, as you would want me to. In fact, I
have been accepted here, have made many friends and am doing well. As
an example to show you how well I have been doing, today I was honored
and picked out as one of only three girls from the entire student body to
represent them. A condition of being able to represent the Szczuka's school
is that I must obtain your permission to go on the two-week trip around
the Balkan countries, chaperoned by Miss Zofia Szczuka. Costs associ-
ated with the trip I have covered by a fraction of my milk money and
I believe that you, Papa, will agree that this is a wise use of my money.
I always have good luck in my life and was chosen for this trip. Now I
am without doubt that my luck will continue and that you will give me
your blessing to go on the trip. I need your permission immediately, ide-
ally by telegram.*
Your loving daughter,
Terenia

To this letter was added a short itinerary for the trip. I also enclosed the school's letter supporting the trip. Carefully folding them all, I put them in an envelope and sealed and addressed it. My heart beat audibly, racing in apprehension and hope, when I dropped the envelope into the school post box.

For the next few days I dreamed about preparations and what I would need with me during the trip. I did not even consider the possibility that my parents would refuse me permission to go. I didn't even utilize my usual trickery for obtaining permission from my parents. My system included first preparing Papa. I would work on him until I was confident that he would agree to whatever I wanted and only then make my request. Having Papa on my side, I then went to Mama. I would present her with my request, asking permission. When she would say that I needed to obtain Papa's permission, I would say that Papa already agreed. This system had always worked in the past. Now, I was so confident and there was so little time, that I did not consider the need for my "system."

With the two non-uniform dresses that I had with me, I would not need anything from home for the trip. The two other girls picked out for the adventure were some of my closest friends. One was Chouquett Chamiec, daughter of the director of Polish Radio. The second was Wanda Szymanowski, daughter of a surgeon. Chouquett was very pleasant and quite cultured. She had often been a part of high society functions related to her father's work. She had a charming approach to people. Wanda was of a completely different nature. She was the most beautiful girl I had ever encountered. What was curious was that she was completely unaware of her beauty. She was wonderfully built, had long blond hair and light skin always tanned to a golden glow. Her facial features were as if carved from Italian marble. She was a truly natural girl, without pretenses and my favorite companion for our trips into the mountains, playing sports, or attending games.

Only a few days after I had sent the letter to my parents, Zofia Szczuka approached me saying that she had important information. She had a telegram from my parents. Observing me closely, tilting her head slightly, peering at me through concentrating eyes, she softly asked if I wanted to read the telegram myself, or would I prefer that she read it to me. Not exposing any reaction, I stated, "I am sure that they have given me permission for the trip."

Miss Zofia was unable to suppress her surprise at my confidence. Smiling kindly, handing me the telegram, she replied, "You are right, Terenia. The telegram gives you your permission. Congratulations!" Taking the telegram offered from her extended hand, I looked at it and read:

```
W  E  A  R  E  H  A  P  P  Y  T  H  A  T  Y  O  U  W  E  R  E  O
N  E  O  F  T  H  O  S  E  C  H  O  S  E  N  S  T  O  P  W  E  A
P  P  R  O  V  E  Y  O  U  R  T  R  I  P  W  H  O  L  E  H  E  A
R  T  E  D  L  Y  S  T  O  P  P  A  R  E  N  T  S  S  T  O  P
```

It is a good thing that Miss Zofia told me what was in the telegram. Initially I couldn't even read it. I feared that I might reveal my apprehension if I was to read it in front of her without first knowing what it said. Slowly, I was able to make out the message: "We are happy that you were one of those chosen. Stop. We approve your trip wholeheartedly. Stop. Parents. Stop."

After giving me a chance to work out the message, Miss Zofia said, "You must now start preparations for the trip."

I replied, to her obvious surprise, "I have already prepared a list of what I need." Continually working on the list, I had it with me constantly and showed it to her. After briefly examining my list, she indicated that it indeed looked comprehensive, without extraneous items and that I had done a good job preparing it. She also expressed her surprise that I had everything prepared when I did not even know if I was going. She then asked how I knew so well what I did and did not need for such a trip. I told her about my previous summer's experience going to the two camps.

Quite impressed and interested in my experience, she said that she was happy to have me along on the trip, that at least one of our party was experienced in such adventures. The four of us started meeting regularly, preparing for our upcoming departure. We studied maps, looking at where we would traverse following our itinerary, looked into what arts and architecture we might encounter, and studied what cultures we could expect to experience. During this process I learned that when we arrived in Sofia, the capital of Bulgaria, we would be split up, each of us living with a different family.

My previous year's travels had taught me to travel light. I packed one small suitcase for the trip. I had less to carry than my three traveling companions. Knowing that we would spend a few days on the Black Sea, I happily added to my packing list the wonderful bathing suit that I had dreamed of for so long. I could just imagine myself sunning by the exotic and fashionable saltwater beaches in the hot, Balkan sun. My parents had given me the suit for Christmas 1935. The world famous bathing suit manufacturer, Jantzen, made it in the far away, small, west coast American town of Portland, Oregon. (Not in my wildest dreams did I imagine that I would one day live there and watch it grow into a large modern city.)

The bathing suit was made of one piece of highest quality, navy blue, wool material. A loop at the top front went over my head. The material went down my front, between my legs and up the back. It was fastened on both sides under my arms with intertwining white and navy blue draw cords laced through white grommets that brought it together on both sides. Low on the left side the company logo patch was sewn on, depicting a woman diving into the water wearing a red bathing suit. It was good that I did not go to a convent school, as they would never have let me wear such a daring bathing suit. Even my parents were rather shocked when they first saw me in it, but I was so thin that the cord brought the two sides virtually completely together.

Preparations were further eased as, anticipating a trip to France, I had coincidentally obtained a passport earlier that year. Somehow all the passports and tickets were quickly arranged and before I knew it, we were in a taxi heading for the Rabka train station. From there we would travel through Krakow and on to Budapest. I sat transfixed, watching the scenery in the warm clear weather as we traversed the country. Everything was refreshed from spring rains and newly grown greenery surrounded us. Initially, we traveled westward toward Katowice through Polish foothills that I knew so well, but then turned south and moved into territories I had never previously experienced. We passed along the Moravian Gate between the Sudetes and Carpathian Mountains. I had anticipated seeing high mountain vistas but from this vantage point we could not see any.

The trip was surprisingly quick despite our eager anticipation. Soon, a number of hours later, having crossed the Hungarian frontier, we viewed Budapest. Upon approaching the city there was a splendid view of the Danube River flowing through the city under ornate bridges. We arrived in our hotel tired from the trip, but more from restless nights of anticipation before our departure.

The next day we toured the city and learned its history. It was originally two ancient cities: Buda and Pest, on the opposite shores of the Danube. In 1872, sixty-four years earlier, they had been united. The old city was fascinating, with wandering gypsies playing their arousing music.

All at once, it started to rain. Seeking shelter, we found ourselves on a street covered over with a high, curved, pane glass roof protecting the many shops on either side. By this time there were many Polish youth gathering at this focal point of our common itinerary. It seemed that no sooner had we taken shelter here then the gypsies struck up the lively *csardas*—"country inn" dance music, to which the youth started dancing spontaneously. Seeing that we were not local and did not know how to dance to this accompaniment, the local young men were quick to take the initiative and invite us girls to dance. Seeing their boyfriends dancing with Polish girls, it did not take long for the local girls to invite our Polish boys to join them, which they did with relish.

Soon they, with their dark hair and faces, were arm in arm with us, with our more often pale complexions and blond hair. It was not difficult to follow eager instructors and the lively beat. Though we could not speak a word of the local language we quickly understood enough to become a part of the lively street scene.

Before we knew it the rain dissipated, and we spilled out through tree-lined boulevards into various wide squares. During the next three days we toured through both of the old cities, now Budapest. We first crossed one bridge, toured through ancient churches, grand museums of fantastic architecture, and viewed awesome artworks. We then returned, back across another bridge. Our days in Budapest were quickly over and we were back on the train, on to the Yugoslavian capital of Belgrade.

I noticed that the character of the people, their dress and the look of villages were very different from Poland. I was impressed with their drum shaped hats—a thick round band, often ornately embroidered, with a flat top. Older men wore the hats straight; younger men wore them at all angles. They had white cotton shirts with colorful embroidery. The women covered their heads with scarves, as was also common for peasant women of Poland. The villages looked impoverished, the fields poor, but the climate was like a dream with a warm, fragrant breeze.

We only spent one day in Belgrade, which, after the wonder and excitement of Budapest, did not make any special impression on me. After only this short break, we crossed into Bulgaria and traveled on to Sofia where we had more adventures before us. By this time we were accompanied by crowds of Polish youth, each with their own itinerary. When we arrived in Sofia with the numerous other Poles, we were matched, one for one, with local families. After an official welcome where we were told that we were guests of Bulgaria, we each went our separate way with our host family.

I found myself with a family made up of the mother, father and two children near my age, one girl and one boy. We arrived at their modest apartment. After putting my things in a room they had designated for me, we all sat down to a meal. Luckily I was matched to a family that spoke French and we therefore were able to communicate, at least at first.

I was by this time looking forward to a meal. Always enjoying something new, I was not put off by the different foods. It looked nutritious, appealing and appetizing. Not waiting, I took a hearty serving of the goulash like dish onto my fork and nearly died when it hit my mouth. My eyes watered and started to bulge. My mouth burned! Even the breath I took in seemed like fire to my lungs. The food must have been laced with an ample portion of hot pepper.

Looking for escape, I lunged for the glass of cool water I spied before me to douse the inferno that was now engulfing me, but to no avail. The water did little but redistribute the live coal like contents in my mouth. Somehow I swallowed the objectionable food, but faced the ample portion I had served myself. Not wanting to appear ungrateful for their hospitality, somehow, I managed to finish the meal, for which I was to pay with a burned mouth through the next several days. I was unable to talk much that evening and went to bed early wondering what I would eat tomorrow. Luckily, the woman of the house noticed that the food was somewhat spicy for me and toned down the servings the next day. Toned down, but still spicy hot. By this time my mouth was so burned that everything felt as though it were made of acid.

The next day while touring the city I purchased some chocolate. I thought that I would at least have something to satisfy my appetite. I could simply eat little or nothing at the meals they served. However, I was not to be rescued by this plan. Having been raised on the excellent confectioneries made by the Wedel family in Poland, I was disappointed. The chocolate was almost liquid within its wrapper in the heat, but the taste was worse than disappointing.

As we wandered the city streets I was struck by how the Byzantine school influenced Sofia architecture. Churches, primarily Orthodox, were mostly built in this style, topped with enormous golden onions. Once again, the city compared poorly to Budapest. The girl and boy of my local host family were released from school to allow them time for escorting me around the city. They tried very hard to satisfy my curiosities, questions and needs, and generally succeeded without fault.

I saw many things that I considered buying. Mindful of my small luggage, and the length of the trip ahead of me during which I would have to carry everything myself, I only purchased two of the unique local hats. I was able to pack them with my lingerie and, therefore, they took next to no space.

The day was hot. I was pleased every hour to host my guides, inviting them to share with me in some ice cream or cool juices. My ulterior motive, of course, was not only to satisfy our thirst but also to quell the fire that burned in my mouth from that first meal and then every one that followed while in this city.

Saying farewell to my hosts, I was reunited with Chouquett Chamiec, Wanda and Miss Zofia at the train station for our trip to Varna, Bulgaria. We had much to compare about the three days spent separately in Sofia. Their experiences mirrored my own. All had tales to tell, particularly about the hot food.

Crossing east toward the Black Sea, the Bulgarian countryside was dry and the temperature was oppressively hot. We looked forward to our arrival at the sea. We eagerly anticipated swimming in cool refreshing waters. Arriving in Varna we found our rooms in a small resort on the seashore.

Quickly changing into our bathing suits, I into my glamorous and exotic treasure, we grabbed towels from the room and raced down toward the water along what appeared to be a cordoned pathway. We noticed signs along the way written in what was, to us, the strange Bulgarian language. Ahead we could see the wide, white sand beach that was absolutely tantalizing.

Taking the right fork in the path toward the water, we found ourselves sharing the beach with women walking about completely naked! Shocked, we froze! I had never seen women naked like this before. Many of them were enormously heavy. In their nakedness they were almost black from repeated total exposure to the sun. Dancing among them were exquisitely shaped girls and young women, also totally naked. While the older, heavy women were to me grotesque, the younger ones were almost as if Greek goddesses; bronzes come alive from some museum.

We, particularly Miss Zofia, did not know how to react. No one uttered a sound, each totally within her own thoughts at this unexpected encounter with the naked women. We wondered what the others were thinking. We hardly dared even to draw a breath thus exposing our shock. Suddenly we noticed that all the women were looking at us. We felt embarrassed in their focus, realizing that we were wearing clothing while none of them were. We were the ones out of place. Zofia saved us from the moment by saying, "Let's go swimming." We ran for the water seeking relief.

Swimming was refreshing after our long trip and our most recent experience. The water was not cool, as we had been anticipating. It was almost too hot. We frolicked about, noticing that we could swim very easily, buoyed by the high salt content. None of us allowed our eyes to venture shoreward.

Miss Zofia kept warning us that we could not stay outside too long for fear that we would be burned. She stood waist deep in the water, facing the sea and watching us swim. Refreshed, we deferred to Miss Zofia's insistence that we return to our hotel before we burn, and hungrily started back.

Following Miss Zofia, I bumped into her when she suddenly stopped short in her tracks. She said in an odd tone, "Don't look. Keep your eyes to the ground and let's quickly get back to our room." I looked up to see what was going on and saw, there in front of us, exposed for everyone to see, a man. Naked! Totally naked! He stood in front of us, apparently oblivious to his nakedness and our shock. Following Zofia's example, eyes cast down, in a tight group, we hurriedly shuffled up the path to our room.

Once in our room no one spoke. Not a word. Everyone pretended that they had not seen anything peculiar. Suddenly Wanda uttered, "Oh my God!" I turned toward her. She was looking, big eyed, at Miss Zofia. I then also noticed that Miss Zofia was as though afire. Her skin was a bright pink, red color. She was intensely burned and now, as she started to be aware of her burn, started feeling the pain. While we were swimming she had been standing unprotected in the sun. While she was watching out for us and warning us of the danger of getting burned, she was the one who was most exposed. She was the only one to burn.

Remembering first aid discussions from the previous year's camps, I told everyone that I would be right back. I quickly put on a blouse, grabbed my coin purse and ran out. Finding the resort kitchen, I luckily found a few cucumbers. Pointing them out and holding out some money, I purchased them. Running back to the room, taking out the knife I always carried with me on trips, I sliced the cucumbers into long slices and started placing them on Zofia's shoulders, back, neck and arms. The result was incredible. It looked as though steam arose from the cucumber lined, burned skin. Zofia was obviously relieved by the layered cucumbers. The pain was arrested and this treatment seemed to even alleviate the burn. Asked how I knew this method of relieving the pain and damage of sunburn, I told them of learning it at camp.

After having treated Miss Zofia, still hungry, we went to dinner. Being a resort area, we were able to talk with our waitress in French. Miss Zofia brought up the question paramount in the back our minds, asking, "Where would we find a normal beach?"

Looking surprised at the question, the waitress nodded toward the beach through the window and replied, "The beach is right here below the resort."

"But when we went down there," replied Miss Zofia, "we encountered a nude beach."

"Oh, did you take the wrong turn, turning left where the path branches? You must take the right path to the women's beach." We were confused by her instruction to take the right fork as, per chance, we had taken the right fork. Having taken our order, thinking that she had answered all of our questions, she left.

We all looked at one another and, knowing that there was only one trail to the beach despite it forking, thought that we had inadvertently found ourselves at a nudist resort. Upon this shocking realization we decided to finish our meal quickly. We were glad that we had decided to eat early. There were no others eating yet, thus we had not been exposed to the nudists during their dinner hour. Thankfully, our food came quickly. We took as little time as possible eating it, after which we all returned to our room. Miss Zofia then told us to wait while she found out more about our situation and, as we desperately wanted to go swimming some more, she promised that she would ask about a "normal" beach.

Returning from her mission, Miss Zofia told us her findings in a calm even tone. "This is not a nudist resort and we can stay here. The beaches are all open to nude swimming. The resort people are proud to offer a beach segregated for men and women. The fork limits the beach in front, where we went, with men going to the left and women to the right. However, here, as long as they don't stop on dry sand, men and women can traverse each other's beaches as long as they remain on the wet sand. All of this is apparently explained on the signs we passed but were unable to read."

We were all shocked and dismayed, thinking that we would not be able to swim. Sitting down on my bed, with a sigh of dismay, Chouquett said dejectedly, "We came all the way to the infamous Black Sea, maybe the only time in my life, and we cannot even go for a swim."

Miss Zofia replied, "No, there is an option. I found out that farther down the road is a trail to the beach that is open exclusively for women. We'll go swimming there." For the next three days we swam there frequently. Salty waves lolled us about while Miss Zofia, covered, sat upon a towel on the beach, watching us. The sun warmed us as it tanned our bodies to a glowing, light bronze color. The pleasant water cooled us and kept us from being too hot. One advantage of this beach was that, apparently, it was not as popular as the nude beaches and it was relatively underutilized. Here, occasionally a nude woman would come by; more often we shared the beach with others who preferred to wear swimsuits.

It seemed that our days on the Black Sea were too few. Rested and well-tanned, except for Miss Zofia who avoided more sun exposure, we traveled on to Bucharest. The train took us there in only a few hours. My impression of the city was that it was very modern. It did not have the endless, ancient, architectural wonders as did the previous cities, but rather modern, tall, less-ornate structures on straight, planned streets.

Once again it was hot. We decided to go swimming. Arriving at a huge pool, we encountered something that astonished me. The pool had waves! They seemed like the waves in the Black Sea, or even larger, but these were artificially created. It was great fun. We were very refreshed and then went on a tour of the city. Of particular beauty was an extensive art gallery that I enjoyed viewing very much. This was our last stop in the Balkans. On the third day we headed almost due north, toward Lwow, back to Poland.

Having paralleled the previous legs of our trip with other Polish students and their teachers, we alone had plans to extend our trip. Lwow was very prominent in Polish history. With no direct family connections there, I had never envisioned visiting this city. I was happy and eager for this opportunity. The trip from Bucharest to Lwow was the longest leg of our trip. This was due not only to the actual distance, but also to the fact that we were all tired by this time.

Arriving in the morning, after a day and nightlong train ride, we went to our hotel. We were not able to check in at that early hour. Leaving our bags with the porter, we decided to take an initial walk around and get our bearings. The city immediately made a great impression on me. Perhaps this was because we were once again among our own, Polish people. People who spoke our language, had the same customs and ate familiar foods. Each beautiful building seemed to have its place in history. I was particularly impressed with the three cathedrals: Roman Catholic, Greek, and Eastern Orthodox. Each was completely different from the other and offered so much to see that it was difficult to leave when it was time to visit something else. Tired from the train trip and hours of viewing the marvelous city sights, once in our rooms we collapsed and slept soundly in our Polish beds.

After eating a large breakfast of wonderfully familiar foods, we went to see the Raclawice Panorama painted by Jan Styka and Wojciech Kossak. Painted after 1893, following the creation of several other paintings of this style, it depicts a battle during the Kosciuszko[30] Insurrection on a sunny afternoon on the 4th of April, 1794. The unique style of painting had the viewer on the inside of a special circular canvas.

---

[30]Thaddeus Kosciuszko (1746–1817) was an American hero of the Revolutionary War, though he is largely a forgotten figure in America today. He was born of the Polish aristocracy and became a military engineer. In 1776 he served the Continental Army of the North. While under General Horatio Gates, he was a major factor in the victory at Saratoga. He built fortifications at West Point and designed a 60 ton chain to block the Hudson River. The US

The viewer looks around as if in the center of the scene: a participant in the midst of the battle. The painting depicts the first time that peasants, not previously considered an integral part of the nation, fought for their country. It exemplifies a crucial moment during the battle when Polish "scythe men" capture Russian cannons. Other events occurring at the moment, at various locations around the scene, include peasants waving their caps in greeting to Commander Kosciuszko. He gestures from upon his horse, arm stretched in the direction of the attack. Russian soldiers are running and hiding from their overrun emplacements. Flags and banners flutter in the wind. Dead and wounded are scattered about. Terrified horses are rearing. A church is in flames. Defenseless women and children, an old man with a lyre, and a cripple are frightened and distraught. Women lament the dead. Shells explode and the hoofs of horses kick up clouds of dust, their riders involved in individual duels.

I had two main impressions. The perspective was done so well that it seemed that you could reach out and touch those things nearby, yet see events unfolding at great distances. The second factor that so captivated me was the superb depictions of horses by Wojciech Kossak. The horses are so alive in the battle, in all aspects, actions and expressions. Heads, eyes, hooves, manes, tails and muscles move in every imaginable form. The depictions are painted so realistically, so real and alive and full of motion as well as emotion. Upon exiting, I had to stop and take a second to return to the moment, outside the intensity of the depicted battle scenes. (Sixty years later I was to see this panorama again, now in Wroclaw, in southwestern Poland, after it was reconstructed there. Once again my impressions were as strong as the first time I had viewed it. Again, upon exiting, I was drawn to look back for a moment at this scene that so captures me with its drama.)

We went to the great Lyczakowski Cemetery where many great Polish patriots, artisans and writers are buried. It has many impressive individual and family monuments. However, of greatest impact on me were the graves of the youth, the "Polish Eaglets," who died defending Lwow in 1918. So many boys and young men died for their country, having experienced so little of life. Many were scouts, as was I. They had formed their own detachment and made the greatest sacrifice for their country, for my country—for Poland!

Congress named him Brigadier General. When he returned to Poland he led the 1794 revolt and defeated Russian and Prussian troops at Raclawice. Thomas Jefferson, a close companion, said of Kosciuszko: "He was as pure a son of liberty as I have ever known, and of that liberty which is to go to all, not to the few and rich alone." Jefferson was the executor of Kosciusko's will, which utilized all of his American assets to buy and free slaves.

On our last day in Lwow, the last day of our trip prior to taking the train back to school, we decided that we did not have to scrimp with our money. During the entire trip we had been frugal with our limited funds. We decided to splurge. Going to the best hotel in Lwow, Hotel George, we treated ourselves to an excellent dinner. I remembered being told by my parents how, when they attended Michal's wedding here in 1929, they had stayed at this hotel. Sitting in this fine hotel we enjoyed every bite as we celebrated our successful trip. We braced ourselves for the return to school at Rabka.

CHAPTER 21

I T SEEMED as though no sooner had we returned from our Balkan trip that the school year ended and I found myself back at home. Home was but a brief interlude as I soon departed for France with one of the women, Miss Krystyna Popiel, who took care of us during after school hours.

She was ten years my senior, and I had been pleasantly surprised at her suggestion that we tour France together during the summer of 1936. Once again Papa agreed with my utilizing my milk money.

I purchased a train ticket to Paris and Rennes, then Brest to Mont-Saint-Michel and then back to Poland. Exchanging into French francs the maximum two hundred Polish zloty[31] allowed to be taken out of the country, we prepared our backpacks and departed. Miss Krystyna and I decided at the onset that we would limit our baggage to one backpack, with a weight limit of ten kilograms, as we anticipated doing much walking.

She was from the vicinity of Krakow so we decided to meet in Warsaw. I would come from home, near Grodno. Meeting as planned, we departed westward by train. Arriving in Berlin where the train made a stop, we decided to get off, stretch our legs and get a cup of coffee. Accustomed to a good cup of coffee at home, I was sorely disappointed by what we were served and expressed as much to Miss Krystyna. She leaned toward me and told me, in a conspiratorial voice, that we were in Germany and that the nation was undergoing a period of impoverishment and self-sacrifice to support the development of a superior army, and that we must be cautious about any criticisms.

---

[31]The pre-WWII Polish currency "zloty" had an approximate equivalant value of 20 cents ($0.20 US). Two hundred pre-WWII zloty would come to be worth about $365 US sixty years later toward the end of the twentieth century.

With this counsel, my awareness of our surroundings was heightened. I had noted the large number of young, well-outfitted soldiers and the general atmosphere, but these now suddenly hit me with more ominous implications.

When we arrived in Paris, Miss Krystyna—always well organized and prepared—ordered us a cab which she instructed to take us to the convent where we planned to stay. The sisters offered student housing to girls and women visiting Paris while on summer vacation. Our reservations included room and board. Rooms were usually shared with several students, but we had a room to ourselves. Nuns served excellent breakfasts and dinners in a large communal dining room.

While we were seated at dinner, one sister came to me and introduced herself quietly. Almost whispering in my ear, she said that the Mother Superior of the convent requested that I come to see her. Quite surprised, I did not know what to make of this. This was my first trip to Paris. Why would a nun be asking for me? Telling Miss Krystyna that I would go see what this was about, I followed the nun through a small door. We entered a quiet hallway lined with little visiting rooms.

In one of them sat the old Mother that I was told wanted to speak with me. My curiosity was heightened, as surely I had never met this nun. I was more puzzled when she slowly stood on her feet and embraced me saying, "My dear Karolina." I told her gently that my name was Terenia, not Karolina and that she must be confusing me with another person.

"You don't remember spending time with me as a little girl when you were chased out of Italy by Mussolini?" she asked. Suddenly it came to me that she was confusing me for my grandmother Karolina. This turned out to be correct. She said that she had recognized me from a distance. She continued, in her confusion, telling me that I had completed school not that long ago, that I had not changed at all and that she was very pleased to see me once more. This was the first of many incidents in my life where I was told how much I resembled my grandmother Karolina.

The next morning Miss Krystyna, using her Michelin self-guide tour book, led us toward the Louvre Museum. I was immediately impressed with just how well Miss Krystyna was prepared. She had an exact timetable of when and where we were to go, with all the necessary maps and timetables, including those for the Metro subway and bus system. Knowing exactly where and how we were going, we were able to arrive at our destinations without delays, or potential extra cost.

At the Louvre, Leonardo Da Vinci's *Mona Lisa* made the greatest impression on me. I stood before the painting entranced by her world-famous smile.

The Louvre had so much to see that it would take many days, if not years, to view the exhibits properly. We did not have the luxury of sufficient time to do it justice, but thoroughly enjoyed our cursory visit.

Next was a visit to Notre Dame Cathedral with its flying buttresses and fantastic gargoyles; we ascended many steps to view them up close. Taking two bus tours to get an overall impression of the city, we were struck with the international tone of the Montmartre district where people spoke in what seemed every possible language from around the world. We took in the obligatory, though impressive, view of the Eiffel tower, passing by the many wide, well-designed boulevards. To soak up a little Parisian ambiance, we stopped at a street-side café. Ordering glasses of wine and cakes, we sat and talked while observing the lives of those who passed by. We had three wondrous days in this city of all cities. Our time here ended all too soon. We experienced only a glimpse of what Paris had to offer.

We departed for our *"Tour de La Bretagn"*: northwestern France in Brittany, facing the Atlantic Ocean. Our train took us as far as Rennes, where our walking tour started. We headed west toward Brest, on the peninsula near the westernmost point of France. This portion of France's population is strongly influenced by its once being the capital of a Celtic tribe. It was interesting to see the people dressed in black, the women with special white headdresses, slightly different and distinguishable in each village. The people were poor, living primarily off the sea. We observed how women lined the shores waiting to see when, and if, the fishermen returned. They fished primarily for sardines. The catch was taken to canneries or sold fresh in markets. Much of French poetry is based upon the tragedies of these people's lives.

Walking, we appreciated what we saw far more than we would have traveling by any other mode, even by bicycle. We observed the unique and strange lines of rock pillars called menhirs and the large, flat, table-like rocks called dolmens. We searched for the meaning and purpose of these rocks, but there was no adequate explanation, as these rocks had been constructed in pre-historic times.

It was difficult conversing with the local people as they were not outspoken. One felt safe amongst them and when a conversation was started, they were very pleasant.

Walking about twenty-five kilometers each day, toward late afternoon we would simply ask someone we came across where we might spend the night. Most often we would find some simple accommodation in a small village. There, they would tell us about their lives during family evening meals that we shared. We observed many sunsets through the masts of their fishing boats. We listened to the sounds of mothers and wives exclaiming their happiness, or lamenting the loss of loved ones. The womenfolk never had idle hands; they were always occupied with repairing nets or making lace. I was entranced by this, my first visit to the ocean and the solid, calm, poor but full and honest lives these people lived, accustomed to the proximity of tragedy that life on and by the sea caused them. I learned to appreciate the delectable taste of fresh sardines, which was a staple of their diet. Each morning when we departed, we would pack some food with us to enjoy during noontime, when every French person stops to eat. We would often stop and sit in a field at the side of the road, pulling out bread, cheese, canned sardines and chocolate, along with some cold coffee to drink. The weather was ideal, warm with a cool breeze off the ocean. The clean, clear air allowed us a great view of vistas as we passed. Thus we walked for two weeks before arriving at Brest.

Taking the train we arrived in Mont-Saint-Michel in Normandy. It was fascinating that during low tide the city was connected to the continent by an expanse of sand, though at high tide it was an island in the English Channel. To me this was surely one of the great wonders of the world. On this "island" was a monastery where one could observe the various architectural ages by looking upward to the next successive level that was built upon an earlier epoch's work. The streets were composed of stairs, as there did not appear to be any flat area. Along the stairs were innumerable shops and small cafes within the sprawling city.

One of the most fascinating things about Mont-Saint-Michel was the water. After a day of exploring the island, we decided to spend some time on the beach by the mainland and to enjoy the water and fine weather. Dressing in our swimsuits, we took some towels to spread on the soft yellow sand. The water was far out and we started walking toward it when some people stopped us, warning us that the sand was unstable in places and to take care where we went. Apparently the water was a kilometer out and we were warned that the water comes in quickly and again, that it could be dangerous. This answered a question we had as to why people were taking boats out to the island rather than just driving out over the sand while the tide was out. Giving up on swimming for now, we stretched out our towels and started to sunbathe, thinking that when the water came up we would have ample time to swim.

Not long afterward, we noticed the nervous movements by others around us. People would anxiously look at their watches and out over the expanse of sand toward where we thought the water was, though it was still out of sight. Suddenly one, then another, then most of the people left. Puzzled, we asked one woman what was happening. "The tide will come in momentarily!" she replied and then she, too, hurriedly departed.

Still puzzled, but taking seriously the adage "When in Rome, do as the Romans do," we started collecting our few things to follow them. Looking out I saw that, indeed, far off, the tide was coming up. I could see water at a distance where there had been only sand a short time ago. Picking up our towels we started walking toward a heavy, long set of stone stairs that led to the seacoast above the beach. Suddenly, the water was upon us, swirling about our feet and rising rapidly! Realizing that we were in danger, we rushed for the stairs and made it just in time as the beach was completely inundated with rising water that was now pounding the shoreline. Had we been just a little slower we would have been caught in the deep rough sea. Fascinated, hearts beating, we stood on the safety of the turf with the others. We looked out at this startling change, sharing our surprise. Several people nodded their heads seriously, understanding our reaction completely. One man told us that a horse at a gallop could not outrun the advancing water. With this excitement we departed not only for our hotel, but the next morning we left Mont-Saint-Michel, taking the train back to Poland.

Miss Krystyna and I parted in Warsaw on the way home, but upon seeing each other again in September for the start of the school year, we were so happy about our trip together that we immediately started planning another trip for the next summer. The year went by busily and actively, but Miss Krystyna and I were always able to find time for making plans, which we indeed were able to put into effect, this time to Italy. I received permission for the trip during the Christmas break. I had noted at that time that my parents were not even surprised at my wanting to go on another trip. They commented that it was unusual to go to Italy in the summer, in the height of the hot season.

Miss Krystyna and I met once again in Warsaw, this time in July. The year was 1937. The train traveled through Vienna where we stopped for a short three days. We had planned ahead and had tickets already purchased for the theater to see Wilhelm Wagner's romantic opera *Tannhauser*. We toured the beautiful city, and Miss Krystyna was pleased that I did not complain about the coffee as I had in Germany, for here the coffee was delicious.

Leaving this wonderful city, passing through the Austrian Alps, we agreed that one day we would have to come back here to do justice to this beautiful area. We toured Pisa, Rome, Venice and Florence, where I saw the cathedral in which my parents were married. In Rome, we stayed at the Polish Ursulen convent run by the same order that ran the school in Poznan that I had attended. The convent rented student's rooms out, as was common in many of these private schools during the off-school months, which provided a low cost, safe haven to young travelers with the advantage of including healthy and bountiful meals as a part of the lodging. We were introduced to a young Polish nun, well versed in the arts, who gave us wonderful tours of Rome and its museums. She did this so well and gave me such an appreciation for art, particularly sculpture, that while I did not say so, I decided to come back here to Italy, to this convent to study art in another year after I completed high school.

Many things in Rome impressed me. Once, while visiting the Vatican City, we attended a very ceremonial mass at Saint Peter's Cathedral with hundreds of priests and bishops. I was taken with how piously Bishop Eugenio Pacelli said mass. Remarking on this to the Ursulen Mother guiding us, she looked at me coyly and said, "Yes, he is very popular. Did you know that your father worked with him for Pope Pius X? The Bishop was the Pope's secretary and your father was chamberlain." Two years later, to my delight, Bishop Pacelli was elected Pope Pius XII.

We toured catacombs, the Coliseum, museums, ancient Roman sculptures and endless ornate churches including Santa Andrea Della Fratre. We visited the parish Papa attended while he lived in Rome, where he had miraculously regained the use of his hand. I was infatuated with Rome and its arts. Throughout the visit I thought about Henryk Sienkiewicz's book *Quo Vadis* and Siemiradzki's painting hanging in the grand salon back home.

From Rome we went to Venice, which was as though a dream. Traversing the canals in gondolas, we learned that all gondoliers are from one clan. Tanned, dark eyed, slim and romantically dressed in their identical garb, they told us many tales of the city, continually pointing out one interesting sight after another. (When back home, I was incessantly teased by my brothers and sisters that I had fallen madly in love with one of these gondoliers.) We sat in the Plaza San Marco, built upon columns, eating fantastic Italian *gelato*. This was where I, for the first time, learned to appreciate ice cream. (I did not appreciate what they passed off as ice cream in Poland.) While eating this rich, sweet, creamy delicacy, I had to fight off the numerous pigeons relentlessly begging for any tidbit. Above us, every fifteen minutes and particularly on the hour, figures emerged from an enormous intricate clock in the tower, playing out their scene accompanied with music.

CHAPTER 22

ONLY EWA AND I went to Rabka in the September of 1937 as Ela had graduated the previous year. We were all proud of the fact that she had passed her matriculation and was going on to Poznan to study business at the same university from which Michal had graduated. Meanwhile, Krzysztof was in Belgium studying agriculture. Jas, Andrzej and Piotr continued high school in Grodno. Adam was in the Polish army officer's school in Rawicz. Jozek and Kryla were still at home, too young for school yet. Marysia was gone with her husband.

As always, at departure from home, Ewa was crying. She was very tied to home. She so enjoyed taking care of things there that she had for the last several years practically taken over running the household for Mama. I could never quite understand how someone so practical and so good at running things could be such a crybaby. Embarrassed and frustrated by her flood of tears, I threatened her with a severe beating if she continued crying on the train.

As we approached Rabka, I joyously opened the train compartment window and leaned out to see everything with great anticipation. Suddenly a coal ash from the locomotive steam engine flew into my eye. I ducked back into the compartment trying to eradicate the ash; the eye watered and soon my face became covered with tears. It was with a wet face and swollen eye, still unable to remove the ash, that I arrived at the Szczuka's school. Seeing both Ewa and I in this condition they tried to console us both. I was furious to think that they would even consider that I, like the crybaby Ewa, would behave so emotionally. The more I tried to tell them that I had an ash in my eye and needed help removing it, the more they tried to console me. Ewa, watching this embarrassing spectacle, had stopped crying and was looking at me, gloating. Here I was, after threatening her for her behavior, with a swollen eye and tear smeared face, being consoled by the Szczuka sisters.

In spite of my less-than-ladylike arrival, I was determined to study seriously this year. I planned to complete my last year in high school with good grades. Then I had to pass the matriculation examination that would allow me to enter the university of my choice. Each of my older siblings before me, for various reasons, had difficulty in passing their matriculation. I was determined to be the first one in the family to pass without problems.

Although never previously overly concerned with grades or my standing at school, this year, for the first time in my life, I really studied. As it happened, I was tremendously aided in my desire to do well by having excellent teachers. The year went well. I studied hard and felt well prepared for the examination summarizing my last eight years of school.

This happened to be the last year in which the exam would cover the full eight years of study. Starting the following year, the exam was to review only the previous four years. Grade school was to be extended from four to eight years and high school was to be shortened from eight to four years. The purpose of this new system was to allow children to proceed into trade school after finishing grade school, rather than having the requirement of completing the eight years to matriculation. Under the old system, many students did not pass the difficult matriculation examination. They were hampered with the stigma of incompleted studies as they ventured fourth in their lives. Students, upon completing grade school, would choose whether to enter a trade or to select a high school specializing in either liberal arts or the sciences.

Wanting to lessen my parents' tension about my matriculation examination, I told them the date of the examination was two weeks later than the actual date. This would allow me to complete the examination and have the results before they started worrying themselves, or me, about last minute preparations for the exam.

The examination had two components: written and oral. The written component was further divided into four parts. We would complete a part in each of four successive days. The first day we had the choice of writing about one of three topics written on the board: summarize our knowledge about Polish literature; write a comparative argument on a given subject from literature; or, write freely on an arbitrary subject that they provided. The purpose was to test us on our overall writing skills, grammar, and knowledge of Polish literature. On the second day we were given a specific historical epoch to write about. The third day was a math exam. The fourth day was on our choice of a foreign language we had studied, or Latin or Greek.

The examinations were corrected over the next few days while we awaited results. If we passed with the top score, 5, then we would not be required to take the oral exam in that subject. Everyone's grades were posted and we would crowd to the board with hearts in our throats to see the result. Cheers, yells and groans were heard upon reading the various results. I received a 5 in math and foreign language where I had chosen French. I had only to pass orals in Polish and History.

Oral examinations were taken the next week. The orals were presented before four individuals: a representative from the ministry of education; our principal, Miss Irena Szczuka; the school director; and the appropriate teacher who was responsible for the subject being discussed.

Each of us could present ourselves whenever we wished. Deciding that I wanted to get it over with as fast as possible, I entered the examination room early Monday morning and was the first in my class to be examined. The night before, I had a dream that I had passed all my orals well and, although disappointed upon wakening that I still had them before me, I was in a good frame of mind.

Entering the room, I was invited to sit down and was introduced. One of my teachers then said that we would review Polish first and held out three cards. I was asked to pick one and told that I could go to the other end of the room for five minutes and prepare myself on the question indicated on the card.

The card indicated that I would need to analyze the poem written on the card and talk about the writer. Reading the poem, I realized that I did not know it or its author. I decided to try to analyze the epoch in which the poem was written, and both my reactions to the poem and the author's intent when writing the poem. I was able to identify which group of poets it came from, so this gave me something to go on. Jotting down a series of notes on the card for reference, I returned to my chair.

Admitting at the onset that I could not remember the author, I told them that I could place the poem within its group and proceeded to analyze it in a very positive manner. Once started, my various experiences at public speaking helped me greatly. I was able to speak without fright or uncertainty. Observing my teacher, who obviously completely disapproved of the approach I was using, I nevertheless continued with my plan for responding. The delegate from the Ministry of Education seemed to like my monologue and started asking some questions to which I was able to give some reasonable answers, turning the exam from a presentation to almost a general discussion with him. My teacher's eyes grew more and more disapproving, but she did not say anything.

Later, I was to learn that the Ministerial representative was greatly impressed and wanted to give me a 5. My teacher strenuously objected and refused. In any case I passed well. The next subject was history, with a change in teachers. This time the card I chose asked about the Polish insurrection of 1830, one of my favorite subjects and epochs. Greatly relieved, I again jotted a few major points on my card to be sure that I covered them. I returned to my seat and delved into the subject. I was so enthusiastic and obviously knowledgeable on the subject, that they interrupted me halfway. After asking another quick question or two, they told me that I was done.

Thus my orals and therefore my matriculation examinations were complete. Exiting the examination room, I could see all my friends, the poor souls, waiting anxiously to be called. Immediately surrounded, they questioned me how it went, to which I replied, "Very easy," perhaps cheering them a little. Extremely happy to be done, not even waiting for acknowledgment of passing, I sent the following telegram home:

```
N O N E E D T O W O R R Y S T O P M A T R I
C U L A T I O N P A S S E D S T O P P L E A
S E C A L L 1 7 0 0 H O U R S S T O P T E R
E N I A
```

That evening, at the appointed hour, Papa called. Congratulating me, he asked how it was possible that I had completed the matriculation. Telling him that I gave them the later date to lessen their worry, he laughed, saying that this was typical behavior for me. He congratulated me once more and passed the phone to Mama who was very pleased. Asking if I could spend a few more days in Rabka, then come home via a visit to Michal, they replied that on a day with such good news they could not refuse me such a small request.

Later in the evening we all learned that our entire class of twelve had passed! We spent the evening celebrating. We were graduates with our matriculation passed; our lives had taken a turn. The next day all left Rabka except for me. We took leave of one another elated at our success, but with the realization that, in all likelihood, we would never all be together again.

Obtaining the rare permission to take Ewa out of classes for three days, one month prior to her completing her school year, we headed for the Tatry

Mountains. Taking the train to Zakopane we started out with backpacks on our backs. Once in the mountains we stayed two nights at mountain retreat hostels. I had always wanted to make this well-known hiking trip around the small mountain chain. Having completed my matriculation, I was in good spirits. Ewa, happy to be out of school, shared my enthusiasm. We enjoyed the mountains during the budding spring season.

Upon returning to Rabka, both of us were happy, tanned and refreshed. Ewa went back to finish up her school year while I prepared to go home. Making last minute plans with Miss Krystyna for our next adventure through northern Italy later that summer, I headed for my brother's home.

I spent a week with Michal, Dusia and their two boys. One was about three and the other a year old. This was the first time that I had met the boys. I was very favorably impressed with their home, undergoing final stages of being remodeled. It was pleasant to be treated as an adult and was seated, for the first time in my life, at the honorific place, to the right of the woman of the house. As guest, I was served first. The atmosphere here was very positive, pleasant and happy. They were a successful, young, noble family with little concern. We had a lot of fun together. The time was filled with laughter, jokes and good-natured teasing. The week went by quickly and soon it was time to leave for home. I was very glad to have had the opportunity to visit my eldest brother, my godfather, and to be with his family, even if for just a short while.

Stopping in Warsaw for a few hours, I visited my beloved Aunt Maria "Teresa" Zamoyski, my Mother's younger sister. She was a Sister, a Nun, a member of the order called Kanoniczki. Never married, she had for years taken care of my grandmother Karolina after the death of my grandfather Andrzej Zamoyski. He was the same one who had taught me an early lesson about crossing myself at my brother Andrzej's baptism.

Aunt Teresa and Grandmother lived together within their little apartment at the convent. They hosted me joyously. After lunch Grandma went for a rest. Aunt Teresa, with a surreptitious glance, told me that she had to show me something. Taking out a book from her library she removed a letter from among its pages and said, "Listen to my story." We sat together comfortably, each with a cup of rich coffee, as I listened curiously to her animated voice.

"Seventeen years ago I received this letter from a very good friend, Jerzy Jezierski. At the time, I was reading this book and was somehow distracted. Putting the unread letter in the book, I never came back to read the letter. Recently I happened to open the book and discovered the long-forgotten letter. I read it then for the first time." Her hand trembled slightly as she handed

SISTERS AND POSTULANTS OF THE KANONICZKI ORDER.
TERENIA'S AUNT, MARIA "TERESA" ZAMOYSKI, IS AT LEFT.

MARIA "TERESA" ZAMOYSKI AS A YOUNG SCOUT.
AFTER A 17-YEAR DELAY DUE TO A MISPLACED PROPOSAL LETTER,
SHE WED JERZY JEZIERSKI.

me the letter to read for myself. The letter started out about some general family news, but soon turned into a love letter. I looked at Aunt Teresa with a coy smile. "Keep reading," she said in a quiet, patient voice. Wondering what more there was beyond uncovering this secret romance, I suddenly read his proposal to her.

"Oh, Aunt Teresa," I cried. "Why did you not marry him?"

"I told you," she replied, "I read this letter for the first time just recently."

"And you never knew of his proposal?"

"No. Not until recently," she sighed, with a radiant smile upon her face.

"What do you plan to do?" I asked.

She told me that she had written back to him, belatedly accepting his proposal—should he still be interested. She then told me that he had immediately repeated his proposal. During the seventeen intervening years he never loved another. They planned to marry in the fall.

I was shocked! Totally unprepared for this news, I started blurting out my reactions and questions: who is he and what is he like, what about your commitment to Kanoniczki, and what will happen to grandmother? She calmed me down with a smile and said that everything had been arranged. She said she was still free to leave the convent. Jerzy, her betrothed, knew and loved grandmother and had anticipated that she would live with them.

I asked, wide eyed, if all of this was really true. She merely sat back in her chair, crossed her fingers together, smiled at me, and nodded. I jumped into her lap and kissed her on both cheeks. We laughed together. She then admonished me that I was not to tell anyone, because she wanted to spread the good news herself. Agreeing, intoxicated with the events of the last week and this exciting news, I left for my train home.

CHAPTER 23

THE WEATHER on the way home was gorgeous. It was warm, almost hot but not quite. Flowers, fields and trees were in full bloom and heavily laden with multiple shades of rich green leaves. Birds, gathering nesting materials or going through mating rituals, were evident everywhere. Storks were already seated in their massive nests, caring for their broods. Having left Warsaw in the afternoon, I arrived in Grodno toward evening. I decided to spend the night in our family's Grodno apartment. Niula greeted me warmly. She was ecstatic at the news of my passing my matriculation.

I immediately noticed that Stasia (the servant girl brought from Poznan), who had always called me Terenia, was now calling me by the formal form, "Miss Terenia." I queried her about this, asking why she was not calling me simply by my first name to which she answered, again formally, "Miss Terenia, you have passed your matriculation and are now an adult. It is my duty, as per instructions given me in my service school in Poznan, that I address you correctly. From this time forward, I will address you in such a manner. Please understand, Miss Terenia, this does not in any way reduce my love for you."

"Of course not," I replied, unsure of how to respond to her statement. I felt honored, and understood that I now had new and additional responsibilities. Furthermore, I was no longer perceived as a child.

I was inundated with a deluge of questions. Andrzej and Piotr were both at the apartment and were envious that I could go home. "First Jas finishes early and then you come to rub your luck in our faces. We still have over a month of school and all our exams yet," teased Andrzej, half seriously. "I sup-

JAN BISPING, "PAPA," CA. 1939

pose you will be taking off on another adventure even before we are done! Won't you?"

"Oh, don't worry," I replied. "We will have plenty of time to see one another at home. I don't plan to leave until July."

"Where to?" they both asked excitedly.

"Northern Italy, I think," I said with exaggerated nonchalance, to which we all laughed.

Asking where Jas was off to, they told me that he was in Wilno applying to the university where he planned to study mathematics. He had originally hoped to study engineering in Warsaw but the university there was not accepting any more applicants. He had, therefore, decided on the alternative in Wilno. This then gave him a better opportunity when reapplying next year to Warsaw.

On the bus home the next day, the fragrance of the fields made me extremely eager to arrive. The trip seemed endless. Finally, the bus driver turned into our entrance drive and dropped me off at our doorstep. Thanking him, I stepped off and was announced by a cuckoo bird. The folk custom of young maidens was to ask the cuckoo bird how many years before marriage. The bird answered my question with many repeated coo-coos. I thought, humorously to myself, that I must have many years of freedom in front of me prior to having the responsibilities as a lady of the house. As I considered this, the house staff came out of the manor to greet me. After I spoke with them briefly, they took my bags and I ran inside to see Mama and Papa.

The next month at home was delicious. I had no worries, no studies, no responsibilities, and was continually congratulated on the honor of having passed my matriculation. I was given a room in the guest wing. This was my first time to have a room outside of the children's wing. As guests arrived and the house filled for the summer, I would be back in the children's wing. Until then, I was going to enjoy the special status.

I got up early each morning, somewhat surprised that I was not tempted to lounge in bed. I went to the stable and had my horse saddled for me. Each day I would ride out to different fields and forests and soak up the peace and calm of my beloved home. The smell of trees and grasses, leather and horse sweat, was like no other aroma in the world. At the edge of the forest I frequently spotted deer with fawns nibbling on tender clover shoots. As I was home earlier than in previous years, the scythers were not yet at their harmonious labors. Crops still had much growth ahead of them. Papa had introduced pheasant the previous year. They could be seen out collecting bugs in the southern park, followed closely by their brood of chicks. After my ride I would change out of riding pants and into a dress. Mama and Papa would be in the small salon at that early hour and I often joined them in a morning cup of coffee and relaxed conversations.

One morning, the subject of continuing my education came up. I indicated my interest in studying the arts in Italy, which they accepted congenially. They asked how I planned to set myself up there. I replied that this summer while in Italy, I could stop in Rome and make arrangements with the Ursulen convent school—for next year.

"Next year?!" both Mama and Papa exclaimed in unison, with raised eyebrows. Expecting this reaction, I was prepared with an answer. I told them that it was my hope to spend one year with them here on the estate. As there would be no children left at home, other than small Jozek, we would have plenty of time together and would have ample opportunities to spend evenings talking, during which I might learn more about the family and its history. Very surprised, but pleasantly so, they wondered if I was not concerned about "losing" a year in this way. I told them that, on the contrary, rather than losing something, I considered having a year to get to know them as an adult would be a lifelong treasure. And so we agreed.

CHAPTER 24

HAVING AGAIN met Miss Krystyna Popiel in Warsaw for the journey to Italy, we traveled to Rome with our now-familiar backpacks. Joining us on this 1938 trip was another student from Rabka, Krystyna Szebeko, two years my junior. When Miss Krystyna first approached me about bringing Krystyna along, I thought to myself, humorously, that Miss Krystyna, realizing that I was now graduated, supposed that I would no longer have time for further travels together. She was training her next traveling companion. Miss Krystyna, anticipating these thoughts, told me that she was deeply intent on studying the route of St. Francis of Assisi. She was worried that her contemplations would make her a boring companion. Rather than having me be lonely, since she knew that I liked Krystyna, she thought that I would enjoy Krystyna's good company.

Passing through Vienna, we noted that the city was absolutely covered with red flags emblazoned with the swastika of Hitler's German Fascist party. Surprised, and wondering as to the meaning of this ostentatious display of foreign colors, we asked a passenger that boarded the train there. "Haven't you heard?" he intoned as if it were impossible that someone not know, "Germany has annexed Austria!" Withholding any comments, we looked at each other in concern. The train moved on.

Arriving in Rome, we immediately went to the Ursulen convent where once again rooms awaited us. I spoke with the Mother in charge of student housing, and made arrangements to live there starting in October of 1939. Locating the young Mother who was our guide the previous year, she agreed to sign me up and reserve my place for next year at the University School of Arts. Having arranged all of this, I felt as though a burden was taken off of me and I was now prepared to enjoy myself. We departed for Sienna the next morning.

In Sienna, situated within the ancient historic Tuscany region, we walked among the ruins of ramparts built to protect the city from ancient marauders. We were fascinated by how successive builders of the cathedral had built it: first in Roman and then in Gothic styles. Also interesting to me was the primitive art of the 13th century Siennese artists, Giotto and Loretti. The character of their woodcarvings was new to me and represented a unique style.

Walking around this small, old city gave me the impression of taking a step back in time. Everything seemed primitive, without the development or utilization of the conveniences which modern life offered. Open sewers ran through small, crooked, irregular streets. It amazed me that this, one of the birthplaces of culture and civilization, was so backward in appearance. It seemed as though its population had never stepped out of the city—and never would.

While giving me the impression of being backward, it also had a romantic appeal. Young and old mingled about. Women gossiped over the street from windows above, while in the evening they might sit singing songs together before their homes on high stone steps. Mailmen wandered about the streets handing the mail to individuals they knew by name, or placing the dispatches into baskets lowered on lines from upper stories. Everyone knew every other person's business. There did not seem to be any personal privacy. If we inquired about something or someone across town, they all had much to contribute.

Renting a room from a family, they would follow us in, not letting us rest or change. They wanted to learn everything they could about us and to see what we had packed in our bags. It was as though they wanted to know everything there was about us, and we had a hard time ridding ourselves of their overwhelming company for a little privacy. After sharing a common evening meal, we excused ourselves and retired to our room. At last, some privacy! We needed sleep after an exhausting day. The heat was oppressive. We opened the windows for some relief. The sounds of the street and the smell of cooking assaulted us. The city had come alive for evening social interactions, penetrating the darkness of our room. These sounds, together with the relentless drone of flies and mosquitoes, kept us from sleep well into the night.

Planning to go from Tuscany to the Umbrian region, which was the main goal of this trip, we decided to hire a local fisherman to take us across Lake Trasimena. Finding a fisherman who agreed to take us, we started out. Though the weather was overcast, it was warm. While Miss Krystyna wore a mid-calf length *jupe culotte* (split skirt), Krystyna and I dressed in shorts for the trip across the lake. The water was as smooth as glass. It turned out that the fisherman's boat was just a rowboat. Asking how long it would take to get across, he reassured us that it would not be long. Half an hour out, the shore we left was receding and the other shore was still not in sight. We realized that the trip must be farther than we had anticipated from our map. The fisherman's large arms seemed to have no problem with their regular rhythm. We were fascinated by the efficiency of his rowing. He twisted the oars a quarter turn each time the oars raised out of the water to skim along with minimum air resistance to their forward most point. Then, with a twist back, the oars dipped into the water once again to pull through for a maximum stroke.

A wind suddenly picked up and we soon were dropped into troughs and crested on waves, each set growing larger than the previous. It was not long before the wind was lashing at us. The fisherman no longer rowed efficiently but now just tried to keep on a steady line to prevent the boat from swamping. The lake now resembled a furious ocean. Our fright turned to terror when we heard him praying! Our only consolation was that the wind was driving us in the direction of our planned destination. His strong hands were locked on the oars that bounced around in the oarlocks as his massive, tense arms tried to maintain control. Speechless, we fixed our hands on the gunwales and seats, holding on for dear life.

The wind started to whistle. Water sprayed the length of the boat, soaking us to the skin in a short time. Waves were now deep black troughs and foaming crests through which we crashed. Fearing the worst at any moment, we caught each other's eyes in silent panic, seeking but not finding any comfort. As we bounced around, I was afraid that if my companions became seasick and attempted to clear their stomachs over the side, they might be swept overboard. The fisherman started glancing around, which gave me hope that he was looking for the shore—and not that he was lost. The trip had now lasted over three hours. We were all tired and hungry and dared not inquire how the poor fisherman felt, or how long we still had to go. Glancing ahead furtively while plunging through a crest, for one moment I thought I saw something ahead. Before I could confirm this momentary impression, we were plunging into the well of the next trough. Looking ahead purposely with the next crest, I thought I saw a shoreline and asked the fisherman if that could be so. "I pray so," he replied and I saw a look of hope upon his face. With the third crest he glanced over the bow and proclaimed, "Yes, it won't be long now!" We were all relieved and soon his proclamation proved correct as we came up landing on a beach almost, it seemed, effortlessly.

Joyously we left the boat and stood on firm ground. The fisherman secured the small craft and bade us to follow him. He took us up to a small fishing village and arranged for us to stay where we could have something to eat and a place to spend the night. The arrangements seemed acceptable. We paid him well and thanked him profusely. He said that he was happy we reached the shore without mishap and he departed for a friend's house close by. Our lodgings turned out to be simple, local, layover accommodations for fishermen. It was clean and the fish based food was hardy. Exhausted, more from the emotional turmoil than physical exertion, we quickly fell asleep after a brief meal.

I was bobbing amongst huge waves. My legs were caught uncomfortably under the boat seat. Fearing that I would soon be pulled under the churning waves, I was finally able to get myself loose and fly above the waves to freedom. I observed the small boat below, struggling through the foam topped, dark waves. It was a fearsome sight but the majesty of nature was magnificent. The rapture of flight was marred only by irritation that my legs, now hanging uncomfortably below me, weighed down my flight.

Suddenly fully awake in the unfamiliar darkness, I remembered where we were. I reached down to touch my legs that had caused such trouble in my dream. Upon touching my thigh I knew that the dream had indicated a real problem. My leg seemed hot, leathery and swollen, and was very sensitive to touch. The wind had long died down. The sky was clear, for a full moon lit the landscape outside. Not wanting to light the gas lamp, I walked over to the window, drew aside the simple curtain and examined my legs in the pale glow that filtered in.

I blinked my eyes in disbelief. The skin on my thighs was swollen to the degree that it was stretched and hung down rolling over my knees. Seeing this, I started to understand the degree to which my legs were damaged, and the full effect of pain came upon me. As I sat on the bed, I considered my situation. Here we were, isolated. I did not even have any cucumbers to place on the burn. I realized that the cloud cover during the lake crossing must have allowed some sun rays to penetrate. This, combined with the winds, had caused the effect I now looked at in the dim light. Pulling out some cream from my bag, I gingerly coated my legs liberally, wondering how Krystyna fared, for she too had worn shorts for the boat crossing. I did not want to disturb her sleep to find out. Thankfully, after a while, I was able to fall asleep.

I awoke to Miss Krystyna's and Krystyna's rummaging around and cleaning up. "Are you burned?" I asked.

"Burned! Why?" Miss Krystyna answered questioningly.

I lifted the covers and swung my legs out from under them, exposing my legs in the daylight. My legs seemed better in the full light and perhaps the lotion had helped, but both of my companions gasped and came to my side. I asked Krystyna how she was, but she seemed incredulous at my question and asked what had happened to me. I understood that she, always of a darker complexion and better tanned than I, had not suffered from the exposure as I had. Explaining that my legs were burned during our voyage, I stood as they eyed me in silence.

"Can you walk?" asked Miss Krystyna. I told them that my legs seemed better now than when I had awakened during the night. The skin seemed to be responding to the lotion I had applied. Replying to Miss Krystyna's concern, I told her that I would apply more lotion. If I wore my shorts I should be able to walk without too much problem.

We ate breakfast, quickly packed our bags and were able to continue our trip with only some discomfort on my part. Luckily, a small local train was available, taking us efficiently to Perugia. From there, our tour retraced the life of Saint Francis of Assisi.

St. Francis was born in Assisi, Italy in 1206. He was the son of a wealthy trader. He left his inheritance behind to live in nature with the wild animals, and he helped the poor wherever he encountered them in the region of Umbria. Later, others followed him who knew him for his goodness and his ability to talk with animals. They established the Franciscan Order, serving the poor and sick, and in time developing a series of hospitals.

Perugia, the largest city in the region of Umbria, was a very old, once-wealthy city. Locating ourselves in a small hostel, we started our exploration. Particularly fascinating to me were ornately painted and glazed local terra-cotta statues. These potteries and reliefs were created by three generations of the 15th century Della Robia family. In spite of their age, the colors, detail and finish of the terra-cotta were perfect. The secret method by which they were created was later lost when the family died out.

We visited the first of a number of churches and monuments dedicated to St. Francis. Miss Krystyna was lost in contemplation. She was fascinated with every detail. The significance of every minute detail was soon too much for the younger Krystyna and myself. I now appreciated Miss Krystyna's anticipation that her interest in all the details of St. Francis' life would be too much for me. She had been wise to invite Krystyna to join us. I started spending more time with Krystyna as Miss Krystyna lost herself in St. Francis. While Krystyna and I were not as contemplative as was Miss Krystyna, it was fascinating to see how the entire region was deeply influenced by this one man.

Statues depicting St. Francis, usually in a pose interacting with wildlife, children, or the poor, could be seen everywhere. It seemed as though every street corner, private yard, rural road, as well as many churches were dedicated to his life.

The next ten days were spent zigzagging through the Umbrian Mountains, visiting numerous sites where St. Francis did his good works. Walking extensively, often thirty kilometers in the heat of the day, we traversed through rounded green mountains with their multitude of refreshing, cascading streams. Often pipes had been extended from the streams so that individuals on pilgrimages could refresh themselves as they followed the footsteps of St. Francis. Well tanned (my legs had healed), refreshed and invigorated from our daily meandering in the natural elements, we arrived in Assisi, the center of the Franciscan following. There, viewing the enormous 13th century basilica, our tour was complete. Miss Krystyna was enormously satisfied with her findings and contemplations. Krystyna and I were equally happy to have seen these ancient lands. We soon returned to Warsaw from where we each went our own way.

Returning home I found my parents keenly anticipating my brother Jas' departure to a special school. A Jewish woman, emissary of the synagogue in Grodno, had come to my father wanting, in some small way, to recognize my father's positive relations with Jews of our region. Apparently a member of the synagogue was a doctor who had a successful school and treatment for people who stutter. He offered to treat my brother Jas. Jas had always stuttered, and my parents were concerned that his stuttering was becoming more pronounced with age. They feared that it could well interfere with his further studies and life in general. They had been notified that his stuttering had a detrimental effect even upon his matriculation, which luckily he had passed on the second try, when they had allowed him to answer in writing rather than orally. When my brother came back a month later, stepping down off the train, he proudly pronounced, "No longer do I stutter!" We were all extremely pleased for him. He seemed completely cured. Years later, an outcome of his surviving the bombardment of Warsaw, the stuttering unfortunately returned and stayed with him the rest of his life.

I, as had been discussed earlier, planned to stay the year at home. Ewa would be going to school alone this year. Mama decided that she would accompany Ewa to Rabka and asked me if I would like to join them. We would visit Częstochowa along the way. I had never been to the historic shrine dedicated to the Black Madonna, and was very pleased for the opportunity. In

1657 the Polish army with fathers of the Paulin Order successfully defended against, and defeated, the invading Swedes that had taken much of Poland. The Swedish defeat at Czestochowa was the turning point leading to the eventual eradication of Swedish invaders from Polish soil.

It gave me a peculiar feeling to escort my younger sister to school, not as another student but as an adult. I watched the many students on the train through different eyes. The younger ones, on their first trip, sat quietly. They tried to look grown up, yet they were obviously greatly affected by their journey and the anticipation of what lay ahead. Older students, familiar with the trip, noisily exuded confidence and experience. We took the train to Krakow via Czestochowa, a slightly longer route, but one that would accommodate our stopping to see the famous site.

Getting off in Czestochowa, we checked our baggage at the station and took one of the many available taxies to the monastery. Learning that the Madonna would be shown at noon, we took a tour. Along the way, entering from the back of the church, we saw that a number of priests were offering the opportunity to confess. Mama told us that she would like to go to confession here. We sat in a pew and waited for her. After a while, she joined us again just as the Madonna was exposed above the altar. Each in our own prayers and meditations, we gazed at this holiest of Polish shrines, in awe of its miraculous powers exhibited all around us. After a time, we withdrew from the church to get back to our train, pleased that we had come, apparently with perfect timing.

Taking a taxi back to the station we sat waiting the short time before the train arrived. Mama, glancing about surreptitiously, told us quietly that she had something to tell us. Ewa and I leaned in toward her to listen. She said that she had an unusual experience in the confessional. When she had finished her confession, the Paulin first asked her if she was married. She had replied in the affirmative. Then he asked whether she had any children, she had answered that, indeed, she had given birth to fourteen, but two, Stas and Ludwik, had died young. When asked what kind of man her husband was, she stated that he was a well-to-do landowner, to which there was silence. Mama told Ewa and I that the silence had continued. She had not known what to make of it. Should she leave, or wait for some signal?

At long last he cleared his throat and spoke again saying, "As you are a dutiful wife and mother, the Madonna shall comfort you with the certain knowledge that none of your children shall die of starvation." He blessed her and she left with strange mixed feelings. Why would a priest say such a thing when she had just given him information that should say that we are wealthy? She would have expected, rather, that he would have said that her children would succeed or some other such thing, not that they would escape starvation. On the rest of the trip to Krakow, Mama seemed rather quiet and introspective.

In Krakow we took leave of Ewa who continued to Rabka. Mama and I changed trains to Tarnow to visit Konstancja Sanguszko, Mama's aunt. She lived in a beautiful old palace, of which we were given a tour. Upon the end of the tour, she told us that she wanted to show me one more thing. We were sitting before a large fireplace where several logs were burning furiously. She told me to go over to the left side of the fireplace. Instructing me to push on a specific rock, I almost fell when suddenly the rocks gave way. A recess opened behind the fireplace. It was almost black inside and I could barely see. There was nothing to see inside for it was empty. Going back out to Aunt Konstanc-ja, she told me that during the Polish insurrections of 1830, 1863 and 1894, this recess had hidden, and thus saved, numerous people fighting for Poland's freedom. Shocked that she would show me such a secret, she replied that it was no longer a secret. She hoped that as Poland was now independent, such secret hiding places would never be needed again. Being elderly, she died be-fore she was proved wrong only a few short years later.

Aunt Konstancja had a terrific stable of Arabians. Unique at this home was the fact that they placed felt shoes on one old favorite stallion and allowed him into the house. He would come to Aunt Konstancja where she was con-fined to her chair. She would feed him sugar and stroke his head until he was lead away again. We were given a tour of the stable. It was like no other stable I had ever seen, before or since. It was a large, well-lit structure kept meticu-lously clean. The floors were of wood and corridors led to numerous stalls laid out with sweet smelling hay. Fenced paddocks and pastures surrounded the stable where the horses were exercised and ridden. Unfortunately, we were there only briefly and I did not get the chance to ride. Soon, Mama and I re-turned home.

Adam, Andrzej, Piotr and Kryla all went to school in Grodno that fall. Adam was going to Grodno, having resigned from his previous interest in a military career. Only Jozek, eleven years old, stayed at home. He was the smaller and only survivor of twins born prematurely. Three months after his birth he had contracted meningitis. As a result, he never developed mentally much beyond that of a child of eight years of age. I spent the entire year try-ing to teach him how to tell time. He would learn, then completely forget the next day. This drove me to distraction. He lived the life of a happy child. He had his own special nanny and, as the doctor told us that he would never develop, no pressure or greater expectations were put upon him.

Other than Jozek, no children were at home. I slept in the corner room overlooking the entry drive and lake. This was a most pleasant room with big windows that allowed a lot of light in. Papa and Mama purchased new furniture for my room. That fall I spent each dawn riding my horse.

Mama suggested that I learn bookkeeping. She gave me the records, bills and overall financial responsibility for everything to be prepared for annual plans and taxes for her estate, Krasnik. Once a week I received documentation from the administrator. I had to track the birth or sale of every animal, and the income derived. I maintained inventory over farm equipment and made payments for parts and repairs. Payments to workers and staff were recorded. I tracked these things in a giant ledger, checking and rechecking to be sure that all amounts balanced. It was sometimes frustrating to me that Mama could do the entire week's work in an hour; it took me an hour or more every day to keep on top of it. Sometimes, finding a correction to one small computational error would take me all day! I thought, however, that accounting would be valuable for me to learn. The ability to keep such records was likely to be of benefit sometime later in my life. I learned from my mother, who kept all the records for Papa's estates, how important it was to be on top of these records. From these books they knew immediately whether or not a venture was profitable. They also knew where they stood so far as taxes were concerned. The tax auditor stood to gain half of any discrepancy he found. One time I heard him complain, good-naturedly, that my mother's books were kept so well, with every detail at her fingertips, that there was no prospect of getting something extra from this estate.

Years earlier Mama had discovered that the chief forester was seriously cheating the estate. Mama found that his billings did not match expenses and the funds under his control. He was called in to talk with Papa. A favored employee who had served Papa for years, when confronted he admitted to having skimmed money for years. After a severe discussion, Papa told him that he could maintain his work. He had a large family to support and would never be able to find such work from another estate without a good reference. Papa sternly told him that his records, from that day forward, had better always be kept exact and correct. Unfortunately, the poor man could not face his shame; he committed suicide that night. Papa, extremely upset, gave the forester's wife a house and pension for the rest of her life.

The record keeping took only a part of my day and for the first time I had plenty of opportunity for reading. I took full advantage of our large family library. Having time during long winter evenings, I took it upon myself to put into order this library and the family archives. Utilizing the opportunity to better acquaint myself with the family archives, I read through them closely, developing an even greater appreciation for what they were and what they stood for. Opening one of the locked cabinets, I discovered innumerable baskets and decorations my brothers, sisters and I had been making for decades: gifts for Christmas and special events. Stating that it made no sense to store these things, particularly as the space was needed for books and other valuable records, I suggested that they be disposed of. As Mama and Papa did not disapprove, I burned the lot of them in the library fireplace.

During my rummaging in the library I chanced upon the memoirs published by Lady Puzyna, who lived in this area at the time of my parent's childhood and youth. We took to reading her memoirs after tea each afternoon; Papa read aloud while Mama and I made progress on needlework as we all sat in the small salon. Papa sat reading in his favorite leather chair with an alcohol lamp lighting his pages and our stitching. Seldom were we able to get through a complete page as each sentence, each paragraph evoked fond memories of various characters; Mama and Papa could not help but add another tale or additional story as we went slowly through the memoirs. It was a pleasure to see the smiles that fond memories stimulated. It was so pleasant to be part of the reminiscing of these, often humorous, historical and interesting events of family and friends from this epoch in my parents' youth. Later in life I was to meet many of the individuals I heard about on those comfortable afternoons. My attitude and relationships with individuals we read about were very positively affected by learning about these events of bygone years from my parents.

CHAPTER 25

THE MONTHS before Christmas of 1938 passed very quickly. During the Christmas holiday, Krzysztof, Ela and Jas talked incessantly and excitedly about the upcoming winter Olympics soon to take place in Zakopane, in the Tatry Mountains not far from Krakow. They had rented a small apartment there where we planned to enjoy the festivities. I was joyously surprised when my parents announced that they were providing me with the opportunity to join my brothers and sister there, along with a generous amount of pocket money as a Christmas gift.

Arriving in Zakopane I located the apartment the boys had arranged for us. It was a simple two-room affair with a kitchenette. There were only two beds for the four of us, a sofa, chair and simple kitchen table and stove. The atmosphere around Zakopane was thrilling. Everywhere we met people who we knew, and we made many new friends. As we had no tickets for the various events, we were always scouting for an opportunity to buy tickets. Tickets were often available. Even without tickets, we could many times watch the events from afar. The giant slalom and high jumps were most impressive, and I enjoyed watching the brave young people as they flew down the slopes or over the ramps. The new Swiss style of the alpine slalom looked like a choreographed dance. The skiers, racing down the hill utilizing full body movement rather than the traditional snowplow "Christiania" manipulation, were exhilarating to watch. It was exciting for us to experiment with the new style.

The main street was packed with people joyously and boisterously enjoying the festivities and talking in unison in all the languages of the world. The only means of conveyance were by walking or sledding in the ornately decorated mountain men's sleds that were for hire. Sled drivers were dressed in heavy white woolen pants and coats emblazoned with characteristic mountain decorations. Atop their heads they wore short-billed, round, black felt hats adorned with feathers. Crowds enjoyed the constant carnival-like atmosphere inside packed restaurants that had opened along the main street. People danced to traditional mountain Polish folk tunes and other popular music. *Bigos* and sausage could be purchased from street vendors, satisfying voracious winter mountain appetites. Shops were filled with Olympic souvenirs and folk art of straw, wood and wool made by locals. Events, restaurants and streets were filled to capacity day and night. As my brothers, sister and I had only the two beds, we spent as much time out in the city and at events as we could, alternating which of us would utilize the beds in a "warm bunk" rotation. This worked out quite well. We were not there to sleep, but rather to enjoy ourselves. We therefore had minimal need for the beds in any case.

I ran into my dear distant cousin Hanka (maiden name Popiel) and her husband Rudy Topor, who was a ski instructor. They told me proudly that they had just opened a ski lodge high on Babia Mountain. When I discovered that they had few clients as yet, I proposed that I come and be one of their early customers. They replied that they would be most happy to have me. If I wished, I could come to help them, especially when larger groups came; the rest of the time we could ski and have fun together.

A few days later, sadly, the last day of the Olympics arrived. We watched the closing ceremonies celebrating all the awards, milled about not wanting to believe that our great time together was coming to an end. We said good-bye to our many old and new friends and finally took leave of one another. Krzysztof, Ela and Jas took the train back to school. Ela suggest that I join her later in Poznan for the last week of carnival, which I agreed with wholeheartedly. After calling my parents to inform them of my change in plans, which they seemed to think would be loads of fun, I joined Hanka and Rudy for our trip together to their new lodge.

Mount Babia was known for its excellent skiing. Typically, groups of perhaps twenty people would go skiing together. They would often come to stay at the lower, main lodge and then come up for a day or two at the higher lodge that Hanka and Rudy just opened. We arrived at the lower lodge and Hanka and Rudy donned large, heavy backpacks filled with provisions. I carried my belongings in a backpack. We put on our skis for the long uphill climb up the snowy slope. There was no other means of conveyance from the lower lodge to Hanka and Rudy's lodge.

Arriving there tired, I found the recently built lodge smelling wonderfully of newly cut pine. The first floor was composed of three main areas: a large salon centered on a terrific stone fireplace, a dining room with long tables and benches, and a kitchen. Rooms above were filled with multiple bunks. There was room for almost fifty guests. Hanka and Rudy had an efficiency apartment within the lodge; I stayed with them, sleeping in a small separate guest room. I soon discovered another reason why they were so happy to have me stay with them. Every day we skied down to the village below the lower lodge and purchased supplies for their lodge's guests. Putting these supplies in heavily laden backpacks, we carried them uphill to the lodge, the round trip taking a good part of the day. Hanka would cook a hearty breakfast each morning for whoever was at the lodge, and after cleaning up, we'd leave for the supply run. Arriving back at their lodge in the afternoon, Hanka would prepare dinner for all the lodgers, after which we would all spend an enjoyable, relaxed evening together.

Rudy continually warned all the skiers, as well as Hanka and me, of the dangers of this mountain, with its disorienting fogs and treacherous slopes. The mountain where we skied was largely composed of three similar shelves where he said many people got lost. Early one afternoon, in a heavy fog, we found that one woman had not returned as expected. We went out to look for her, with Hanka's warning that we be careful and not also get lost. I soon discovered why Rudy had so often cautioned us all. Due to the fog, I was unable to discern where I was, though in close proximity to the lodge. The fog and peculiarly shaped slopes combined to disorient me to the degree that sometimes, as I accumulated speed, I did not always know if I was skiing downhill or uphill. Meeting up with Rudy, neither of us having seen any trace of the woman, we returned to the lodge with great trepidation as to her fate.

As we were pondering what to do next, a group of scouts came into the lodge, carrying the woman. They had discovered her not more than two hundred meters away, mostly buried in snow. She was half frozen to death. Luckily we were able to revive her. Hanka, who had been our school nurse in Rabka, was able to bring her around without serious injury or problems. Later, talking with the woman, we learned that she knew she was not far from the lodge but became confused in the fog. Wandering about for some time, getting very tired, she sat down to rest. She woke up in the lodge under our care. Since she was found so close to the lodge, we presumed that she had walked all around it, the treacherously confusing terrain nearly claiming another victim. Rudy later showed me a number of crosses around the plateau, not far from the lodge, where numerous victims had succumbed in similar fashion. I then and there decided never to wander off by myself but to stay in their company, particularly since in my short time there I had seen how quickly and unexpectedly the weather could change and the fog could roll in.

We worked hard, but the atmosphere was very enjoyable and none of us felt as though there was anything to complain about. The skiing down for supplies was great. The trip was a joy. Our interactions with the young and older spirited lodgers were stimulating and always happy. We sang songs by the fire, told endless stories from various skiing expeditions and enjoyed snacks, baked goods and hot beverages that Hanka prepared expertly. The heavy daily exertion, fresh mountain air and agreeable social atmosphere combined to provide a most pleasant and invigorating stay. Unfortunately my season in the mountains came to an end and I left for Poznan.

My sister Ela was waiting for me when I arrived at the Poznan station. Ela had always been one of the quietest in the family. I anticipated a quiet stay in Poznan while she studied. We climbed up the stairs to street level past the taxi stands from the station. We each held a strap from the sides of my bag, holding it by its "ears." Ela said excitedly, "You came just in time! We have to go shopping immediately and prepare for this weekend. We have three invitations to balls."

After a brief stop and snack at her apartment, we went to several dress stores and picked a ball gown out for me. We thought, though it was very expensive, that it would be a practical buy (and I loved it) because it had a lace top and several colored petticoats that I could interchange. It would look as though I had a different gown at each occasion.

We stopped by a friend's house for a second opinion on our purchase. Ela had a friend, Basia Bilyk, whose mother was considered an authority on fashion. She instructed me to put the garment on and to walk about, showing how I looked with each petticoat. I began to worry when I heard her talking to Ela, but said little as I modeled each variation. Finally, thinking that it just wouldn't do and that maybe I should return the expensive gown, Ela's friend's mother proclaimed, "On the contrary, you look positively delightful in all of its variations and by all means you should keep it." Little did I know that this would be my first and last true ball gown that I would ever wear.

We went to the first ball, at which I felt awkward and somewhat uneasy until I met several of Ela's friends. We started dancing and talking and soon I discovered that I, dressed in this splendid gown, fit in just fine. I was having a fantastic time! Everyone commented on my superb tan, asking me where I got it, expressing his or her envy of my adventures.

One of the young men I met, a distant cousin, was particularly handsome and was an excellent dancer. We were soon dancing every dance together and seemed to talk and dance effortlessly. We had fun together and were totally at ease in each other's company. At the next ball we spotted each other again. I was very pleased to no longer feel as though I were alone or a stranger. We spent much of the evening together and arranged to meet again at the next ball, which was to be my last.

Soon, I was to return home. The entire trip had been wonderful. I was totally impressed with the active social life Ela was leading and felt that my stop in Poznan truly capped off the whole trip. Taking leave of all my new friends, particularly my special dancing partner, Ela and I left the last ball late in the night. The next morning, profusely thanking Ela for showing me such a good time, I took the train to Warsaw with bittersweet thoughts.

Papa met me at the train station in Warsaw. I saw him looking for me as the train came to a stop. He looked past me in the crowd several times as though he could not see me. I came up to him and kissed him. He pulled back for a second and looked me in the eyes. "Terenia, I didn't even recognize you with that marvelous tan. You look quite enchanting. You've become quite a woman. I can tell by the expression on your face that you have been having a good time. Tell me all about it!"

Instructing a porter to get my bag, Papa held out his arm for me, which I took and gave him a hug saying, "I had a great time Papa, thanks to you and Mama." Talking all the while, we went to the next *peron*,[32] boarded the train waiting there and arrived in Grodno before I knew it.

---

[32]*Peron:* (Polish) train platform.

Chapter 26

Krzysztof, Ela, Jas, Ewa, Adam, Andrzej, Piotr and Kryla all came home for Easter. It was great to have us all together (except for Michal and Marysia, who were married). Somehow we started plotting for Mama and Papa to leave the estate together on vacation, and decided that we would encourage them to do so. Stating that we could manage the estate for a short time without them, we suggested that they take this opportunity and leave for a couple of weeks. Somewhat to our surprise, they took us up on our offer. They left soon after we celebrated Easter. Our younger, school-age siblings went back to school, leaving Krzysztof, Ela, Jas and me at home.

It was the first time in our lives that we were alone, in charge of the estate. Each morning the various staff or foremen came to the house to present their activities, but for the most part they were well aware of the expectations Papa would have of them and little more was needed than to confirm their plans. We took advantage of the cook who accepted, with tolerance and perhaps a degree of mischievousness, our extravagant requests.

Evenings were spent playing bridge. One evening Krzysztof proposed that he had something special for us to try. Asking what he had in mind, he would not tell us and just said to come into the small salon after dinner. When we arrived there, the shutters were tightly closed. A single candle burned on a small table set in the middle of the room with four chairs set around it.

Sitting down, he started to tell us about what he had read recently about calling the spirits. He claimed that if we all concentrated, we could conjure a spirit. Looking at one another skeptically, we nevertheless followed his example and placed our fingers upon the table. He blew the candle out and instructed us to keep our fingers on the table, but joined in an unending circle. When we did this he bade us to cease our talking and to concentrate in quiet as he invited a spirit to show itself, should one of us prove to be a good medium.

After ten long minutes where nothing happened, becoming bored with this uneventful calling of the spirits, I decided to take action. I nudged the table with my foot. I felt Krzysztof's hand tense. Nudging it again, harder this time, Krzysztof spoke. "I feel a spirit. Who are you spirit?" Silence. We waited.

Holding back any laughter, I kicked the table and everyone jumped. "Who are you? Identify yourself, spirit," demanded Krzysztof! Silence. We waited. Nothing!

I whispered, "Maybe we should make suggestions as to who the spirit is and maybe the spirit will let us know when we are right."

"Shhh!" Krzysztof responded. When I kicked the table again he jumped and said "Maybe you're right. Spirit, are you one of our ancestors?" Silence. "Are you a friend of the family?" Silence. "Are you perhaps an enemy?" Krzysztof asked cautiously. Gratefully, there was silence once again. "Have you ever lived in this house?" At which I gave the table a good kick and uttered a sound as I had hurt my toe.

Everyone jumped and the circle was broken. My contrivance was thus kept hidden. Krzysztof, in despair, cried out "How could you break the circle the moment we make contact?!" Joining together again, we tried once more—to no avail. Lighting a lamp, Krzysztof, looking pale in the clean alcohol light, suggested we try again tomorrow.

The next evening Krzysztof prepared everything again with tremendous ceremony and anticipation. All day we had discussed whom we wished to ask about and speculated who it could possibly be. When the time came, the candle was again snuffed out and put aside, and we joined in a circle. Silence. I dared not repeat my actions for fear of the consequences at the hands of my brother if found out. Silence. Nothing happened. The table failed to react to any of Krzysztof's suggestions and pleadings. Nothing. Finally, disgusted, we gave up. When Krzysztof suggested we try again the next evening, the rest of us, having had enough, refused. I was pleased not to have been caught in my deception.

Mama and Papa came back looking well rested and in very good spirits. They had spent the time rejuvenating themselves in the waters at the Krynica Resort, which was very popular and where they met numerous acquaintances. Finding that nothing drastic had occurred during their absence, they thanked us for the suggestion and opportunity to get away. We never told them about our séance.

Mama chuckled with the cook who reported all of our requests. We had taken the offensive when Mama first came back, giving compliments about the cook. Mama passed these on. All were satisfied. Papa made the rounds and saw that everything was as it should be. Soon, Krzysztof, Ela, and Jas left for their respective studies. Life at home returned to normal. I spent the following weeks with Mama's papers, and quiet evenings in Mama and Papa's company. The days grew longer as I started anticipating next season's activities.

CHAPTER 27

URMOIL GREW from the west. Talk of possibilities for an imminent war was unceasing. Germany, its population having been cajoled into making every sacrifice for the development of its military, now represented the greatest armed force in the world. Having occupied Austria, Germany now threatened to do the same with Czechoslovakia. Hitler's speeches were increasingly fervent, promoting fanatical nationalism. His lightning bolt words thundered fear into every Pole's heart. Poland's government, all too familiar with the possibilities this threat represented, urgently strengthened international ties by signing mutual defense pacts with England and France, and a non-aggression treaty with Russia.

In response to the western threat, Poland's defense forces were activated. The strength of the national army was widely and proudly demonstrated, often through large parades. Polish youth believed in the strength of these Polish forces and supported them. School children raised money to help finance airplanes and tanks. While the youth were exuberant, many of the more practical, older generations were glum. They shook their heads at this optimism, hoping that past experiences they and Poland had would not be repeated. As Polish students completed the school year in the spring of 1939, a common expression heard as each went their separate way was, "Maybe we will meet again—at war," or more grimly, "Maybe we won't see each other next year due to war."

Despite this gloomy outlook, much of life continued as usual. Crops were sown, gardens planted, and summer vacations planned. Having prepared my passport and visa for studies in Italy the next fall, I decided to tour my mother country. It was always said that you toured distant lands because you could always see nearby sights later—often resulting in never getting to know what was nearby. Not wanting to find myself in this situation, having more knowledge of foreign nations than of my native country, I decided to spend this summer touring Poland.

A few of my siblings and I, together with a visiting teacher from Rabka, decided to make an excursion to the nearby Bialowieza National Forest. Taking a series of short train hops through Grodno, Bialystok, and Lewki, we spent the night at Hajnowka in a large tourist lodge.

The next morning we took a tour to view some of the oldest trees in Europe. These old oak trees, which took ten people to circumference with arms outstretched, were said to date back to the earliest days of Poland. I tried to think about what ancient histories and stories these trees could tell. We were told how various historic figures had come by here, often resting under the massive branches of these trees. Seeing our interest and possibly the opportunity to make a little extra money, the guide suggested that we might want to take a night tour, to see how the forest lives after dark. Happily embracing this suggestion, we agreed to meet again at midnight.

After a long day, a hearty meal, and a nap, we met outside the lodge at the appointed hour. Slowly our eyes grew accustomed to the dark as we followed closely behind our guide whom we could barely see. He warned us to keep behind him and to stay on the trail so that none of us would become lost. Following the trails by looking up at stars through breaks in the branch canopy above us, our guide searched for any signs of life in the dark. We could see little. Occasionally, a night bird or the stirrings of an animal would come to us through the dark. We were disappointed in what little could be viewed. Suddenly, the guide stopped in the trail and lay down. He seemed to be listening to something.

We stood quietly, puzzled at what he was doing. Rising, he told us all to hide quickly behind the base of the closest tree and not to move! As we dashed toward the enormous trees nearest the trail, a fantastically loud and haunting sound came from up the trail. Just making it to a tree, my heart now pounding, trying to quell the noise of my quickened breath, the sound from the darkness intensified. Suddenly, I heard a loud thumping on the ground and the whispering of animals brushing past plants. Then, almost close enough to touch me, a large dark figure—a meter in height and over a meter in length—burst powerfully past me. Thinking that maybe my eyes were playing tricks on me in the dark, I opened my eyes as wide as I could, peering intensely into the darkness. Then moonlight glinted off a 30 centimeter long tusk as it too whisked by! Wild boar!

CARMEN AND FERDINAND DE BOURBON,
KAROLINA AND REMIS DE BOURBON, UNKNOWN, AND TERENIA

KRZYSZTOF

ADAM

Boar also inhabited our marshy forestland at home. Fearing the danger I had been warned of all through my life, I dared not stir. I remembered the guide's caution. I wanted to climb into the tree's branches to safety, recalling tales of injured hunters. My limbs would not move! The beast rushed passed me as I held my breath. I thought, hoped, prayed that it did not hear the beating of my heart! I feared that the loud booming inside my tight chest must have been resounding throughout the forest! Apparently he did not hear me for he passed without pausing. Still, I dared not move. Then another, and another of the large, wickedly tusked, ferocious, wild swine whisked passed! There were great-tusked boars and massive sows each followed by a series of piglets. Had this not been such a dangerous situation, I would have been tempted to reach out to hold the piglets.

The noise disappeared as quickly as had the fifty-odd animals that filled the night with excitement. We were more than compensated for the now forgotten boredom that we had started to feel before their appearance. The silence was terrific, nary a bird or animal making any sound until I heard our guide say, "Well, we were lucky tonight to see such a sight; we just witnessed the best there is of the wild night life of Bialowieza." Lucky indeed! I thought we were lucky to have survived. I heartily joined in with all, saying that we had most assuredly witnessed an unforgettable sight. Heading back to the lodge we started telling various boar stories.

One was of the time during a hunt when suddenly a boar attacked one of the hunters. With little time to do anything, he grabbed a branch overhead and pulled himself up. The boar passed under his drawn-up legs and disappeared into the brush. Other hunters laughed at him saying he should have stood his ground and shot it, until they found their four hunting dogs, gutted—tusk-slit from throat to tail.

Another story we shared with our guide was of when Papa was informed of a wild bunch of boars not far from the manor. Company was with Papa, and they immediately decided to take advantage of the opportunity to do some hunting. Sure enough, upon entering the identified forest, they quickly encountered a large group of razorback. Unleashing an ample volume of shots into the swine, they were quickly congratulating themselves on a successful hunt until,the local boys and men, brought along to help, started calling out: "This one's Piotr's!," "That one's Tomasz's!," and "Over there, that one belongs to Marek!"

Puzzled, Papa went to learn what they were talking about, only to discover that his hunting party had succeeded in shooting a drift of pigs. The local pigs, looking like wild boar due to interbreeding, belonged to local villagers.

They had gotten loose and were out happily rooting for food. It turned out to be an expensive hunt! Papa had to pay each villager for his "prize" animal. We never told these details to his guests who, for years, told of the great hunting at Papa's estate. Each time the story was repeated, we just looked at one another trying not to laugh and give it away.

Later that summer Ela, Jas and I joined Uncle Kazimierz Bisping's children, our cousins Zosia, Jozio and Anusia, for a canoeing trip. Jas went ahead to Strubnica where he joined our cousins. They took one day to bring two canoes down the Niemen River from Mosty, near their home Strubnica, to Grodno. We met them with one of our canoes from our lake at home. When Ela and I arrived on the waterfront in Grodno, we found them and were shocked at the sight of Anusia. She was badly sunburned from their one-day trip and could not proceed farther. We packed her off back home and reorganized our strategy: Ela and Jozio would take one canoe, Zosia and I the second, and Jas, the strongest of the group, would paddle his boat alone. Taking our few provisions aboard without ceremony, we started off, the flat bottomed, light craft handling well in the calm river waters.

The Niemen River starts south of Minsk, about one third of the way from Warsaw to Moscow. It meanders in a generally westward direction down to Grodno, about two hundred and fifty kilometers west of Minsk. The river then turns north to Kovno, which lies about ten kilometers north of Grodno, and then flows east to the Kuronski Delta along the Baltic Sea. The river's meandering makes these distances much farther by the waterway then the distances between these points "as the crow flies." But we were not planning to stay on the Niemen River the entire way. We stayed on it up to the point where the Czarna Hancza River flows into the Niemen. Planning to get to the Czarna Hancza River the same day, we took off aggressively.

The Niemen flowed well, being a fairly good sized and deep river, with oft-tall banks, or even small canyon walls on both sides. At times it flooded out onto flat plains. Wildlife was abundant. The weather was mild. The sun shone brightly. Having learned a lesson from Anusia's burns, we donned light clothing over our swimming apparel. Bypassing a number of small villages and hamlets, we made good time through the clean, clear water, arriving and turning into and up the Czarna Hancza River in the afternoon. Here the situation changed entirely.

This river, smaller than the Niemen, flowed faster and we were now paddling upstream. The river, which meandered widely, looked black in color due to the abundant vegetation that lined its unmanaged banks. Much of

ELA AND KRZYSZTOF, 1939

the way was through government protected, virgin forests. Occasionally we passed private forests made up of enormous old trees, reminiscent of *Puszc-za*[33] Bialowieza that we had visited only a short time ago. At one point, Jozio told us that we were now passing through our family estate's forests. Having never been in this area before, I was enchanted by this totally wild forest. It had the appearance as though no human had ever passed here previously. It was tremendously overgrown with plants of boundless variety growing everywhere. We sometimes passed places where enormous trees lay crashed upon the ground or into the water. In some places groves of young trees grew where several hundred-year-old trees had fallen in some storm, providing light and the opportunity for the forest to renew itself. Passing through kilometer after kilometer of these untamed forests, I suddenly understood how, in historical books set within these regions, entire armies, sometimes composed of thousands, if not tens of thousands of men could remain hidden.

The going was hard. Not only were we paddling upstream against the steady and swift flow, but also the river meandered hither and yon. In order to see more wildlife, we worked our way upstream as quietly as possible, but apparently not quietly enough. Perhaps it was because we were passing in the heat of the day, but I was surprised at how little wildlife we saw. I hoped that as evening approached we would observe wildlife as it came to the river's edge to be refreshed before dark.

Without warning, we suddenly found ourselves in open fields, apparently having passed through the old forest refuge. By this time we were all feeling our muscles from the constant paddling. Ela in particular was not accustomed to such physical activity. She was in obvious pain, though she did not sound a peep of complaint. She did not want to appear as though incapable of keeping up with us or, to be taunted as a "baby." The river here broadened out in the flatter terrain. We soon chanced upon a farm. Having had enough for one day, we decided that this might make a good place to stop, particularly since nightfall would soon be upon us. Approaching, we met the farmer who lived there and requested that he allow us to sleep in his barn for the night. He approved without hesitation.

Entering the large cow barn, we climbed up the crude but sturdy wooden ladder into the hayloft that was filled with new, clean, fragrant, fresh hay. We donned trousers and woolen shirts and grabbed something quick to eat from our provisions. Each of us found a place upon the pale yellow hay and fell asleep without a word. It seemed as though I had not fallen asleep yet when

---

[33]*Puszcza:* (Polish) great forest or wilderness.

I heard Ela calling out to me, "Terenia, are you awake?" Not pleased to be awakened, I replied that of course I was awake and asked, curtly, why she was calling me. She replied, "I can't sleep in a standing position." Fully awakened by this statement, my curiosity motivated me to find out just what she was talking about. Moving in her direction through the semi dark twilight of the loft, I found her, sure enough, in a vertical position. She had apparently not padded down the freshly heaped hay and had fallen through it, feet first, up to shoulder height. Totally exhausted from the day of paddling, she did not have the energy to improve her situation and had slowly fallen into this comical position. She looked so wretchedly tired and unhappy that despite my exhaustion, I crawled up to her, patted down a good area, pulled her out of the hole and, after seeing her re-situated, went back to my spot where I immediately fell asleep again.

Once again I was pulled out of my slumber by someone calling my name and asking if I was asleep! Replying, "How could I be asleep with my name being constantly called," and asked what happened this time. It was Ela again. This time she was complaining about how the smell of the cows below us was wafting up to us and that the sound of the cow's dung hitting the ground was awfully noisy. To illustrate, she started mimicking this sound clapping her hands together, which I thought she did with a certain realism. Unable to hold back, I laughed uncontrollably, waking the rest of our party, who also enjoyed Ela's accompaniment. We all started to copy the sound of the falling cow pies. Finally, we all settled down once more and fell asleep again. I awoke a third time, not to a plea from Ela, but due to the cold. I could see the early dawn through gaps in the barn walls.

Getting up to see the sunrise, I quietly climbed down the ladder, observing the cows chewing their cud and looking back at me with their large, soft, brown eyes. Going out into the fresh air, a sight greeted me that pulled at my heart. The view of the broad plains, the quietly flowing river, the soft blue sky, and chirping spring birds drew me on out into the open, despite the fact that the quickly dropping early morning temperature was making me shake all over. I realized my feelings for this land—my fatherland—were like no other. I was here where I belonged, in this my fatherland. How happy I was to be a part of all of this placid natural beauty. As I stood there, the sun rose. It searched out my body and warmed it with its golden rays that felt, oh so good. Basking in the comfort of the sunrays, I stood there. My head and heart were raised. My eyes closed. A gentle breeze caressed my cheeks, but it too was warm against my still frigid body. I could hear as various animals scurried about foraging for food in the early dawn. I could hear as first one and then another of my party awoke. Turning, I observed them stiffly climb down the ladder, stretch, and stomp their feet in the soft turf.

A peasant girl, of maybe fifteen years, blond hair gently blowing in the breeze, dressed in a heavy, richly embroidered woolen vest and full skirt, tall and slender, with a happy smile on her face, quietly and shyly passed me. She carried a three legged stool and milking pail. "May God be praised," she said quietly and shyly.

I replied, a smile also on my face, "For ever and ever."

I could hear her talking to a cow, calling it by its name. She soon came out. The pail was now half full of creamy rich milk, steaming in the cool of the morning. She came toward me, but then observing Jozek, turned in his direction and coyly asked if "we" would like some milk. Reminded of Papa's oft-repeated admonition concerning fresh milk, that it should always be boiled to kill any chance of transferring tuberculosis, he replied in the affirmative. He asked her if she could please boil it for us and that we would be happy to pay for it. "Of course, Sir," she replied, curtsying to him, head lowered demurely. She turned on her heel and scampered to the farmhouse. We could see a number of children peering curiously out of windows as smoke billowed out of the chimney nestled in the roof thatch. As she entered, a rooster jumped out through the door in a flurry, alighting on the fence that encircled the house and garden, crowing in delight at the brilliant morning sun. A moment later the farmer came out, stretched in the sun and headed out across a field.

Zosia and I went to the boats and returned with a basket full of breakfast supplies. Spreading a blanket on some grass, not far from the barn, we made sandwiches for our breakfast. The girl came out once again carrying a steaming porcelain pot and offered us the now hot milk. Hungrily eating we finished the food and milk that quickly warmed our bellies. The girl had disappeared back into the barn where we could hear her talking softly with the cows, milk rhythmically striking the pail. Packing our things quickly, ready to leave, Jozio went into the barn to pay the girl for the milk. She came out with him, then watched as we put out into the water. Waving to us yearningly, she stood there watching us until we disappeared with the next bend in the river.

Our stiff muscles quickly loosened up as we pulled hard on the paddles to gain advantage on the increasingly swift river. After an hour of this effort we were rewarded with the sight of the first canal lock. Having anticipated the canal, which bypassed a number of waterfalls, we entered. Immediately by the gates the canal was lined with concrete; most of the canal was like an earthen ditch. Entering past the first lock gates, the lockmasters above turned a giant horizontal wheel by inserting long pins into the wheel and walking around it until the gate was fully secured. Then walking to the next gate, some thirty meters upstream, carrying the wooden pins with them, they slowly turned the next wheels in the opposite direction. This slowly opened the gates. Water boiled through. We were raised up to the next level of the water of the next higher section of canal. The gates were then opened wide to allow us through. We were lucky that we had arrived just as they needed to pass a barge through from the other side, or we might have had to wait a long time. Later, farther up the canal, we did sometimes have to wait a long time. Occasionally, we would decide not to wait but rather portaged our canoes around. After making our way through or around about ten of these locks along the length of the canal, toward the evening, we were once again rewarded with having passed through the last lock entering Lake Augustow.

We peered into the quickly approaching sunset before us, tired, hungry, and sunburned; we keenly looked ahead to the Lake Augustow yacht club. There we hoped for showers, good food, an entertaining evening and a clean, comfortable place to spend the night. It was not to be so. The club, elegant and beautifully situated, was extremely popular—and full! All of the rooms in the lodge were occupied.

Now disappointed as well as tired, we started thinking about an alternate plan. The club, in addition to having rooms that could be rented for the night, also had several luxury suites that wealthy and influential members kept permanently. General Anders, in command of the first cavalry detachment stationed in our region, owned one of these suites. The cavalry often trained on our fields, with the officers staying as guests in our home, and General Anders was a close friend of the family. Jozio, thinking quickly, asked the person at the desk if General Anders was in. When he replied that no, the general was out, Jozio asked that the general be contacted in order that we get permission to utilize his suite.

As the general was out, his office staff gave the man at the lodge desk permission to provide us with use of the suite for one night. Slapping Jozio on his back for his ingenuity, we headed for the suite, bearing wide grins, already relishing its comforts. The suite was indeed comfortable and we made immediate use of the tub. Refreshed, changed into clean clothes, we went to eat and had a fine meal in the opulent dining room. A trio played festive popular tunes and when some friends of Jozio's showed up, we started dancing and having lively discussions. When they heard that we were staying in General Ander's suite, the topic immediately changed to the possibility of imminent war. One fellow told us that his older brother was in the general's cavalry unit undergoing intense training. Another said that he expected to be called up for military duty at any moment and asked Ela to dance. We all danced without care, though not too late into the night. All the members of our party were quite tired, and soft, clean, comfortable, inviting beds awaited us. After sleeping in and enjoying a rich, hearty, country breakfast, we carried our canoes to the nearby train station and purchased tickets for home.

CHAPTER 28

POLISH FOLKLORE has it that, "Strange signs in the sky and on the earth foretell the advent of war." We were regularly hearing this presage. One day Ela got a phone call from a friend, Lusia Zalewski, in Warsaw asking if she could come for a visit that afternoon. Ela, eager to see her friend, asked how long she planned to stay, expecting that she was coming for several days. "Oh," she replied, "I have to be back in Warsaw this evening, so we will only come over for coffee."

Puzzled, Ela said that surely her friend remembered the distance to our home and that the train takes several hours and that she would miss the train back. Whom did she mean by, "We"?

Laughing, Lusia replied that her young friend was a pilot and that they were going to fly.

"Fly?!" An excited discussion ensued, centering on where the plane could land and how to designate the landing spot. Arrangements were made and Ela frantically told us that we must all help. Papa suggested that the best place to land would be on the flat field opposite the main road from our entry drive. The field, having been recently harvested but not yet plowed, was quite smooth.

Two hours after the call, Ela took us all out to the field. Giving us large white bed sheets, she walked around the field with us, paced off a large rectangle to show each of us where we would have to lay the sheets down to designate the landing strip. Having walked over the designated rectangle, we were talking excitedly when suddenly a storm cloud came over us pelting us heavily with large raindrops. We covered ourselves with the bed sheets for some protection. Soaked through and through, we heard a strange droning sound and suddenly realized that the plane approached. At the same moment, Ela pointed to the southwest yelling, "Run to your positions, they are approaching!"

Sure enough we could see the distinctive two wings of a biplane approaching. Before we could hardly move, it was circling above us. Huddling in the wet sheets we ran to our corners, spreading the sheets out, as were our instructions. The plane quickly and easily landed after nary a bounce. No sooner had it come to a stop than the roar of the engine died and the propeller ceased its rotation.

The two occupants in the open cockpit removed scarves, hats and goggles. Grabbing wing struts, they pulled themselves out of the cabin and jumped out onto the ground, roaring in laughter. Surrounding them we asked what was so funny. Lusia could hardly make introductions, they were laughing so hard, but finally they were able to explain. "You looked like a bunch of scared little white rabbits running around with the sheets over you. We had to circle the field a couple of times to make sure that you were out of the way."

One of us ran over to the gatekeeper's cabin to telephone Papa that our guests had arrived. Mama answered saying that they had heard the plane and that he had already left in the carriage to fetch us. Sure enough, Papa was just arriving at the main road. We all climbed on for the short ride back. In the manor, we all sat down at the dining table where Lusia excitedly talked about the exhilarating ride from Warsaw. We sat, transfixed, eating cakes and drinking coffee. Papa had earlier admonished us that we should not request any rides in the "flying machine." So we withheld our most obvious desire. When we had finished our cakes and coffee, the pilot asked if we wanted to take a closer look at the plane to which several of us heartily agreed. Lusia stayed to talk with Ela. After we left, Lusia told Ela that she had met her handsome pilot recently. Rather than inviting her out to dinner or the theater, he had proposed that they fly to visit a friend of hers. He agreed when she suggested coming here. She was obviously under his spell.

Meanwhile, the rest of us were scrutinizing every detail of the plane. The pilot showed us its instruments, structure, engine, propeller and landing equipment, describing all in great detail. He asked me if I wanted to try out the passenger seat. I was happy to oblige! He put on my safety strap, told me to try on the hat and goggles. Before I could say anything, he sat down saying that he would show me what flying was like.

He started the engine and before I fully realized what was happening, we were in the air! I could barely breathe; the air came at me so fast. The cap flapped against my cheeks. I looked down and could see the lake and trees of our park encircling our manor, which from above looked like a matchbox.

The lake fascinated me as I could look down into its depths and for the first time appreciate the varying depths.

We circled the estate a couple of times, giving me a good look from this new vantage point. Then saying that I should check that my safety strap was fastened tightly, he said that he would show me what flying was really like. Suddenly, we were upside down! I was held in place by only the straps. It was exhilarating! He made a couple of rolls, where I could see only sky and not the ground! After this we lowered down and quickly landed.

"Did you enjoy yourself?" he asked, to which I could barely hold back my enthusiasm. Lusia, Ela, Mama and Papa came to us just as the propeller stopped.

Papa, crooking his finger at me, head tilted, eyes slightly squinting, said to me pointedly, "You were flying!"

The pilot said, "She really enjoyed it." I could do nothing but confirm my pleasure. The local peasants took this first arrival of a plane in our fields as a bad omen.

We were still talking about the airplane and what implications flight would have in the future, particularly considering use of airplanes in war, when Uncle Remis Grocholski called, saying that his family was planning to come to visit for a week. Papa offered to send the carriage for them, but Uncle Remis said that there was no need as they were coming by automobile. The party would include everyone: Uncle Remis, his pregnant wife Basia, their seven children, and his sister-in-law Marjuzia, with her daughter Maryjka. An interesting fact about these families was that Uncle Remis and his brother, Zdzislaw, married two sisters. When Bolsheviks killed Zdzislaw after the Great War (World War I), Remis took on the responsibility for his brother's family. Needless to say, the two families were very close.

The news of their coming was met with great enthusiasm and expectation because we had heard so much about them from Mama, who was very close to them. On the designated day, almost to the minute of the appointed hour, a noisy cloud of dust came down the entry drive and settled in front of the manor. We were barely able to see a car for the gaggle of children draped, seemingly, over every surface. Children swarmed out and off of the car even before it came to a full stop. Then, like well-trained infantry, they formed a perfect line in front of the car facing the manor, as if for inspection.

Somewhat stunned by this unique vision and the extreme change from noisy, joyful motion to instant quiet and still order, we observed the car and the yet-to-emerge passengers. The car was a large old thing, which would have been black were it not for the generous coating of dust. It had ample, old-fashioned fenders and running boards from which the children had descended. Emerging from the driver's door on the far side was a tall, thin, handsome, blond man. No longer in his youth, he carried his middle-aged years well. His manner and bearing reminded one of a distinguished officer.

He opened the doors for the remaining passengers, two women and a young teenager. They got out, turned to face us and were heartily greeted by Mama and Papa who introduced the four to us. Uncle Remis then turned to the seven children still standing motionless at attention, commanding them to introduce themselves to their Uncle Jan and Aunt Marynia and their cousins. One by one, starting with the eldest, each saluted and gave their name in a clear resolute voice. When the line was complete, Uncle Remis dismissed them and turned back to Mama and Papa. Taking Mama familiarly by her waist with a hug, not waiting to be invited, he started into the manor. Papa, bidding the two sisters and one remaining teenager to enter, seeing that the youth were already well engrossed in various greetings and explorations, called them all inside to the grand salon.

Inside, the group encountered Father Mikolajan ("Pomidor") who was visiting us from his duties teaching religion at a Bialystok high school. Upon facing Pomidor, Uncle Remis, with a great flourish and deep bow, sweeping his hand as though with a great hat, introduced himself formally as if to a prominent bishop. Pomidor, uncharacteristically silenced, face immediately turning bright red, looked like he was not at all sure how to respond to this unexpected, elaborate and flattering introduction. Papa, wanting to rescue the situation Uncle Remis had placed Pomidor in, took the initiative and presented Pomidor to Uncle Remis. Peering at Mama, I could see a twinkle in her eye, as though she knew that the jokes had only just begun. This promised to be an interesting visit.

Mama sent Ewa to check if dinner waited in the credenza. When Ewa gave her a sign confirming that everything was ready, Mama invited everyone immediately to the dining room. Leading us all in and going to her place at the far end of the table, Mama bade Pomidor to sit to her right and Uncle Remis to her left. Next, came the two sisters, one on each side and then all of us children who had already paired up.

Papa, not yet sitting in his customary place at the end of the table closest the door, unlocked his Gdansk cupboard, withdrew bottles of wine and poured for all the adults. Asking Uncle Remis if he would not join him in a glass of our Zubrowka,[34] Uncle Remis heartily replied, "Well, of course!" Pouring two glasses, Papa gave one to Uncle Remis, sat down with his own, and with Papa raising his glass to Uncle Remis, they both downed the relished clear liquid.

The butler, who stood by during this time, now brought bowls of soup. At a glance from Papa, Jas and Andrzej helped. Our guests were particularly hungry from their expedition and we were all happy to start the meal. The adults immediately turned to discussions about various family members and debated opinions on the imminence of war.

Leaving the adults to their serious discussions, we children, having immediately sensed the fun loving nature of this family, turned to a variety of jokes. Since we were all hungry and looked forward to other activities, the meal was soon finished. As we stood, Uncle Remis proposed that he take Father Mikolajan for a ride in his car. Cars were still a novelty in our region and particularly here, since Papa did not like them. Pomidor was happy to take him up on his offer and they left immediately.

Looking out over the lake, one of our cousins asked, "Are those chestnut trees?" When we replied that they were, our cousin said that we should go pick chestnuts. We were puzzled. The season was too early for nuts to be ripe, and surely, they recognized this tree variety as having inedible nuts. Our cousins affirmed amongst themselves that this was just what was needed. Noting our perplexed expressions they said that they would explain everything and we started around the lake. Walking along, they asked if our mattresses were of the customary three stuffed segments. They seemed pleased when we said that, indeed, the guest mattresses were the usual kind. We were soon making a large pile of green chestnuts. Not yet understanding their purpose, we asked if we were going to husk the nuts, to which they said, "Definitely not!" Having collected the nuts, which they said they would use later, we were returning to the house just as Uncle Remis' car came speeding down the lane.

Pomidor, uncharacteristically pale, got out of the car and, after somewhat curtly thanking Uncle Remis for the ride, went directly to his room. Looking after him somewhat puzzled, we followed our cousins who asked Uncle Remis mischievously, "How did the ride go?"

Uncle Remis, free to laugh now that Pomidor was out of earshot said, "It was great!" Gesturing expressively he demonstrated the adventure. "As we were first driving out the entry drive, the car started creeping over toward the side of the road. I stiffly fought the steering wheel, muttering that I couldn't

---

[34]Zubrowka: one of the highest quality Polish vodkas, to which a few blades of *zubrowka* grass is added. *Zubrowka* grass, which grows only in limited areas in Polish forests, favored by *zubry*—European bison—adds a particularly desirable distinctive light flavor to the vodka. We were lucky that this grass grew in one place on the family estates.

control the wheel. Just before we were off the road, threatening to hit a tree, I wrested control over the car once again. I brought it to a stop at the entry where the gatekeeper had opened the gate for us.

I started again onto the main road, turned left and then after a while, right onto the Jozefinski road to the forest beyond. The good Father, who had not said a word through the temporary loss of control, was sitting quite tensely, but seemed to relax as we started down that tranquil lane. Suddenly, the car lurched to the right, crossing a small ditch out into the field. Father, crossing himself quickly, uttered a question of concern. I, acting as though I was able finally to control the car to a stop, turned off the engine.

Father asked me, 'Why did you do that?'

I replied, 'I didn't mean to, the car just lost control... I think I can fix it though.' Getting out, lifting the hood, I picked up a small rock and started hitting something inside, as I could see Father quietly praying, having not moved from his seat. Throwing away the rock and getting back in, I told him, 'That should do it,' started the engine and put it in gear.

The car lurched ahead again speeding down the field. It started swaying violently side to side. 'What's happening,' Father yelled in a panic!

'I don't know, hold on tight,' I answered."

By this time we were all holding onto our stomachs, practically falling down in laughter. Uncle Remis could hardly continue his story, laughing with a stream of tears flowing down his cheeks. He regained some composure and continued, "I had the car speed back onto the main road, almost colliding with the back of a wagon and in the last moment went around it accelerating down the road. You should have seen the face of the old peasant driving it. When he saw Father he tried to tip his hat to him, but we were long gone and Father was slumped down in his seat, pale as a ghost, fondling his crucifix, uttering prayers in Latin.

After a little while I spotted a boy on the road and slowed the car down. Father, pleading now, asked that he be let out, saying that he would prefer to walk back. I told him that I couldn't stop the car, at which Father started praying out loud now for our deliverance. The peasant boy walking down the road, looked back at our car as I kept pace just behind him. The boy courteously walked over to the side to let us by, but I just followed his steps. Puzzled, the boy started to cross the road to walk down the other side of the road to let the car go its way, but I just followed him again. The boy looking back with an expression of bewilderment and fright, walked off the road and around a tree. Once again, I followed him around the tree at which the boy cried out and scampered up the tree limbs.

'Please let me out, I wish to walk,' groaned Father, pale, seated low in his seat, his head sunk into his roman collar.

'I can't stop now, but I feel like I'm regaining control,' I replied and thinking that he had had enough, swung the car back onto the road and we returned to the manor."

For several minutes none of us could talk, doubled over in painful laughter. "Pomidor will never accept a ride in a car again," Piotr said, to which we all agreed. We found ourselves chuckling the rest of the day. Later, Pomidor came out, peered at Uncle Remis, shook his finger at him saying, "It was not the car at fault," to which we all laughed again, and this time Father Pomidor joined in the laughter.

Having no mercy, our guests made Pomidor their victim once more that day. While he was in the salon talking with everyone, Uncle Remis with one of his boys crept into Pomidor's room. They removed the center section of his sleeping pad and substituted it with a pillowcase filled with the sharp, spiked chestnuts. Having to remake the bed several times, they even called me to inspect it to see that it was made well.

As always, Pomidor retired early and he bade us a good night. As Father walked toward his room, Uncle Remis, twinkle in his eye, looked around at all of us with his finger over his lips, indicating that we should be quiet, motioning that we should follow him. We all quietly crept toward the guest wing and stood quietly in the hall. After some fifteen minutes, we heard the poor priest preparing for bed. He finished his prayers and Uncle Remis started a silent countdown with his arm. After a count of twelve lowerings of Uncle Remis' arm, we heard a frightful yell! No one could stand it. Trying to stifle our laughter, we all fled, imagining what had happened inside the room. Rushing into the salon we almost collided with Mama and Papa, who upon seeing our faces, sternly asked, "What have you been up to now?"

Uncle Remis imitated Pomidor's yell, which reverberated around the cavernous salon walls. "Maybe you should take him a medical kit," suggested Uncle Remis turning to Mama.

"Remis, shame on you," she reprimanded him. "No more!" she said, but had to turn away, a smile emerging on her face.

Everyone found themselves the victim of Uncle Remis' practical jokes, in which his children, well trained, took part. Soon everyone was double checking everything before touching it. It was great fun, but their departure after a week was a great relief to everyone, though we talked about the misadventures for the rest of our lives. Stories about the car spinning around fields and roads, chasing people about, was told by locals as another bad omen.

One afternoon in the middle of August, a Polish Air Corps officer Gizycki unexpectedly showed up at our manor requesting a conference with Papa. Papa took him to the library where they spent several hours behind closed doors. Papa suddenly called our butler to the library, who after a few minutes emerged with a serious expression. He crisply ordered that a room be prepared for the officer and said that we were all to assemble in the salon. Papa came to the salon with the officer and spread a map of our estate on the table.

"I have some important news for all of you," he said gravely. "The Polish Air Corps has chosen our estate as the third line for the defense of Poland in the event of war with Germany!" We sat in silence, in shock! "Starting tomorrow, the field beyond our main gate will be prepared as an airport." All of us seated around the table took in our breaths in unison. "The trees shall all be cut down, the roots removed and the soil leveled and prepared for a landing strip."

I thought of what a huge change this would be. The plan in front of us showed that the roads, Jozefa and Alexandra, would cease to exist up to the forests. I wondered which way I would be able to ride my horse to the forest, which I still loved to do almost every morning.

Papa's next statements were even more shocking. "All able hands will start to work in preparing the fields. All horses"—my heart stopped—"shall be dedicated to the service of the Air Corps. The estate from this time forward shall cease its normal activities and, as is needed, shall do everything it can for this effort. Adam, go now and fetch Szemiot so that I can start plans with him." Adam left to bring back the foreman. We sat in silence for a moment, then slowly dispersed, each in our own thoughts after Papa and the officer went back to the library. Kryla, tears running down her cheeks in bewilderment and lack of understanding, went to Mama who tried to soothe her. Arm around Kryla, Mama stood there, eyes as if focused on something very far away.

The next morning, life changed for everyone on and near the estate. "Another omen," was heard over and over.

CHAPTER 29

MOBILIZATION! Events of the next weeks were dramatic. They came quickly, one after another. In the days following the officer's arrival in our home, it seemed as if every able-bodied man was called to work on the airfield across the road from the gate leading to our manor. In an amazingly short time the soil was leveled and tamped down where once there had been fields and roads.

The radio, once listened to only in the evening, was on now virtually all day and all night. Suddenly, I heard a commotion. General mobilization! All able-bodied men were called to service. Older women and mothers cried, though silently, remembering the loss of husbands, fathers, sons and sweethearts to various battles. Young women, girls, boys and men were exuberant and excited to participate in the defense of our country. Older boys, chests puffed out, started imagining glories and prepared as though for a scout outing. Older men, still within the age of conscription, started readying their families and homes for their absence. Young couples crept off by themselves to whisper endearments to each other. Supplies were doled out and packed.

After a few hours of beehive-like activity, everything ceased when the confusing information was broadcast that the general mobilization had been canceled. "What did this mean?" was the anticlimactic thought in everyone's mind. Later, we were to learn that Poland anticipated that Germany might act aggressively toward Czechoslovakia. Prepared for this action, taking advantage of the fact that Czechoslovakia would be distracted with Germany, Poland rushed in and occupied the disputed border region near Cieszyn. The mobilization was in preparation for a military response by the Czechs, which never happened due to the quiet capitulation of Czechoslovakia to Germany.

With no independent Czechoslovakia and no aggression by Germany toward Poland—and with a nonaggression pact in place between Poland and Germany—the mobilization was canceled.

The demobilization was short lived. A few days later almost every man and older boy received written marching orders. Each man received instructions as to where and when they were to report. Krzysztof, in Krakow, was called to report to the cavalry in a few days. We received a telegram from him the next day announcing that he and Maryla Konopka had wed. Under wartime dispensation from the need for advance notification, they were able to marry immediately, before he reported to duty. Jas, in Warsaw, was never called up and continued his studies. Adam and the rest of our boys were under eighteen and therefore below the mobilization age.

Our gardener, teamsters, the many field hands and administrators all departed. All healthy horses were taken, including my beloved Orzelek. Luckily, Papa was allowed to keep his old team. I watched, heartbroken, as our horses were taken in pairs from the barnyard past our stables, where the household horses were added to the column and disappeared down the road to Krasnik. Papa followed, as he was responsible for the horses' delivery. When he reluctantly fulfilled this obligation, he received a receipt and was paid for them with freshly printed paper bills. Papa, though realizing the necessity for the military to have horses, also realized that this put a stop to the ability of the estate to continue functioning.

Adam, sixteen years old, was given the keys to all the estate offices and buildings, including granaries, barns, cattle yards and tool and equipment sheds. As the men who normally were in charge were no longer around to do their duties, Adam had to take over all these responsibilities. He was called by the civil defense authority to perform night guard duty of the telecommunication lines between the towns of Olekszyce and Massalany. Every second night, he and Mr. Kucinski, who continued to take care of our dairy cows and the cooperative creamery, walked the line armed with rifles.

Papa was continually optimistic that Poland would not find itself at war. He made numerous decisions to quell any fear in the locals, trying to maintain as normal a life as possible. The estate made no particular preparations for war. As Papa was the best informed and naturally the leader of the region, his example calmed the populace.

Returning one morning from his night duty guarding the phone lines, Adam, over breakfast, told Papa that he had learned some disturbing news. Apparently, earlier in the summer, an emissary from the communist party in Russia had held a secret meeting in one of the teamster's houses. They had recruited another of the teamsters to lead the organization of local communists in case of war with Russia. The two treasonous teamsters were now lodged in jail, thanks to their being secretly renounced by a Polish patriot who did not want to be identified for fear of retribution. This added to the general feeling of disquiet.

Fall was enchanting. The sky was blue. With nary a drop of rain, a drought ensued. It was not so dry, however, that our crops failed. In fact, under the consistent rays of the sun, everything seemed to grow bountifully. The vegetable garden was laden with ripening vegetables, which were not being harvested or sold at market due to the shortage of hands; instead, the produce was falling to rot on the ground. Our orchards were bent down with heavy fruit. Even the nursery, where unsold young peach and apricot trees, never dug up and disposed of by the gardener, were now covered with luxuriant fruit. Eating what we could, the rest rotted.

Fine weather was not enough to lift spirits burdened with a constant threat of imminent war. Much of the population was depressed, and feelings of melancholy were common.

The German border was far away and the safe (so we hoped) border with Russia was closer to the east. While we were already impacted by preparations for war, I never dreamed that war would reach our estate. Being healthy and having been trained to help, I felt that I could not stand to stay here, in the comfort and tranquility of our estate, far from events unfolding hundreds of kilometer to the west. I felt that it was my patriotic duty to be involved in the protection of my nation. Like much of our national youth, I wanted to be part of the patriotic energy, events, and activities happening in other parts of the country. I did not want to be here, lost here on the estate, taking care of picking fruit and vegetables, enjoying the pleasant sun and the coming autumn while others were doing their patriotic duty.

Our various guests departed one by one. Pomidor left for Bialystok in preparation for the next school year and Niula went on vacation. Ela, Ewa, Adam, Andrzej, Piotr, Jozek, Kryla and I were all at home with Mama and Papa. Michal, with his wife and two boys, was on his Kieleckie estate. Marysia, with her husband and two boys, was living near Mosty. Krzysztof was in the army, his new wife in Krakow. Jas was completing his polytechnic entrance examinations in Warsaw. We pretended that life continued as usual, but it was anything but usual. Air Corps officer Gizycki now seemed a permanent resident in our home, supervising the last details of preparing the airfield.

I was awakened early one quiet morning by the sun shining through my unshuttered window and the chirping of birds. A strange sound started intruding on the passive dawn. Opening my eyes, I tried to identify the sound, suddenly realizing that it was airplanes. The sound, although far away, was getting quite loud. Hurriedly putting on my robe to go outside and see what was transpiring, Papa suddenly came into my room, just as the distant drone turned into the loud wail of planes flying above us. "War! Germany has invaded Poland! Those are German warplanes flying above," Papa stated in a serious, controlled tone. Running past Papa, who followed close behind me, I ran out of the house and stood in the middle of the courtyard looking up. Overhead flew several squadrons of planes, swastikas emblazoned on their wings and tails.

"There is no doubt left, war has begun," quietly stated our guest, the officer. "Let's listen to what we can learn from the radio." We all walked dejectedly to the small salon. There we sat silently, listening to radio reports of events as they unfolded.

Life as we had known it up to now had come to an end. We could only imagine what lay ahead for us—the dread, uncertainty, pain and misery of an unknown wartime future.

AFTERWORD

Noble Youth was written from a strong family tradition of writing. My mother, Teresa Maria Gniewosz of the family Bisping — "Terenia" — the principal subject in the book, started writing it in the early 1990s. She wrote her memoirs, first in Polish. In 1994 we decided that if the memoirs were to convey family and Polish history to following generations, many of whose families live beyond Poland, then an English version needed to be created.

It was a rare and wonderful experience for mother and son to spend months working together on a translation — a process we continued for additional works. She masterfully wove the fabric of life through the seasons and years, richly embellished with the exploits of her large and active family. During our cooperation, we discovered that a simple translation in itself was not satisfactory. Language, technology, lifestyle and customs had changed so dramatically that a translation would not suffice to convey her life during this period. We settled into a routine where my mother would read a page, paragraph, sentence or sometimes a single word, which we discussed at length to arrive at a common understanding and appreciation. I would then seek to surround my mother's dissertation with a verbal scene sufficient for others to understand, though they perhaps had never experienced a similar situation and were unfamiliar with the environment. She unexpectedly passed away just prior to publication of *Noble Youth*. I greatly miss her steadfast support and our frequent and extensive interaction.

Terenia's true life story continues in *Noble Flight*, as she and her family are overcome by war. Abandoning their beloved Massalany Estate through dark, perilous forests, they encounter terror, pain and loss. Family members are separated, some never to be seen again. Yet through wanderings across Europe, impoverishment and starvation, Terenia's spirited nature is shared as she experiences what man, nature and God bestow during times of war.

CHECK WWW.NOBLEYOUTH.COM FOR AVAILABILITY

BIBLIOGRAPHY

Arnold, Stanislaw, Zychowski, Marian. *Outline History of Poland,* Polonia Publishing House, Warsaw, 1962, 246 pages

Bernier, Brenneman, Giloane, Keefe, Moore, Walpole, *Area Handbook for Poland,* The American University, Washington, 1972, 335 pages

Better Homes and Gardens, *New Cook Book,* Des Moines, Iowa, 1989, 480 pages

Bisping, Adam. *Nasze Massalany—Wspomniena;* Adiutor, Warsaw Poland, 1993, III pages

Bisping, Ewa. Personal Diaries. Gniewosz Archive

Bisping, Jozef. *The History of the Bisping Family;* London, 1988, 81 pages

Debski, Henryk. *Contemporary Polish Cookbook, A,* Interpress Publishers, Warsaw, 1990, 475 pages

Davies, Norman. *God's Playground—A History of Poland—Volume I—The Origins to 1795,* Columbia University Press, New York, 1982, 605 pages

Davies, Norman. *God's Playground—A History of Poland—Volume II—1795 to the Present,* Columbia University Press, New York, 1982, 725 pages

Gella, Aleksander, *Development of Class Structure in Eastern Europe—Poland & Her Southern Neighbors,* State University of New York Press, Albany, 1989, 326 pages

Gieysztor, Aleksander; Herbst, Stanislaw; Lesnodorski, Boguslaw; *A Thousand Years of Poland,* Interpress Publishers, 260 pages

Glowny Urzad Statystyczny, *Historia Polski w Liczbach,* Warszawa, 1993, 206 pages

Gniewosz, Teresa Maria. Remeniscences. Gniewosz Archive

Krzyzanowski, Julian, *History of Polish Literature,* PWN-Polish Scientific publishers, Warszawa, 1979, 807 pages

Magocsi, Paul Robert. *A History of Ukraine;* University of Washington Press, Seattle, 1997, 784 pages

Matejki, Janna, *Poczet Krolow I Ksiazat Polskich / The Gallery of Polish Kings and Princes,* Wydawnictwo Interpress, Warszawa, 1996, 165 pages

Novakowski, Tadeusz. *The Radziwills—The Social History of a Great European Family,* Del Publishing Co., Inc., 1974, 325 pages

Panstwowe Wydawnictwo Ekonomiczne. *Kuchnia Polska,* 1985, Warszawa, 799 pages

Panstwowe Wydawnictwo Naukowe. *Polska—Wielka Encyklopedia Powszechna PWN,* Warszawa 1967, 231 pages

PKP. *Rozklad Jazdy Pociagow PKP;* Wydawnictwa Komunikacji i Lacznosci, Warsaw, 1990, 1056 pages

Pogonowski, Iwo Cyprian. *Poland—A Historical Atlas;* Hippocrene Books, Inc., New York, Revised edition 1988, 322 pages

Polish World's Fair Commission. *Poland—New York 1939, Official Catalogue of the Polish Pavilion at the World's Fair in New York 1939,* Drukarnia Polska Ltd., Warsaw 1939

Radziwill, Michael. *One of the Radziwills;* Latimer Trend & Co. Ltd Plymouth, Great Britain, 1971, 221 pages

Stoye, John, *Siege of Vienna, The* Birlinn Limited, Edinburgh 1964 and 2000, 226 pages

Sienkiewicz, Henryk, *Quo Vadis,* Translation by S.A. Binion; Altemus, 1897

Zamoyski, Adam, *The Polish Way,* Franklin Watts, New York, 1989, 422 pages

Index